THE MAN WITH THE BATON

"KOUSSEVITZKY CONDUCTING"

John B. Sanromá

THE MAN WITH THE BATON

The Story of Conductors and Their Orchestras

by
DAVID EWEN

*"There are no bad orchestras;
there are only bad conductors."*
—GUSTAV MAHLER.

Essay Index Reprint Series

BOOKS FOR LIBRARIES PRESS
FREEPORT, NEW YORK

First Published 1936
Reprinted 1968

LIBRARY OF CONGRESS CATALOG CARD NUMBER:

68-57316

MANUFACTURED
BY
HALLMARK LITHOGRAPHERS, INC.
IN THE U.S.A.

To H. F.

FOREWORD

I SHOULD like to make it clear that it was not my intention in this book to discuss every prominent conductor of the past and present. My primary purpose, here, was to throw some light on the mysterious art of conducting and, with it, upon the greatest personalities that this art has produced. However, to discuss every name in baton history that has earned distinction would have cluttered these pages with repetitious material that would have bored the reader to tears. Therefore, I have followed the procedure of selecting from the mass of outstanding conductors those who require special mention either in lengthy chapters, in several pages or paragraphs; others I have pointed to in passing. There are, to be sure, some eminent batonists whose careers and art do not contribute any new material to our general thesis; their omission from this book should not reflect unfavorably either upon their competence or their importance.

The use of excerpts from an essay by Doctor Koussevitzky for the first chapter should not be interpreted as an indorsement of the opinions expressed in this book.

CONTENTS

LIST OF ILLUSTRATIONS

CONCERNING INTERPRETATION
By Serge Koussevitzky

CONCERNING INTERPRETATION

1.

AS AN auxiliary art, interpretation is, above all, most closely connected with music. Interpretation manifests itself in two directions. On one side, it serves as a link, becomes the intermediary step between hearer and author. Its most important aim, here, is the creation of a *contact* between author and public. In this direction, interpretation only then reaches its goal when it produces a real, living contact, when it becomes that vehicle through which the aesthetic value established by the author is transmitted to the public directly and with greater power. The greater receptivity the interpretation arouses in its listeners, the more perfect will it be. The power of conviction will dominate in the struggle and victory over indifference, and passive receptivity peculiar to the public, generally formed of a casual assembly of people of heterogeneous culture, different tastes and artistic habits.

Good interpretation leads the public to one denominator, seeking to make homogeneous the mixed crowd, bringing it to one level of receptivity. The impression is that the mass is transformed into one single listener. The first instant of contact created by the good interpreter is the moment of smoothing, of bringing the listener's mind to some single artistic level. It is the gathering of all the heterogeneity and motley of artistic tastes into one focus, which, in this meaning, resembles the interpreter himself. If that aim is not immediately reached, one must consider the interpretation to have failed and all that follows later is destined also to failure—the contact cannot arise.

The performance will go in one direction. The listeners' receptivity, instead of yearning towards unity, will diverge more and more from interpretation and will be scattered in the audience itself, provoking, at last, a complete discordance between interpreter and audience. What is called mutual misunderstanding will then happen. The reason is not at all in the fact that the performed music or the interpreter is bad. The cause is quite different: It is the absence of a *will* in the interpreter, the absence of that power which urges the public to submit itself *willingly,* or even *unwillingly* if this is necessary. The performed work may be excellent, but the contact does not arise if the will of interpretation is absent in the interpreter. And the inverse: The performed piece may be of low artistic quality, but if the interpreter's will is obvious the contact with the listeners will arise in any circumstance.

The matter of second moment in interpretation is the attraction toward the interpreter of the listeners brought to one level of receptivity. This attraction must increase with such strength that, in the end, it has brought the hearer to a complete subordination. If this complete subordination is reached, it gives birth to what is called an immediate receptivity which overcomes both satiety and indifference and even the peculiar, professional feeling—that is, puts the listener into an immediate contact with living music and expression. This is the interpreter's great victory—creating such receptivity on the part of the audience. Then happens the "awaking"—the listener trying to return to his customary state. If this is easy for him, the whole matter is concluded; if the return to the previous state becomes difficult, sometimes impossible, then a very important thing has happened. Awaking from his musical sleep, the listener faces reality, which takes a new shape, an unusual one. As if the world had partly changed, life possesses a new value. A spiritual enrichment has taken place. For the interpreter this is the highest reward, the highest step to which interpretation may ascend.

2.

Interpretation is not an art by itself, but an auxiliary one, greatly dependent on the general conditions of musical creation in this or that epoch. What we consider a stylistic performance is the link between musical performance and musical creation —this link being determined in relation to some definite epoch. A stylistic performance, of any quality, can always be only more or less precise. There is no solid basis to the argument that this or that style of our period coincides with previous performances. It is always a matter of guess-work and conventions. The quality of a stylistic performance always depends not so much on traditions as on the sagacity and culture of the interpreter himself.

A good interpreter commands not only the styles of different epochs, but also the composer's styles of one period. At the same time he does not copy anything at all. An interpreter, who possesses a style of his own, creates his performance by uniting past traditions in the shape they reached us with the techniques of our time. Neither Bach's nor Beethoven's *tempo* and dynamics is in accordance with our *tempi* and dynamics, and to copy servilely the previous performance would mean to retard modernity forcibly and artificially, achieving only dullness; for it is not possible to turn life backward. In a performance of classical works, seeming sometimes free, the departure from the past serves more to transmit the character and meaning of the work than a servile imitation of this past. To speak the truth, one must consider interpretation a very young art (in the sense of orchestral conducting). It was born at the end of the nineteenth century and really flourished only in our time. It is a mistake to think that the great conductors of the past were better than the contemporary ones. There is much more solid ground to suppose that such excellent conductors of the nineteenth century as Hans von Bülow or Hector Berlioz would be unable to do anything with the modern orchestra and modern music. Their techniques are indivisibly connected with the romantic period, and in our time they would be weak, helpless, just as some winner at a London Derby in the nineteenth century, were he even the most marvelous jockey of his time, would not be able to use an aëroplane instead of his horse and replace Lindbergh.

If in Wagner's and Berlioz's time the techniques of orchestral conducting were not clear, in such measure as it was then possible to contest the independent part played by a conductor, now these techniques of orchestral conducting have reached such fruition that they may, with justice, be considered

17

an independent musical science. Wagner and Berlioz, had one to judge by the testimony of their contemporaries, were excellent conductors; but both,
trying to confine to a definite theory the techniques
of orchestral conducting, could write only a few pages
about it. Now, the development of these techniques,
and their explanation, would need the writing of
great scientific and theoretical works. The techniques
of a modern conductor are not less complicated and
precise than the techniques of a modern virtuoso, and
the quality of orchestra playing does not depend any
less on the fingers, wrist and hand of the conductor
than a violinist or a pianist depends upon his instrument. The art of a virtuoso is in the submission to
himself only of one instrument, on which he plays,
and in his union with it. The conductor's techniques
are not connected immediately with the instruments,
but with two groups of living men, toward whom
his will is directed. His art is to transform the first
group into one vibrating instrument, sounding as if
he played on it, not conventionally, but with his own
hands and fingers; and the second group, which is
the public, the conductor yearns to change into one
listener. Thus, in the form in which it now exists,
interpretation is a new kind of art. It is a product
of our time, appearing to be one of the achievements
of the twentieth century. The conductor's creation,

today, is an offering to the treasury of spiritual values of mankind, on an equal basis with the work of the scientist, the architect, and the painter-creator. The musician interpreter causes the fusion of all the manifestations of the modern man's activity, out of which modern culture is built. Being a painter, he is at the same time an organizer and an educator in the world of the beautiful. He belongs to those happy promoters of mankind who help to vanquish everyday gray existence, lifting it to the ideals towards which life tends.

Written on receiving the degree of Doctor of Laws conferred by Harvard University, June 20, 1929.

Book 1

INTRODUCTORY COMMENTS: HISTORICAL AND ANALYTICAL

I

THE CONDUCTOR'S INSTRUMENT
The Symphony Orchestra

1.

SIR FREDERIC H. COWEN, the eminent
English composer who for many years conducted the Royal Philharmonic Orchestra of London, once referred to the art of conducting as "the
greatest and the most subtle in all the executive
branches of music." If this is so—and there are few
to dispute this contention—the reason should not be
difficult to uncover. The conductor performs upon
the most complex musical instrument in the world:
the symphony-orchestra. This is a gargantuan organism which, like some mythological monster, has many
bodies but one mind. To understand so complicated
an organism it is imperative to reduce it to its component parts, and to analyze each part separately.

We can separate this tonal monster into four distinct bodies: there are the strings, the woodwinds,
the brass and the percussion. Of these, the most
important, not merely in size but in expression as
well, is, without a doubt, the string section. Com-

prising more than three-fifths of every orchestra, the strings cannot be equalled by any other body in the symphony orchestra for range, dynamics and tone-quality.

The string-section is reducible into still smaller segments: the violins (which, in turn, fall into two classes—"first" and "second"), violas, violoncellos and double-basses. The violin is too familiar an instrument to require comment. The viola—which, like the violin, is played under the chin and supported by the shoulder—is somewhat larger in size than the violin, has strings that are thicker and that can produce a tone of much greater mellowness and depth, and is tuned one-fifth below. The violoncello is one octave lower than the viola; and the double-bass, in turn, is one octave lower than the violoncello.

Over each of these groups presides the "first-desk man" (the "first-desk man" of the first violins is the only one possessing a special title, that of "concert-master"). Usually a virtuoso of distinction, the "first-desk man" not only performs the solo passages of every musical work that calls for them (Rimsky-Korsakoff's *Scheherezade,* for example, requires a solo violin, and Richard Strauss's *Don Quixote* demands a solo viola and a solo violoncellist) but he also assists the conductor in explaining technical problems to the men by direct illustration.

Since the time of César Franck, the harp has been added as a prominent member of the string-section. Composers like Wagner and Richard Strauss have used the harp with sensuous effects in their orchestration.

In a symphonic-body like the New York Philharmonic Symphony Society there are eighteen first violins, eighteen seconds, fourteen violas, twelve 'cellos, ten double-basses and two harps. It is customary, in performing Haydn and Mozart, to reduce the strings to less than half the number. The position of these groups upon the platform is by no means definitive. Most conductors prefer to keep the first violins at their left hand, the seconds at their right, with the violas and 'cellos behind the violins and the double-basses in one line in the very rear of the orchestra. A few conductors, however—Willem Mengelberg in New York was one example—group the first and second violins together at their left hand, combine the violas and the violoncellos at the right, and range the double-basses at the extreme left-hand corner of the platform.

The woodwinds, so called because they are wind instruments constructed out of wood, represent the second important body of the symphony-orchestra, and can usually be found on the concert-platform in two rows behind the violas and violoncellos. The highest register in this group is voiced by the flute and the piccolo[1] (the piccolo being nothing more than a "little flute," half the size, and one octave higher than its parent). The soft, tender, dulcet tones of the flute are familiar to all lovers of music, and are utilized by the composer for his most expressive passages; one brings to mind particularly the unforgettable flute solo in the last movement of Brahms' *Fourth Symphony,* or the repetition of the opening melody for violins in the poignant *Adagio* of Beethoven's *Fourth Symphony.* The flute—as well as its child, the piccolo—differs from all other woodwinds in one very important respect: its mouth is a flue through which the performer blows, whereas with all other woodwinds the mouth of the instrument holds a reed (or double reed) which, when breathed upon, quivers delicately, setting the air-column into motion.

The oboe, next in register to the flute, has a conical-shaped tube, and holds a double-reed in its mouthpiece. Its tone is of such poignancy that the oboe is often enlisted by the composer for elegiac effects as, for example, the funeral march of the *Eroica Symphony* of Beethoven where the oboe re-

---

[1] Although the flute is today made of metal, it comes under the category of "woodwind" instruments because originally it was constructed of wood.

peats the opening march melody first announced by the violins, endowing it with an altogether new tenderness. Directly related to the oboe-family is the English horn (curiously named, for it is neither "English" nor a "horn"!), tuned one-fifth below the oboe. First brought out of comparative obscurity by Rossini, the English horn suffered neglect until Richard Wagner brought it prominence by utilizing it for his shepherd's pipe music in the third act of *Tristan* and César Franck introduced it in the second movement of the *Symphony in D-minor*.

Somewhat more robust and masculine an instrument is the clarinet, whose tube is cylindrical instead of conical, and which utilizes a single, instead of a double, reed. The clarinet is often spoken of as one of the most expressive instruments in the orchestra, by virtue of its four-octave range and its lavish tone. Those who are interested in comparing the tone qualities of the oboe and the clarinet can do so very effectively by referring to any recording of Schubert's *Unfinished Symphony* where the second theme of the second movement (bar 66) is first expressed by the clarinets and then repeated with some amplification by the oboes.

There exists an entire family of clarinets. The one most usually employed in the orchestra is the Clarinet-in-A, and less frequently the bass-clarinet, tuned one octave lower. Other clarinets, called upon from time to time, include the E-flat and B-flat clarinets. All of these instruments are identical with one another as to keys, holes and fingering; they differ only in the scale upon which each is built. Why should there exist such varieties of clarinets? Why should not one clarinet be capable of playing all clarinet music? The answer need not elude us. When there are many accidentals (sharps or flats) in a musical work, fingering becomes extremely complicated; and the technical facility of the performer consequently decreases considerably. In such cases the composer has been taught by experience that it is much more expedient to use another clarinet—the E-flat or the B-flat instead of the one in A—which, since they are tuned to a different scale, will eliminate most of the accidentals.

The lowest register of the woodwind section is assigned to the bassoon, and its relative the contra-bassoon, which is one octave lower. Like the oboe, the bassoon has a conical shaped tube, and a double reed. Its tone is very deep, heavy, somewhat vulgarly rakish in quality, and is therefore eminently satisfactory for humorous passages. Beethoven well realized this, in his depiction of a village band, when he composed the third movement of the *Pastorale Symphony.*

In the classic symphony, one pair of each of the woodwinds—with the exception of the piccolo, of which only one is essential—is sufficient. It is only in later symphonic music that the woodwinds increased in numbers and importance. Today, a large symphonic body requires the services of no less than four flutes, one piccolo, four oboes, one English-horn, four clarinets, one bass clarinet, four bassoons and one contra-bassoon.

Seated directly behind the woodwinds on the symphony-concert platform, are found the brasses—the muscle and sinew of every orchestra, the resonance and sonority of every orchestral composition. The French horns—with tubes coiled into circles from one end of which expands the wide bell, and from the other, a funnel-shaped mouth—have the noblest voice among the brasses, a voice of mellow majesty. Wagner used the French horns for his most grandiose utterances—the opening of the Good-Friday music in *Parsifal,* for example. The trumpet and the trombone are familiar instruments both as to shape and sound. The tuba has a conical tube with a deep funnel-shaped mouthpiece, and because of its low register is often felicitous in expressing passages of masculine strength. Wagner employed the tubas when he wished to give voice to his most heroic conceptions; and it is for this reason that in

the opening pages of the death music for Siegfried
in *Götterdammerung* the tubas are so prominently
utilized.

Although in the classic symphony four horns,
three trumpets and three trombones suffice, the demands of a modern orchestral work are much more
exacting. A major symphony-body employs, therefore, six horns, four trumpets, three trombones, one
tuba and one bass-tuba.

We come, finally, to the last of the orchestral
bodies — the percussion instruments which are
grouped directly behind the brasses. For variety of
instruments, and effects they can produce, the percussion is unique. The most important of this family
are the kettledrums (or the tympani, as they are
more frequently known)— those three bulging
stomachs of sound so essential to the dramatic climax
of every musical work and sometimes even used as
major instruments (as Beethoven did with such
telling results in the *Scherzo* of the *Ninth Symphony*). The three drums of the tympani represent
three different tones which, in turn, can be raised
or lowered by adjusting the screws. It has frequently been commented upon that, of all orchestral
performers, the tympanist must possess the most
sensitive ear. Often, in the midst of the performance, he must change the tones of his instrument;

and his aural perception must be so keen that, with an entire orchestra playing, he is able to adjust his instrument to the correct pitch.

The bass-drum (the drum which is usually found in brass-bands), the snare-drums and the cymbals are likewise employed to heighten and intensify dramatic climaxes. A few other percussion instruments, exotic in their origin, are called upon to suggest foreign countries: the gong, for example, to speak of China; the castanets, of Spain; and the tambourine, of the Orient. Still other percussion instruments are utilized both to enrich tone-colors or to produce the most delicate effects. The triangle, a steel-rod bent into triangular form and beat upon with a spindle-shaped piece of metal, has a metallic ring of delicate quality (e.g. the *Alla marcia* section of the choral movement of Beethoven's *Ninth Symphony*). The celeste, which in appearance resembles a harmonium (steel-plates are struck by hammers, directed by the keys of a keyboard) can produce a quality so ethereal that Tschaikovsky brought it out of obscurity to depict a fairy dance of the sugar-plum in his *Nutcracker Suite*. The xylophone (a series of horizontal bars of wood, struck by a hammer), and the glockenspiel (resembling a xylophone, with the exception that a series of steel bars are used instead of wood) can produce the most exquisite tones of tinsel. More robust, and more drenched with color, are the sounds produced by the bells (a series of horizontal metal bars) and the chimes (long perpendicular tubes of steel), both struck with hammers.

The modern symphony orchestra requires five percussion players, one performer often called upon to employ several instruments.

Besides the instruments mentioned above, enumeration should be made of others, less frequently in use. The piano has become a member of the modern orchestra because it is used so extensively by such contemporary composers as Respighi, Stravinsky, Shostakowitch, etc.; and, less frequently,— as in Saint-Saëns' *C-minor Symphony*—a modern score calls for an organ. Occasionally, a composer, searching for new colors, will utilize the most unorthodox instruments. Berlioz, for example, called for a bass-trumpet, a contra-bass trombone and a contra-bass tuba—none of which is in general use. A symphony of Gustav Mahler, or an orchestral work of Richard Strauss, will sometimes require a mandoline, a guitar or a saxaphone. And there are modern composers whose imaginations are so limitless that they demand unusual instruments for the expression of their musical ideas; and in this way complete strangers often find their way into the sym-

phonic family. Respighi employed a gramophone
in his *Pines of Rome,* Richard Strauss a "wind-
instrument" of his own invention in *Don Quixote,*
and Joseph Schillinger a Thereminvox ("ether
music") in his *Airphonic Suite.*

2.

Many years of experimentation, of trial and
error, have been responsible for the present-day
organism of the symphony-orchestra. In its slow
evolution from an inchoate group of instruments to
the greatest vehicle for musical expression, its numbers were at times increased and at other times de-
creased; effects were first tried and then eliminated;
old instruments were discarded and new ones introduced. So through centuries of musical progress
the symphony-orchestra has undergone growth and
change as a human-body might—and its evolution
was marked by an increase in its physical resources,
development of its personality, strengthening of its
muscles, tissues and sinews, and enrichment of its
voice.

A glance at this growth and evolution of the
orchestra can be illuminating in giving us a more
complete understanding of the structure of our present-day symphonic organizations. It is not essential for us to trace the development of the orchestra

with the meticulous diligence of a theoretician; there exist many distinguished treatises on instrumentation—need we mention Gevaert and Berlioz?—which cover the ground with penetrating thoroughness. For our purposes it is sufficient to point out merely the milestones in the march of the orchestra towards present-day maturity, and to designate only the essential changes in its organism.

It is generally conceded by the musical historian that the father of our modern symphony-orchestra was Claudio Monteverde (1567-1643), likewise the parent of modern opera. It is true that before Monteverde's day there existed groupings of instruments into orchestral bodies. There is documentary evidence of orchestras giving performances of instrumental music in the courts of Edward IV (14th century) and Francis I (15th century), orchestras which included an ill-assorted assemblage of trombones, lutes, viols, drums, flutes, and a virginal. It is equally true that Monteverde's contemporaries— Peri in *Eurydice* and Cavaliere in *La Rappresentazione dell'Anima e del Corpo*—employed groupings of instruments (usually a violin, a guitar, a lute, a cembalo and a lyre) to accompany the voices. But, without exception, in all of these instances the orchestra lacked a definite character; it was disproportionately assembled; its resources were poverty-stricken.

With Monteverde, the orchestra was brought for the first time to something approaching artistic importance. In his musical expression of dramatic effects, Monteverde leaned heavily upon the orchestra for support. He increased its size, and introduced an assortment of instruments more varied than had existed heretofore. The orchestra of *Orfeo* called for thirty-nine players, with a rich assortment of string, brass and wind. Monteverde inaugurated effects in orchestral technique which, at the time, must have stung the ears of musicians; in *Tancredi e Clorinda* the use of *tremolo* and *pizzicato* for strings were first introduced. He enriched orchestral color, strengthened sonority, and increased technical resources. What is, perhaps, even more important is the fact that, for the first time, he established definitely an instrumental style of composition as opposed to the vocal. And for the expression of this "instrumental style" the orchestra was in his hand a supple and pliable instrument.

After Monteverde, experimentation with the orchestra became a favorite pastime with composers. Jean Baptiste Lully (1633-1687) first gave the strings the prominence they deserved by employing them to voice his exquisite melodies. Alessandro

Scarlatti (1659-1725) suggested strongly that the string-quartet would soon become the nucleus of the orchestra by accompanying his airs with two violins, two violas and a bass. With Vivaldi, Handel and Bach, the string-quartet became the very backbone of the orchestra. The marvelous polyphonic fabric that both Handel and Bach wove for the string-section, in their *Concerti Grossi,* broadened the horizon of the strings immensely, and for the first time definitely established them as the all-important body of the orchestral organism. From this time on the physiology of the orchestra begins to assume recognizable features.

The orchestra during the day of Haydn and Mozart already presents a familiar aspect to our eyes. Comprising about thirty players, it included first and second violins, violas, 'cellos, basses, two flutes, two oboes, two clarinets, two bassoons, two horns and the tympani. With Mozart, the flutes, oboes, clarinets and bassoons received flattering attention and their scope and importance increased. It was Beethoven, however, who brought the orchestra to almost present-day development.

With Beethoven, many orchestral instruments which, until then had been used solely for accompaniments, achieved full importance in the symphonic scheme for the first time. That awkward

fellow—the double-bass—began to acquire nimble-
ness, and was even utilized for solo passages (as in
the trio of the *Scherzo* of the Fifth Symphony).
The brasses were given an individuality they had
never before possessed. Moreover, Beethoven inserted new voices into the orchestral throat. Such
instruments as the piccolo, contra-bassoon, trombone
now became permanent members of the orchestral
body; and the percussion propagated into a veritable
prolific family—now to include the triangle, cymbals,
bass-drum as well as the tympani. And, finally, in
its resources for artistic expression—its dynamics,
sonority, technique, color—the orchestra had taken
gigantic strides across the pages of the "immortal
nine symphonies."

After Beethoven's *Ninth Symphony,* new instruments persistently made their appearance in the
orchestra, introduced by composers indefatigably in
search of new colors and timbres; and many of these
instruments were to become of permanent importance. Mendelssohn first employed the tuba in
symphonic-music—and with Richard Wagner the
tubas were given an unparalleled importance;
Meyerbeer brought with him the bass-clarinet;
Rossini, the English horn; and Berlioz—dismissing
so many of his unimportant innovations—several
varieties of the clarinet, particularly that in E-flat.

Of even greater importance was the rapid increase of the technical equipment of the orchestra after the time of Beethoven. Berlioz's introduction of keyed woodwind instruments into the orchestra—an invention of Boehm—virtually revolutionized the entire technique of woodwind playing. As Mr. H. C. Colles has explained in the *Oxford History of Music* (volume 7), before the invention of the keyed woodwinds "certain scales were very difficult to play in, rapid chromatic passages were uncertain, and many chromatic shakes impossible. Moreover, the holes had to be placed where the players' fingers could cover them and not in the exact positions which acoustical laws dictate. And the result of this was uncertain intonation which the player had to correct as far as possible by his manner of blowing. A composer asked that he should play accurately and in tune; the player set himself to improve his instrument and his technique, his efforts finally resulting in the Boehm action."

Equally revolutionary for the horns and trumpets was the introduction of valves and pistons, making it possible for these instruments to master any scale with equal flexibility.

Finally, the orchestra after Beethoven developed a much more opulent palette of colors. With the use of divided strings (first employed by Weber,

Schubert and Mendelssohn) which splits them into
many more groupings than the traditional quartet,
their polyphonic texture became richer and more
complicated—Wagner's prelude to *Lohengrin,* for
example. And under Berlioz and Wagner the brass
and woodwinds learned how to blend into brilliant
combinations of tonal hues; and the percussion to
produce pyrotechnical displays of aural fireworks.

3.

Of the major symphony-orchestras in existence today, the most venerable is the Leipzig Gewandhaus
Orchestra, whose distinguished career reaches as far
back as the days of Johann Sebastian Bach. The
Leipzig Gewandhaus orchestra dates from 1742, and
its concerts—known as *"das Grosse Concert"*—were
given in an ancient market-hall, from which the orchestra derived its name. The first director was
Johann Friederich Doles—the same Johann Doles
who succeeded Bach as cantor of the St. Thomasschule and who introduced Mozart to the music of his
great predecessor when Mozart visited Leipzig in
1789.

The early career of the Gewandhaus Orchestra
was marked by uncertainties and vicissitudes. With
the Seven Years' War it passed out of existence,
returning to life in 1763 with Johann Adam Hiller

as director. Once again its life span was short. It was not until a final reorganization took place, in 1781, that the Orchestra was firmly planted upon its two feet and prepared for its long, consecutive march through musical history.

The first of the great conductors to bring the Gewandhaus to importance was Felix Mendelssohn who, directing the orchestra from 1835 until 1843, brought the performances to an artistic level it had never before approached. Mendelssohn first introduced a scrupulous fastidiousness in the interpretation of every work he performed with the result that the concerts under him passed from mere lethargic routine and became endowed with new life. By beginning to exercise judgment over *tempo,* by becoming meticulous at rehearsals about the quality of performance, and by consciously striving for new effects and nuances, Mendelssohn introduced a new standard for symphonic performances at the Gewandhaus that was unequalled in Germany at the time.

With Karl Reinecke—who, if not so imposing an artist as Mendelssohn, was even much more efficient as a disciplinarian—the orchestra acquired a command of its technique that became the wonder and awe of contemporary musicians. A solid musician who was almost pedantically fastidious about "correct playing," Reinecke—during his thirty-five years (1860-1895) as head of the Gewandhaus orchestra —remedied the imperfections that had previously existed in the orchestra and brought it to a technical efficiency that was almost machine-like in its precise perfection.

There followed the greatest chapter in the history of the Gewandhaus Orchestra. Artur Nikisch— combining the artistry of Mendelssohn and the technique of Reinecke—assumed the conductorship in 1895, and held the position for twenty-seven years, establishing the Gewandhaus firmly as one of the great orchestras of the world. Upon Nikisch's death, in 1922, Wilhelm Furtwängler was selected as successor—and nothwithstanding his youth, he proved to be so well equipped for the task of carrying on Nikisch's work that the great artistic standard of the Gewandhaus did not suffer deterioration. More recently, the Gewandhaus has been permanently directed by Bruno Walter.

The Royal Philharmonic Society of London bears upon its shoulders an age of more than one hundred and twenty years. It was founded in 1813 as a group of thirty performers—with Johann Peter Salomon as "leader" (or concertmaster) and Muzio Clementi "at the cembalo." For several years, the Royal Philharmonic functioned under a system that called for two conductors at the same time: the musician "at the cembalo" designated the *tempo* by movements of his hands and head to the "leader" who faced him, and the "leader," in turn, relayed the beat to the musicians of the orchestra. But, as George Hogarth—the distinguished musicologist of the early nineteenth century—observed, this system was as clumsy as it was complicated. "The 'leader' could not execute his own part properly, and at the same time attend to, and beat time to, the whole band; while his colleague at the cembalo could scarcely exercise any influence on the 'going of the performance' without coming into collision with the 'leader.' "

It was Ludwig Spohr who overturned this method of conducting. In 1820, he was invited to be the "leader" of the Royal Philharmonic Society, after a conductorial experience in Germany where the authority of his performances created a favorable response. At the first rehearsal, he startled the musicians by his revolutionary attempt to dispense with the services of the cembalist and to direct while standing upon the platform with a little stick in his hand. His triumph with this new method [2] inaugurated an altogether new era for the Royal Philhar-

[2] For a full description of Spohr's triumph with the baton, see the next chapter.

monic Society, in which the conductor was to be in full command of the artistic destinies of the orchestra; and the baton was henceforth to be his regal sceptre.

During the next decade, the importance of the Royal Philharmonic as a musical institution rested primarily in its relations with Ludwig van Beethoven. Much to its credit, the Royal Philharmonic perceived the full artistic stature of Beethoven, even from the limited perspective of contemporaneity, and attempted to bring him encouragement and compensation. In 1816, it offered Beethoven seventy-five guineas to compose expressly for it three new overtures—and although Beethoven pocketed the money and dumped upon the doorstep of the orchestra three "pot-boilers" which he had previously composed (the *Overture in C-major,* the overture to *Ruins of Athens,* and the *King Stephen Overture)* the Philharmonic did not lose patience. In 1822, it paid him another fifty pounds to compose a new symphony, the exclusive rights to which were to rest with the orchestra for eighteen months. Once again Beethoven could be capable of dishonesty. On April 1824, the manuscript of the *Ninth Symphony* reached the London Philharmonic, and one month later Beethoven permitted a performance (the world's première, incidentally) to take place in

Vienna. It will reflect everlasting glory to the Royal Philharmonic that, notwithstanding this shabby treatment it received at the hands of the great composer, it could be capable of a gesture so sublime as that of sending Beethoven—when he was on his sickbed, in 1827—a gift of a hundred pounds.

During the next hundred years, some of the greatest conductors of the world came to direct the Royal Philharmonic and to place it among the great orchestral organizations of all time. Felix Mendelssohn came in 1833 and again in 1842 and 1844, to give London a glimpse of his scholarly readings. For nine years (1846-1855) the Royal Philharmonic underwent a rigorous technical schooling under the conscientious direction of Michael Costa. From then on, it developed rapidly—both technically and artisically — particularly under the régimes of Sterndale Bennett (1856-1866) whom Felix Mendelssohn admired so enormously, and Sir Frederic H. Cowen (1900-1908). In recent years, the Royal Philharmonic has performed under such world-famous conductors as Artur Nikisch, Sir Edward Elgar, Willem Mengelberg, Safonov, Sir Thomas Beecham, Sir Landon Ronald, Albert Coates, Felix Weingartner, Wilhelm Furtwängler, Sir Henry J. Wood, Paul von Klenau and Ernest Ansermet.

The Queen's Hall Orchestra, which originated in

SIR THOMAS BEECHAM

1895 under the sponsorship of Robert Newman and with Henry J. Wood as conductor, was the parent of the present-day B. B. C. Symphony Orchestra in London. Beginning with a series of summer Promenade concerts, the Queen's Hall Orchestra— guided by a young conductor of high integrity and ideals—outgrew its summer schedule and became a fitting rival to the Royal Philharmonic. In 1904, a fierce dispute within the ranks of the orchestra threatened to bring to a sudden end the rapidly flowering career of this young organization. But after a large number of musicians resigned to form a new competitive orchestra, the remarkable organization talents and discipline of Henry J. Wood were instrumental in restoring unity, cohesion and artistry to the Queen's Hall Orchestra. For more than twenty years it enjoyed a fertile existence; and it established its dynamic and versatile conductor as an interpreter of importance. In March 1927, the Queen's Hall orchestra disbanded, but the following autumn it reappeared under the new name of the B. B. C. Symphony Orchestra, with the long-familiar and welcome baton of Sir Henry J. Wood still its directing spirit.

The rebel group that deserted the Queen's Hall Orchestra in 1904, organized itself into the London Symphony Orchestra and gave its first concert at

Queen's Hall on June 9, 1904, under Hans Richter. Richter's genius brought the orchestra to a marvelous efficiency in a short time, and the right of the orchestra to an important position in England's musical life could not be doubted. In 1912, the London Symphony Orchestra toured America with Artur Nikisch, and since that time has been instrumental in introducing such eminent conductors as Sir Hamilton Harty, Enrique Arbós, Serge Koussevitzky and Eugene Goossens to London's music audiences.

Crossing the Channel, we discover that the oldest of contemporary symphony orchestras in Paris is that of the Conservatory, which today performs regularly under the sensitive direction of Philippe Gaubert. The first of the *Concerts du Conservatoire* took place in 1828 (the principal work performed was Beethoven's *Eroica Symphony*) under the baton of François Antoine Habeneck, who remained the conductor of this organization for twenty years. Habeneck enjoyed an enviable reputation, and in his method of conducting was said to have been many years ahead of his time. Fastidious about correct performance, he was a stringent taskmaster, and his temper could be cataclysmic in the face of mistakes. He brought to music an enormous zest and enthusiasm, and his performances were said to have been characterized by a tremendous vitality;

Berlioz and Wagner spoke of his art with the highest praise. Not the least of Habeneck's achievements was his presentation, for the first time in France, of all of the Beethoven symphonies in chronological order.

Among the more important conductors who succeeded Habeneck at the *Concerts du Conservatoire* were Narcisse Girard (1849-1860), Paul Taffanel (1892-1901), A. Messager (1908-1918) and, finally, Philippe Gaubert.

The *Société des Jeunes Artistes du Conservatoire* (not to be confused with the *Concerts du Conservatoire*) was the parent of the present-day Pasdeloup concerts, which enjoy such distinction under the direction of such outstanding French conductors as Rhené-Baton and Albert Wolff. The Pasdeloup Orchestra was founded in 1851 by Jules Etienne Pasdeloup who, unable to find an orchestra willing to perform his works, was driven to create a symphonic organization which would bring to public attention the music of younger French composers. It cannot be said that Pasdeloup was a great conductor; contemporary criticism informs us that he was not always meticulous about correct performances. But as a force in French music, his importance cannot be overestimated. His programs were always alive with modernism, and the young French composers (Gounod, Vincent D'Indy and Saint-Saëns, for example) found Pasdeloup a vigorous ally. For several years, the *Société* of Pasdeloup struggled in comparative obscurity. Then, in 1861, its conductor brought the orchestra to *Cirque d'Hiver* for regular Sunday afternoon concerts known as the *Concerts Populaires,* and for a while it performed to crowded halls. But competition among symphony-orchestras, on Sunday afternoons, was very keen, and one of its first victims was the *Concerts Populaires.* In 1884, the conductor regretfully announced that public indifference to his work was too great for him to continue, and the orchestra passed out of existence. In 1886, an attempt to revive the *Concerts Populaires* proved unsuccessful. It was not until 1918, that the concerts returned to become a factor in Parisian musical life, when Rhené-Baton brought them back to life and—in honor of their valiant founder—called them the Pasdeloup concerts.

Two other symphony-orchestras of Paris have more recent origins. In 1874, Edouard Colonne—who had served a short apprenticeship as a guest-conductor of the *Concerts Populaires* of Pasdeloup—inaugurated the *Concerts du Châtelet.* Like Pasdeloup, Colonne was motivated by a driving desire to provide a haven for the vigorous young voices in

French music—and for many years he stubbornly fought the battle for the unknown composer. Massenet, Lalo, Bizet, César Franck—and, finally, Berlioz (all of whose works for chorus and orchestra were performed with scrupulous diligence)—asserted themselves as important composers of the day in the concerts directed by Colonne. Fortunately, Berlioz's star as a composer was soaring in Paris at the time, and the elaborate programs of his music that Colonne had prepared, soon brought tremendous popularity to these concerts. Until his death, in 1910, Colonne's concerts enjoyed unparalleled success in Paris; and their conductor was generally recognized as the foremost in France at the time. Romantic by temperament, Colonne was uniquely fitted by nature to give expression to the music of his contemporaries; and what his baton lacked in perfection of details it supplied with enthusiasm and devotion. He was succeeded by Gabriel Pierné.

The Lamoureux concerts, directed today by Paul Paray—one of the less important of modern French conductors—originated on October 23, 1881, when Charles Lamoureux inaugurated a series of orchestral concerts, called the *Nouveux concerts,* at the *Château d'eau.* For eighteen years, Lamoureux brought distinction to his orchestral concerts by virtue of his profound musicianship, devotion to the

49

musical art, and a fine sincerity. Not the least of his accomplishments was the wide recognition and appreciation which he aroused for Wagner's music, the bulk of which he performed in concert-form. Upon his death, in 1889, his son-in-law, Camille Chevillard, inherited the orchestra, and he carried on the eminent work of his predecessor with considerable success. There were critics to maintain that, in his freshness of approach and enormous vitality, many of Chevillard's performances surpassed those of his father-in-law. However, with the death of Chevillard (1923) the importance of the Lamoureux concerts began to decline; today, Lamoureux's formerly significant organization is only one of the less important orchestras in Paris.

There are two other important symphony-orchestras in Europe whose histories should be traced, and both of these can be spoken of in a few lines. The Berlin Philharmonic Orchestra was organized in 1882, its first conductors being Joseph Joachim (whose baton was never so potent as his violin-bow) and Karl Klindworth, an efficient, although not particularly inspired, director. The history of the Berlin Philharmonic duplicated that of the Leipzig Gewandhaus Orchestra in that its richest period began under the baton of Artur Nikisch (1897) and continued with Wilhelm Furtwängler (1922), both of whom divided their time between Leipzig and Berlin.

In Vienna, the Philharmonic Orchestra began its career in 1842, under the direction of Otto Nicolai, as a subsidiary of the Opera. For many years, its performances were not particularly impressive, and failed to attract very much attention. When, in 1875, Hans Richter was appointed its permanent conductor, the history of Vienna Philharmonic became an important one. From 1897 until 1901, the orchestra took further strides towards greatness, driven by the indefatigable artistry of Gustav Mahler. Then came its greatest epoch. Karl Muck (1903-1906) and Felix Weingartner (1908-1927) brought the orchestra to the very front rank of modern symphonic-organizations. Since 1927, the more permanent conductors of the Vienna Philharmonic have been Franz Schalk and Clemens Krauss, while some of the principal guests have included Furtwängler, Richard Strauss, Mengelberg, Toscanini and Weingartner.

4.

The history of music in America, as James Gibbons Huneker wrote many years ago, is the history of the New York Philharmonic.

In 1842, the New York Philharmonic Orchestra,

comprising fifty-three members, gave its first concert
at the Apollo rooms in New York City, and no less
than three batons were enlisted for the occasion:
U. C. Hill, a pupil of Spohr, directed Beethoven's
Fifth Symphony; H. C. Timm conducted the Kalli-
woda *Overture in D,* and D. Etienne the *Oberon
Overture* of Weber. The early years of the Philharmonic were not crowned by any substantial success—artistic or financial. Carl Bergmann, who
conducted the orchestra from 1855 until 1876, was
never a great conductor, even in his best performances, but he was a good musician, and his long
régime was characterized by a vigorous and indefatigable struggle to overcome the apathy of his public
to great music, past as well as present. It is
paradoxical, perhaps pathetic, that victory in this
bitter struggle should have meant at the same time
personal defeat for Bergmann; with the growth of
music appreciation among the audiences of the Philharmonic came a growing dissatisfaction with the
conductor's stereotyped performances. In 1876,
Carl Bergmann was compelled to resign from his
position. After a transitory year—which saw Dr.
Leopold Damrosch as conductor (two years before
Dr. Damrosch organized his own New York Symphony Society)—the orchestra passed into the hands
of Theodore Thomas.

The history of music in America would today depict a different story if Theodore Thomas had never been in our midst. He was never esteemed as an outstanding conductor, even in his own heyday; but, I feel confident, musical history will find few forces who have shaped it so unmistakably as Thomas did in America. Born in Esens, in Hanover, in 1835, he came to this country as a boy of ten. From the time he attained manhood he consecrated his life, with an almost priestlike fervor, to developing musical taste in America. In 1864, he gathered a group of musicians into a symphony-orchestra which he directed in concerts at Irving Hall and Steinway Hall and, somewhat later, every evening in Central Park Garden. A born teacher, Thomas realized that an appreciation for great music is not inculcated overnight; that the method adopted by Carl Bergmann, with the Philharmonic —forcing great music upon audiences without a preliminary training—can lead only to failure. As a result, he cluttered his programs with "light" music —waltzes, polkas, quadrilles; and then, somewhat surreptitiously, inserted movements from symphonies and great overtures into his concerts. It was not long before more and more good music asserted itself on his programs, finding a rapidly growing audience.

In 1869, Thomas took his orchestra upon an extensive tour through the East and West, insidiously planting the seeds of propaganda for great music wherever he went. It is said that several orchestras in America today owe their origins to the fact that Thomas came to the important cities and introduced vast audiences to great symphonic-music for the first time.

His reputation was rapidly expanding, and when the New York Philharmonic Orchestra searched for a successor to Carl Bergmann, it came upon Thomas. From 1876 until 1892 (with the exception of one year), Thomas was the principal conductor; and it was largely through his efforts that the Philharmonic developed during these years into an outstanding symphonic body. The high artistic standard of its programs was unquestionable. Thomas felt that the time for discarding popular music from his programs had arrived, that the audiences were now ripe to appreciate the greatest music; and from this time on only the greatest composers received performances at his concerts. The modernist of those years found in Theodore Thomas a staunch defender, even though there were occasions when the audiences began to show signs of definite rebellion against the preponderance of unfamiliar Berlioz, Liszt, Wagner and Richard Strauss that so frequently made their appearance on his programs. One concert was particularly illustrative. When Thomas introduced Liszt's *Mephisto Waltz,* the resentment of the audience against new music had grown to such proportions that it noisily refused to permit Thomas to begin conducting the new work. Thomas, however, could be stubborn. Angrily, he tore his watch from his pocket and, holding it in the palm of his hand, announced that he would allow five minutes for all dissenters to vacate the hall; and that after that time he would perform the work irrespective of what attitude the audience adopted. And his battle was not fought in vain. It is generally conceded that—although much of Berlioz, Liszt and Wagner had been introduced to New York by Bergmann—it was Theodore Thomas who made these composers popular.

By the time Theodore Thomas left the Philharmonic for Chicago, the orchestra had grown in artistic importance (and had firmly established itself financially); it was now pliant and flexible, ready for the great hands that were soon to bring it new greatness. These great hands included those two preeminent Wagnerites whose performances, always built upon grandiose outlines, so often approached the majestic—Anton Seidl (1891) and Emil Paur (1898)—who, in turn, were succeeded by Felix

Weingartner (1903), Safonov (1904) and Gustav
Mahler (1909). From 1911 until 1923, the Philharmonic relapsed under the lethargic and uninspiring leadership of Josef Stransky. But it has since
roused itself from its temporary slumber. After
merging first with Artur Bodanzky's New Symphony Orchestra (1922) and then with Walter
Damrosch's New York Symphony Society (1926),
it not only returned to its former magnificence but—
under the batons of such great conductors as Mengelberg, Furtwängler, Toscanini and Bruno Walter
—went further and assumed an undisputed position
at the side of the two or three greatest symphony-
orchestras in the world.

The name of Theodore Thomas is even more
closely linked with the history of the Chicago Symphony Orchestra than with the New York Philharmonic. In 1891, an orchestra arose in Chicago—
largely through the indefatigable drive of Charles
Norman Fay, a music-lover—and Theodore Thomas
was promised full command over its destinies if he
would accept the post of conductor. On October
17, 1891, the first concert took place, with Beethoven's *Fifth Symphony* as the principal work.

For fourteen years, Theodore Thomas worked
under ideal conditions in Chicago. His word was
law, and he was given full freedom to develop his

orchestra and to shape its artistic program. When he died, on January 4, 1905, the orchestra had been installed in its new concert-hall, and was firmly established as the most important artistic institution in Chicago. There was no dissenting voice in the opinion that it was Theodore Thomas' sincerity, musicianship and passionate zeal that had brought the orchestra permanency and distinction.

Theodore Thomas' baton passed on to Frederick Stock, his young assistant, who has since continued Thomas' work with competence and uncompromising integrity. Unfortunately, Stock has never been a spectacular figure; and he has never courted the front-pages with eccentricities of personality and temperament. The result has been that the fame he so well deserves has never been fully his. It is true that his is not the gargantuan stature of Toscanini or Muck, and his performances do not scale Olympian heights. But he is a musician to the tips of his fingers, a forceful leader, and a fine and sensitive interpreter. His performances are always solidly musical and sincere. It is largely because of his efforts that the Chicago Symphony Orchestra continued its artistic growth and assumed importance among the major symphonic bodies in America.

In Boston, the great symphony orchestra that

bears the name of the city was the realization of a
dream long nursed by Henry Lee Higginson, a
sincere music-lover, and one of Boston's most prominent art-patrons. On March 30, 1881, Higginson
announced that he was prepared to support such a
musical project, and the following autumn an orchestra of sixty players gave its first concert in the
Boston Music Hall under the leadership of Sir
George Henschel.

George Henschel, a fine musician and a refined
interpreter, remained with the orchestra for the first
three years. The command then passed on to Wilhelm Gericke (1884-1889), a firm disciplinarian,
who immediately assumed the thankless task of
improving the orchestra. New faces persistently
appeared in the organization during Gericke's régime, and after five years of careful experimentation
and replacements, Gericke succeeded in producing
an orchestra of such technical and artistic attainments that even a musician like Artur Nikisch was
astonished when he came to conduct the orchestra in
1889. With Karl Muck (1905 and 1912) the orchestra's preeminent position among the symphonic
groups of the world was fully established. The passing of Muck brought about a sharp decline to
the orchestra's reputation. Neither Henri Rabaud
(1918-1920) nor Pierre Monteux (1920-1924)

could walk gracefully in the tremendous footsteps of their distinguished predecessor. Moreover, during Monteux's régime, a strike among the musicians —in an unsuccessful effort to establish a union in the orchestra—resulted in the resignation of more than twenty musicians, including Frederic Fradkin, the concertmaster, thereby weakening the structure of the orchestra immeasurably. In 1924, however, a new conductor was brought to Boston, with full authority to reconstruct the organism of the orchestra as radically as was necessary. And in a much shorter period than anyone could dare to hope, this new conductor—he was Serge Koussevitzky—succeeded in restoring dignity and prestige to the concerts of the Boston Symphony Orchestra.

The birth of the Philadelphia Symphony Orchestra took place at the turn of the twentieth century. While its initial conductors—Fritz Scheel (1900-1907) and Karl Pohlig (1907-1912)—were both excellent organizers and distinguished musicians, it was not until Leopold Stokowski was brought from Cincinnati that the Philadelphia Orchestra began to acquire individuality and importance. As H. E. Krehbiel has written, the Philadelphia Orchestra "owes its singularly perfect ensemble to the genius of Stokowski."

"The genius of Stokowski" was equally responsible for bringing the Cincinnati Symphony Orchestra to front rank. Created in 1895 and launched upon a successful first season by Frank van der Stücken and Anton Seidl, the orchestra did not rise to eminence until 1909 when, after a radical reorganization, the young Leopold Stokowski was appointed its director. By the time Stokowski resigned from this position, in 1912, the orchestra's significant position among American orchestras was quite apparent. That position was considerably fortified from 1918 until 1922 with Eugene Ysaÿe, the world-famous violinist, proving that his profound musicianship could express itself felicitously with the baton. Since Ysaÿe, the conductors of the Cincinnati Orchestra have been Fritz Reiner and Eugene Goossens.

5.

In concluding a resumé of the rise of the symphony-orchestra in America, a few pages should be devoted to one who has long been considered the "dean of American conductors" and who was destined to carry on the work of Theodore Thomas in increasing the musical appreciation of American audiences. Dr. Walter Damrosch—the fortieth anniversary of whose first public appearance as a conductor was celebrated by the musical world on April

WALTER DAMROSCH

12, 1935—has been, one must confess, a far greater personality than an artist. Even his most devoted admirers would hesitate to call him a great conductor, or even a very good one. Competent, he was, and a fine musician as well; and we have yet to see a program-maker who could repeatedly fashion concerts that possessed, for so long a time, such variety, freshness and perpetual interest.

However, even in his prime and youth, Damrosch never attained performances of outstanding merit. His baton too often touched the surfaces of a musical work without penetrating very far into the depths; and it could frequently evoke no more than a stereo-typed reading from the players—a reading in which the inner voices, the subtle threads of sound that course and intertwine into a musical fabric, were usually completely absent. Moreover, it was true that Dr. Damrosch never possessed that scrupulous artistic conscience that inevitably belongs to the great conductor. He was not above hurrying a symphony on occasions to twice its *tempo* when the orchestra had to catch a train; and he never hesitated to give a performance without preliminary rehearsals when rehearsals, for one reason or another, could not be obtained. Casual and superficial in his preparation of most musical works, Damrosch was usually quite satisfied, at the concert, if his orchestra played correct notes, and no more.

And yet, in the history of American symphonic-music his name looms large; and, though he cannot be linked with the great conductors of his time, his importance as an influence should not be hastily dismissed. Through his travels with the New York Symphony Society, at the dawn of the century, he spread music to Western audiences that had never before attended a symphony-concert. These voyages to the hinterland (often marked by disagreeable incidents such as the one in Nebraska where a music-lover in the balcony insisted upon diverting himself by spitting upon the bald heads of the bass-players!) were enormously successful in spreading a genuine love for great music, and it was not unusual for a clumsy farmer to accost Damrosch at the end of a program—as one did in Fargo, North Dakota—to express his enthusiasm with these robust words: "God dammit! I don't know why I like this music —but I do!"

Even greater importance rests with Damrosch because of his valiant battle for the modern composer at a time when he stood virtually alone on the battle-field. With plodding perseverance, Damrosch performed the works of the most important younger composers, despite the chilling indifference of his audiences to this music, until he finally succeeded in establishing a permanent place for the modern composer on every symphony-program in America. For Damrosch—like some musical Voltaire—may have disapproved violently of what the young composers were saying, but he fought vigorously for their right to say it.

Walter Damrosch, who was born in Breslau, Germany, in 1862, is the son of that eminent conductor Dr. Leopold Damrosch (1832-1885). Leopold Damrosch's prolific musical activities spanned many decades, and two worlds. In Europe, as the personal friend of Wagner and Liszt and as the director of the Orchesterverein of Breslau, which he himself organized in 1862, his influence in the musical world was strongly felt, and his baton was an important factor in bringing further appreciation to the music of his two great friends. In America, he attained even greater significance. As the founder of the New York Symphony Society and the choral Oratorio Society of New York, and as the first Wagnerian conductor at the Metropolitan Opera House, he was to be an important pioneer in our musical life. Young Walter, therefore, not merely inherited Dr. Leopold's baton, but his artistic mission as well.

On the day of Walter's birth, the foremost musicians of Germany gathered at Leopold's house to commemorate the event. Richard Wagner was elected godfather, but at the last moment Wagner demurred because—having christened another son of Dr. Damrosch, who died shortly thereafter—he maintained that the same misfortune that pursued him through life would curse whomever he came into close contact with. A substitute godfather, therefore, was hurriedly enlisted—and the child who was to have been called Richard Wagner Damrosch was now named Walter Johannes.

When Walter was five years old, his family migrated to America whither Dr. Leopold had come to conduct the *Männergesangverein Arion* in New York. It was shortly after his arrival in America that Walter made his debut, somewhat inauspiciously to be sure, as an orchestra member. His father was at that time rehearsing Schubert's *Der hausliche Krieg* and a passage, in the "March of the Crusaders" required the crash of a cymbal. To hire a man merely to crash a cymbal was at that time considered an extravagance. Dr. Leopold, therefore, enlisted the services of his bright six-year old son. For several hours the father trained Walter how and when to crash the cymbal. Then, at last, he felt that young Walter had learned his lesson well. The excitement of the concert, however, proved too great for the little musician and, when his moment arrived, his hands simply would not move. He saw his father give him the signal once again, looking at him with the fire of anger in his eyes—but nothing, not even the greatest effort on the boy's part, could raise those two stiff hands to crash the cymbal!

It required the tragedy of Dr. Leopold Damrosch's untimely death to bring Walter his first assignment as a conductor. In 1885, Dr. Leopold's death found the first Wagnerian cycle at the Metropolitan Opera House on the threshold of realization. A substitute was needed to carry on the deceased conductor's work and—it having been known that Dr. Leopold had been personally training his son—young Walter was called to the post. He had mastered the lessons his father had taught him, and he performed his duty competently. The ease with which the baton rested in his hands inspired him to carry on the other work of his father as well. And so, although he continued as a Wagnerian conductor at the Metropolitan Opera House for several years, his indefatigable energy and idealism drove him to assume, at the same time, the leadership of the New York Symphony Society and the Oratorio Society of New York.

It was as conductor of the New York Symphony Society—a position he held for thirty years—that

Walter Damrosch assumed a leadership among our native conductors. Some of his achievements during this long reign with the baton have been relegated to the history-book. He was the first conductor to perform in America Brahms' *Fourth Symphony* and Tschaikovsky's *Symphony Pathétique*. He introduced America to Wagner's *Parsifal,* which he gave in concert-form; and as an appreciatory gesture Wagner sent the young conductor the last act of *Parsifal* as a gift. He featured the most representative of modern composers on his programs at a time when their names were only vaguely familiar and their work complete strangers: among them Mahler and Bruckner, Vaughan Williams, Stravinsky, Saint-Saëns and Sibelius. Finally, he was the first American conductor to acquire an international reputation—so much so that, in 1919, he was invited to bring his orchestra to England and France where his concerts were outstandingly successful.

Thus, for thirty years, Damrosch's genial and warm personality, and his own devoted enthusiasm for his art, were powerful propaganda for great music in America. Then, when the battle had been won and America had become more and more the musical center of the world, Damrosch realized that his life-work as an orchestral conductor had ended.

The Symphony Society was, therefore, dissolved in 1926, and Damrosch discreetly withdrew from the orchestral limelight, knowing as he did that hands much more capable than his, were now on the American scene to carry on the work; henceforth, he was to devote his energies to the less exacting requirements of the radio. He retired with grace and dignity, even though during the last few years of his conducting—particularly in his farewell appearances with the New York Philharmonic Symphony Society when he shared the season with Mengelberg, Toscanini and Furtwängler—it had become painfully apparent that Damrosch's day as a conductor had passed. Despite his present radio performances on the weekly "Music Appreciation Hour" and an occasional appearance at a charity concert, Walter Damrosch's career belongs essentially to the past history of American music.

II

THE CONDUCTOR ASSUMES ARTISTIC SIGNIFICANCE

1.

IN AN article on Walter Damrosch published several years ago in a popular radio monthly, there appeared an anecdote about a young man who came to visit this veteran conductor for the purpose of inquiring into the secret of great conducting. Inured to absurd questioning by a lifetime of popularity and the limelight, Dr. Damrosch—far from losing his customary poise and grace — quietly listened to the query and then reached to the bottom drawer of his desk to withdraw a baton. "Beat three-quarter fast time," Damrosch was reported to have said to the young man. The aspiring Toscanini waved the baton in mid-air to the imaginary strains of a Johann Strauss waltz. "Now beat two-quarter time," Damrosch continued. Humming to himself the *Allegretto* of Beethoven's *Seventh Symphony* the young man fashioned the required rhythmic pattern with the stick. "That," Dr. Damrosch announced, "is all that there is to it, my young man."

"Only,"—there followed as an afterthought—and there must have been a mischievous gleam in his eyes as he spoke, "don't give away the secret to anyone when you are world-famous!"

This anecdote is amusing only because it is read by twentieth century eyes. A musician of the eighteenth and early nineteenth centuries hearing this story would not only fail to recognize the humor implicit in it but would also, in all probability, consider it, in an amplified form, very sound advice. For the conductor as a great artist, is essentially a phenomenon as modern as wireless telegraphy and the telephone.

Until the middle of the nineteenth century, the conductor of orchestras served only one preëminent function: He was the human metronome, beating time for the musicians so that they might play together. Conducting required no special talents or extraordinary equipment, and the conductor — as Artur Nikisch pointed out in an interview many years ago—"had no opportunity in years gone by to develop an individual conception or an artistic individuality." The work of the conductor consisted of the mere mechanics of enunciating rhythm and *tempo*. Every composer and every virtuoso, therefore, considered himself eminently qualified to become a conductor when the occasion demanded. A correct performance—a performance, in other words, in which the musicians played together in time—was all that was expected or desired of both the conductor and the orchestra.

But while the conductor as artist is essentially a product of the past fifty years or so, the conductor as time-beater—*"Taktschläger"* the Germans called him—is as old as music itself. We read in Sir John Gardner Wilkinson's *Manners and Customs of Ancient Egyptians* that in the orchestras of ancient Egypt it was customary for one or two musicians to beat time by clapping their hands at regular intervals. In ancient Greece, one of the musicians wore on his right foot a special heavy-leaden shoe to enable him to stamp the time loudly enough for all the other musicians to hear and follow. From the music of ancient Egypt and Greece to that of sixteenth, seventeenth and early eighteenth century Europe is a leap over many years, and a vast expanse of musical growth and development; this broad span failed, however, to change very radically the essential status of the conductor. He remained a time-beater—that, and no more.

The method, or means, of beating time occasionally underwent slight variation with different *Taktschläger* during these passing years. "One man conducts with the foot," Johann Bähr, concertmaster at Weissenfals, wrote in a book published in 1719, "another with the head, a third with the hand, some with both hands, some again take a roll of paper, and others a stick." Johann Bähr might have gone still further. Some utilized a handkerchief tied to the end of a piece of wood; others hammered a key on the organ bench. In the Sistine Chapel of Rome in the sixteenth century, it was the custom to beat time with a roll of paper called the "sol-fa." One century later, Jean Baptiste Lully, in conducting, used a heavy stick—in all probability his walking stick—which he pounded upon the floor to emphasize the time.[1] Progressing still another century we learn from the section on *"Battre la musique"* in Jean Jacques Rousseau's *Dictionnaire* that, in his day, it was habitual for the conductor, at the performances of the Opéra, to strike a stick on one of the desks with metronomic regularity, thereby so often disturbing the performances with his persistent and indefatigable knocking that contemporary writers maliciously nicknamed the conductor of the Opéra a "wood-chopper."[2]

[1] Lully's premature death is, as a matter of fact, attributed to this method of conducting. Lully, in the opinion of many musicologists, accidentally struck his foot with the heavy stick until he developed a fatal gangrene of the leg.

[2] "How greatly are our ears disgusted at the French Opéra with the disagreeable and continual noise which is made by the strokes of him who beats the time, and who has been ingeniously compared to

THE MAN WITH THE BATON

In the eighteenth century it was generally the custom to couple conducting (since it was esteemed an insignificant task) with the playing of either the organ, or more especially the harpsichord, which sounded the ground bass.[3] A practice said to have been first introduced in Dresden by Adolphe Hasse in the early seventeenth century, it was employed by such eminent *Taktschläger* as Handel, Johann Sebastian Bach and his son Philip Emanuel. From Philip Emanuel Bach we derive a graphic description of the benefits resulting from this method of conducting. "The notes of the clavier,"—he is quoted by Philip Spitta—"which stands in the middle surrounded by the musicians, are clearly heard by all. If the first violinist stands, as he should, near the harpsichord, it is difficult for any confusion to ensue. If, however, anybody begins to hurry or drag the time, he can be corrected in the plainest possible way by the clavier; while the other instruments have enough to do with their own parts because of the number of passages and syncopations; and especially the parts which are in *tempo rubato*

a woodchopper felling a tree! But 'tis an inevitable evil. Without the noise the measure could not be felt!"—Rousseau's *Dictionnaire*.

[3] At times conducting was coupled with the playing of an instrument other than the harpsichord or organ, such as the flute, or the violin, for example.

by this means get the necessary emphatic up-beat of the bar marked for them."

Today, we can get a very illuminating conception of this manner in which the *Taktschläger* of yesterday functioned by attending a performance of a Handel *Concerto Grosso* or a Bach *Brandenburg Concerto* conducted by Otto Klemperer or Willem Mengelberg. These conductors adhere to tradition by directing these works while playing upon the harpsichord, precisely as the composers did two centuries ago—beating time with abrupt movements of the head and body, and with hurried gestures of the hand when the harpsichord is at rest.

Sometimes time-beating was much more complicated than the process mentioned above. In the early nineteenth century, the conductor would sit at the harpsichord, signal the beat with his head to the concertmaster who faced him and who, in turn, would designate the *tempo* to the men with movements of his violin while he was playing, or with his bow when he was at rest. Sometimes, too, there was both a time-beater (at the piano) and a leader (who was the concertmaster). In Vienna, Haydn's *Creation* was performed with Kreutzer at the harpsichord and Salieri as conductor; and, as we have already seen in the preceding chapter, in the early history of the Royal Philharmonic Orchestra of London this method was used exclusively.

2.

Although at this time the conductor was an unimportant time-beater, he was slowly beginning to assert himself as a personality, and as early as the seventeenth and eighteenth centuries we find temperament already entering into conducting. Lully used to break violins in a demoniac fit of rage when the orchestra played out of time. The usually placid Handel once threw a kettledrum at his orchestra. Gluck was a tyrant when he directed, and it is reported that at one rehearsal he crept under the desks on his hands and feet in order to pinch stingingly the calf of an offending double-bass player. And Beethoven, his biographers inform us, was an unleashed tempest in the face of mistakes—although, we are also informed, he was by no means an efficient conductor.

Conductors, as a matter of fact, were making their tempers and whims so strongly felt that, by the end of the eighteenth century—as we are told in Schünemann's admirable history of conducting—a code of personal conduct was drawn up for them by the musicians in the orchestra. According to this code, a conductor was never to be "abusive"; he was never to be "behindhand in his praise"; he was to be "sociable and companionable with his men," and he was to make his interruptions as infrequently as possible and always with the utmost amount of discreetness, courtesy and tact.

But the conductor was soon to assert his own personality in directions other than temperament. Johann Sebastian Bach, by virtue of his profound musicianship, brought to his time-beating a keen sense of musical values which first suggested that the personal element in conducting was not much longer to be absent. He would preside over "thirty or more players all at once"—so we learn from the writings of Gessner, a contemporary of Bach, and the rector of the St. Thomasschule in Leipzig— "recalling this one by a nod, another by a stamp of the foot, another with a warning finger, keeping time and tune; and while high notes are given out by some, deep notes by others, and notes between them by others, this one man, standing alone in the midst of the loud sounds . . . can discern at every moment if anyone goes astray, and can keep the musicians in order."

The personal element, to a limited extent to be sure, manifested itself as well in the conducting of the Kapellmeister in Mannheim, Johann Wenzel Anton Stamitz, contemporary of Bach. It was principally the rigid discipline that, as first violinist and *Taktschläger,* he imposed upon his fellow musicians that brought the Mannheim orchestra to a virtuosity bewildering for the time—the Mannheim orchestra amazing contemporary musicians by its ability to play *crescendo* and *diminuendo!* Today, the musical historian concedes that in Mannheim our modern symphony orchestra was born; to a certain extent, the modern conductor was born there as well.

3.

But we are, as yet, a long distance from the conductor of the twentieth century, and his evolution was by no means an overnight one. The conductor of the eighteenth century was not over-meticulous about perfection of performance, and in the interpretation of a work his own opinions were rarely voiced. Rehearsals were superficial, and only the most cursory preparation was demanded for every concert. We know, for example, that the first performance of Beethoven's *Ninth Symphony*—a work which technically, as well as artistically, was so many years ahead of its time—received only two hurried rehearsals; today, with our amazingly proficient symphony organizations, a great conductor would not undertake a performance of the *Ninth Sym-*

phony unless he were given a full week of thorough rehearsals.

It was not until the baton fully established itself as the vital staff of life in the hands of the conductor that his importance and prestige began to soar.[4] For the baton was to free the conductor from the slavery of performing upon an instrument, and at the same stroke was to direct all of his attention and effort upon the business of training performers.

The baton has been in existence for many centuries. In Emil Naumann's *History of Music* there is an illustration of a fourteenth century minnesinger, Heinrich von Messen, who is shown employing one in the direction of a group of singers and players. And the "sol-fa" of the Sistine Chapel, already commented upon, was after all a baton of paper. In 1807, Gottfried Weber, a distinguished musical theorist of Mannheim, spoke vigorously on behalf of the baton, stoutly maintaining that it was the only effective instrument for the hand of the leaders. Others—like Spontini—likewise pledged their allegiance to the stick. But in the early nineteenth century, the baton was still something of a

[4] In recent years, several conductors have attempted to dispense with the baton, particularly that eminent Russian conductor Safonov, and Albert Coates and Leopold Stokowski. But it is still generally recognized by conductors that the baton is infinitely more effective in clearly outlining rhythm than the bare hand.

curiosity—and when Spohr visited England in 1820 to direct a few concerts of the Royal Philharmonic Society, he bewildered his musicians into stupefaction at the rehearsal by pulling from out of his breast-pocket a small, heavy, stumpy stick and attempting to direct them by waving it over their heads.

He has written about the event—an all-important one in the history of conducting—in his Autobiography: "I took my stand . . . in front of the orchestra, drew my directing baton from my coat-pocket, and gave the signal to begin. Quite alarmed at such a novel proceeding some of the directors protested against it, but when I besought them to grant me at least one trial they became pacified. The symphonies and overtures that were to be rehearsed were well-known to me, and in Germany I had already directed their performances. I, therefore, could not only give the *tempi* in a very decisive manner, but indicated also to the wind instruments and horns all the entries, which ensured to them a confidence such as hitherto they had not known. . . . Incited thereby to more than attention, and conducted with certainty by the *visible* manner of giving the time, they played with a spirit and correctness such as, until then, they had never before been heard to play. Surprised and inspired by this result, the orchestra immediately after the first part of the symphony expressed aloud its united assent to the new mode of conducting, and thereby overruled all further opposition on the part of the directors. . . . The triumph of the baton as a time-giver was decisive."

The baton had now firmly asserted itself; it was henceforth to be the all-important instrument for the hand of the conductor. The first conductor to realize this fully was Felix Mendelssohn, the famous composer, who directed the Leipzig Gewandhaus Orchestra for eight years. It is probable that, according to modern standards, Mendelssohn would be accepted complacently as a third-rate conductor. Richard Wagner made many derogatory comments on the rigid formalism and straightjacket conservatism of Mendelssohn's conducting (Mendelssohn, for example, could not tolerate the use of *tempo rubato*[5] in his performances). But his historical importance is imposing. Because of his work with the Gewandhaus, the conductor began to personalize his performances, to make them a reflection of his temperament and genius; the conductor, for the first time, began to tear from his wrists the chains of the *Taktschläger*. He was beginning to give a definite

[5] In the next chapter, *tempo rubato* is discussed and defined.

79

shape and quality to every performance, and to make it a creative expression.

4.

It was in England that two conductors now made their appearance who suggested, even more strongly than Mendelssohn did, what the present-day conductor would be like.

The *bizarre* conductor was born with Louis Antoine Jullien (1812-1860). A Frenchman by birth, Jullien fled from his native country because of insolvency and came to England in 1840. From that time on he established a remarkable reputation as a conductor, primarily at the European Opera House where for a long time he led annual performances of orchestral music.

It was Jullien who first made of orchestral conducting something of a circus-spectacle which, a century ago, surpassed the wildest antics of our modern baton exhibitionists. He was perhaps the first conductor to be fastidious about his personal appearance, and when between numbers he would sit upon the stage facing the audience it was only to impress his attractiveness upon its consciousness. His shock of curly hair always revealed the unmistakable touch of the *coiffeur*. His dress was the last word in elegance; he always wore an elaborately embroidered shirt-front, and was lavishly bedecked with gold chains, diamond rings and pendants.

During his conducting, Jullien stood upon a crimson platform etched in gold; in front of him was a carved music-stand, gilt-stained, and behind him an ornately decorated gold and velvet armchair which, in its ornate splendor, resembled a throne.

In his performances, Jullien was no less ornate. His concerts were always characterized by the most absurdly exaggerated histrionics. For example, before conducting Beethoven, he would have a pair of kid gloves ceremoniously brought to him on a silver platter, and these he would put on and wear during his conducting. For signally important music he utilized a special jeweled baton. He would direct with such a flourish and elaborateness that even a contemporary newspaper — the *Courier and Enquirer*—was tempted to make the facetious comment that "he used the baton to direct the audience." And even his performances themselves were said to have been marked by the most curious eccentricities; all the music that Jullien conducted bore the unmistakable fingerprint of its conductor.

But Jullien was not entirely a mountebank. By introducing into his orchestra the foremost musicians that could be found, he improved the quality of orchestral performances immeasurably. And, although many of Jullien's programs were devoted to the popular music of the day—polkas, quadrilles, waltzes—he was a powerful agent on behalf of great music by introducing into his programs the masterpieces of Haydn, Mozart and Beethoven in small doses, thereby slowly educating his audiences into appreciating these great composers. No less an authority than Berlioz has referred to Jullien as a "clever and intelligent musician." The truth was that Jullien was a strange combination of charlatan and genius, of clown and artist.

In view of his strange antics during his lifetime it may, perhaps, come as no surprise to the reader to learn that Jullien died in an insane asylum.

A much more serious musician than Jullien, and a more important conductor, was Michael Costa (1808-1884). Costa was born in Italy, a descendant of a proud, old Spanish family. As a very young man, he came to England to direct his own cantata in Birmingham. In 1883, he was appointed director and conductor of the King's Theatre, and from that time dates his successful career with the baton. "From the first evening when Signor Costa took up the baton," wrote H. F. Chorley, "it was felt that in him were combined the materials of a great conductor; nerve to enforce discipline, readiness to the second, and that certain influence which only a vigorous man could exercise over the disconnected folk which made up an orchestra in those days."

Although Costa was not above utilizing display, he was not half so exhibitionistic as Jullien, and twice as important. In his performances with the Royal Philharmonic — which enjoyed under his baton a celebrated régime—and with his important Handel festivals, Costa introduced an efficiency into orchestral performances which, up to the time, was virtually unknown. He brought the orchestra to a high degree of technical skill, and his temperament colored all of his performances. Individuality was marked in his interpretations of great music. Under Costa, another significant step was made in the history of orchestral conducting.

5.

It should not be assumed, however, that even with the remarkable strides made by Jullien, Costa and Mendelssohn, conducting had as yet attained the full stature of manhood. Certain growth and development had taken place, to be sure, but conducting was still in the rompers of infancy. Baton technique, for example, was not as yet widely developed. In Berlioz's book on *Instrumentation* (1848) we find an excoriation against audible time-beating, and as late as 1880 Hermann Zopff, in his section on conducting in the *Musikalisches Lexikon,* advises the leader to nail a piece of metal upon the upper edge of the conductor's stand and to tap the beat lightly upon the metal. The conductor, morever, was not, as yet, expected to know his score intimately; François Antoine Habeneck, one of the foremost conductors of his day, directed from a violin part! Rehearsals were still inadequate and superficial. And the function of the *Taktschläger* was still the conductor's paramount task, for even Richard Wagner, in *Über das Dirigiren,* wrote that "the whole duty of a conductor is comprised in his ability to indicate the right *tempo.*"

With Berlioz in France, and in Germany with Liszt and Wagner, conducting took further healthy strides towards artistic liberation. Separately, and in different cities, these three great musicians were going in one definite direction with their sticks. By assigning greater importance to the baton than it had enjoyed heretofore, and by devoting minute pains and effort in rehearsal to phrasing, nuance and dynamics—far more than was formerly customary—Liszt, Wagner and Berlioz definitely brought into being the new era of orchestral conducting.

The orchestra, moreover, had by now developed into that complicated organism perfected by Wagner and Berlioz. New colors had been deftly etched upon its palette; new tone qualities had been discovered; new voices introduced. The conductor could no longer concern himself merely with the correct *tempo*. Problems of sonority and balance now became pressing. It was essential now to have many more rehearsals, and to devote much more fastidious attention to the details of performance. This fastidious attention was given by Berlioz, Liszt and Wagner—and it is because of this that they definitely ushered in the new age of orchestral conducting.

We are informed by those who heard Berlioz, Liszt and Wagner conduct that, from a modern viewpoint, there were obvious defects in their performances. That supreme mastery of the orchestra known by the modern conductor, was not yet in their possession: that ability to command and execute the slightest and the most complicated desires with a gesture and a nod. Moreover, too many exaggerations and dramatics distorted their performances. However, with all their faults, they definitely pointed the way; and an entire school of conductors now arose to follow their footsteps. Beginning with Hans von Bülow—and continuing with such "perfect Wagnerites" as Hans Richter, Gustav Mahler, Anton Seidl, Felix Mottl, Hermann Levi and Dr. Leopold Damrosch—an altogether new type of conductor was now to emerge upon the musical scene. He was no longer a mechanical accessory. He was now the soul and life's breath of the orchestra, its dynamo of energy, its sensitized heart, its contemplative mind. He was now the medium between the music and the performers; and the music, as it coursed through his fingers, now began to acquire new depth, new shapes and new meanings.

"I am now making a thorough study of *Der Freischütz* so that I may know it by heart," Hans von Bülow once wrote before beginning to conduct the Weber opera. "Only when one has thus mastered an opera . . . in which each nuance, each instrument has its special determination and importance, is it possible—so at least I think—to rehearse and conduct it. And this can only be done when one is not obliged to bury one's head in the score."

With these words the new conductor officially makes his bow. He has definitely ceased to be a mere *Taktschläger*. He has now become a fine and sensitive artist.

III

WHAT IS THIS THING CALLED CONDUCTING?

1.

IT IS not an accident that, of all the branches of musical expression, conducting is the only one that has not been kind to the child-prodigy. The baton has never gone well with velvet knee-pants and flowing bow-ties. Violinists like Jascha Heifetz and Yehudi Menuhin, pianists like Josef Hofmann have played the concertos of Bach, Beethoven and Brahms—the profoundest expression that the art of music has produced—with maturity and bewildering comprehension at an age when most children have only just outgrown their diapers. In the creative field, musical history abounds with tales of *wunderkinder* composing penetratingly beautiful music before they have even learned to read or write; need we go further than the case of Wolfgang Mozart who, at the age of ten, could compose an *Adelaide Concerto?* And yet, the times when the conductor's podium was invaded by the child-prodigy have been amazingly few and far between; and, as yet, there exists no instance in which it has been invaded with any convincing degree of artistic success.

Several years ago, musical England was stirred by the feat of Willy Ferrero, the son of a clown, who seemed—while conducting Wagner's *Meistersinger Overture*—to possess such remarkable instinct for orchestral direction that even so eminent a conductor as Sir Landon Ronald was deeply impressed. Further acquaintance with Willy's performance, however, soon revealed that he did not possess any significant musical knowledge, nor even an unusual talent for musical expression but merely an intuitive gift for rhythm. Willy returned to obscurity almost as quickly as he had soared to fame. More recently, tales have floated out of Soviet Russia singing high praises of Margaret Heifetz, a girl of nine (no relation to the violinist) who, on one program, conducted Schubert's *C-Major Symphony,* Rimsky-Korsakoff's *Scheherezade* and Beethoven's *Fifth Symphony* with a surprising degree of competence. But here, once again, there proved to be nothing more than a keen ear and a fine talent for beating time; of musical penetration and interpretative talent there seemed to be practically none.

Why, of all the branches of musical art, have we had no precocious orchestral conductors to impress us with performances as deeply as so many prodigies of the violin and piano have done? The answer should be apparent. Conducting—unlike composition, or the playing of any instrument—demands not merely a native talent for musical expression, but a broad and thorough musical education, an intellectual background, maturity, experience, and integration of personality. It is a subtle and complicated art that can be mastered only—even with all the talent in the world—after arduous training and intensive study.

The music-lover well recognizes the fact—especially in New York and Philadelphia where the system of guest-conductors frequently brings a great and a mediocre conductor to the same platform within a few weeks—that one and the same symphony-orchestra changes its soul completely under the hands of different conductors. Through what means does the conductor cause this transformation? Precisely what are his approach and technique?

Before considering the technique of the conductor it should be remembered that methods often vary with different temperaments, that each conductor, if he possesses individuality, will have his own approach to the task. Who is there to pronounce which is the more potent? There are some conductors who are severe autocrats of the baton who, refusing to recognize that they have human-beings in front

of them, will manipulate their men as though they
were pieces of machinery. These autocrats will
insist that on the concert-platform they be masters of
all they survey, and that their word be the final law.
Thus every phase of the performance, no matter how
negligible, is controlled by them. This, of course,
often leads to marvelous mechanical efficiency in the
technique of an orchestra's playing, and to a conception of interpretation that is unified and whole.
However, our present-day concertgoer, fed with
stories of the despotic rule of Toscanini or Stokowski
over their men, should not be tempted into believing
that this is the only efficacious method for the conductor. Others, whose temperaments do not permit
them to be so dictatorial as Toscanini or Stokowski,
have been equally successful with a far less stringent
policy. Felix Mottl and Artur Nikisch—to point
to two giants of yesteryear—always adopted a more
democratic method with their men. Not merely was
their relationship with their orchestra poised on a
much more human basis, but even in their interpretations the individuality of the players under them
would be taken into account. Felix Mottl, for
example—when the brass section of the orchestra
had a solo passage—would invariably permit the
group freedom in phrasing within certain limitations,
and it is said that in the trombone passage of the first

fortissimo section of *Tannhäuser Overture,* for example, he achieved the most marvelous results. In solo passages of a single instrument, Artur Nikisch would always tell the player how he himself felt the solo part should be performed, but he would always add that "you are perfectly free to play it in any way you wish"; and those who have heard Nikisch conduct the last movement of Brahms' *Fourth Symphony,* the prelude to the last act of *Tristan* or the second movement of Tschaikovsky's *Fifth Symphony* have written of how efficacious this method can be. These conductors—rebelling strongly against the tyrannical rule of other directors—were convinced that, by assigning a certain individuality to their men, they not merely attained a finer cooperation with them but they also succeeded in achieving a much fresher performance.

Methods may vary in other respects as well. A conductor like Toscanini calls for the utmost tenseness on the part of the players when they perform, both at the rehearsal and at the concert; in his opinion, playing tends to become lackadaisical unless the men are nervously rigid throughout the performance of a work. On the other hand, Wilhelm Furtwängler has attained some of his most poignant performances by advising his men to remain completely relaxed and flexible while playing. Some conductors—Karl Muck and Mahler are excellent examples—complete all of their work at the rehearsal to the minutest detail, and at the concert merely beat time and give essential cues. Other conductors—we can point out Stokowski and Koussevitzky—will, in rehearsing a standard symphony or a thrice-familiar symphonic-poem, touch only on important phrases at the rehearsal, and complete the carving of their interpretations at the concert itself. These conductors know well that too much rehearsal can frequently be as dangerous as too little; the orchestra-men, after all, cannot be expected to approach with enthusiasm and zest a piece of music that they have played and replayed at rehearsals until every theme begins to scrape across the nerves.

2.

But although the method that conductors may utilize to exercise their technique may vary with different temperaments, the technique itself always remains the same—calling for certain qualifications, certain proficiency and background, certain aptitude and talent, certain training and education that every outstanding conductor must possess.

At the outset, it might be illuminating to quote what one eminent conductor has said about his art. "A great conductor," in the opinion of Pablo Casals, "must first of all be a great interpreter. The main thing is to have a full, clear comprehension of the works to be performed; perfection can only be reached with hard and constant labor. . . . The important thing is to communicate one's own sensations to the players, and to make one's ideals understandable. To know how to get in touch with others, to be able to convince one's men and impress one's own originality upon them, is in the highest degree a mark of capability in a leader."

To fulfil happily such functions as Pablo Casals has outlined above, the conductor must be endowed with certain qualifications without which he cannot hope to raise a baton successfully. First of all, he should have the faculty of "hearing with his eyes and seeing with his ears." In other words, his aural and visual senses should be so coordinated that, in reading an orchestral score, he should be able to hear it clearly with his mind's ear and know precisely how it should sound in performance; and in performing a work, he should be able to translate the sounds he hears from the notes upon the printed page. This requires a very comprehensive musical background and training that embraces every phase of musical theory. In addition to this faculty, the orchestral conductor should know something of the potentialities and capabilities of every instrument in the orchestra. It is imperative for him to have an insight into its technique so that, in working out his effects, he may know precisely what every instrument can and cannot do, and can explain his intentions much more lucidly to his men. A knowledge of the various instruments gives the conductor the ability to develop sonorities, to attain solid balances and to etch in subtle tone-colors with a much surer and a much more cunning hand.

This, of course, does not imply that the conductor should be able to play every instrument of the orchestra with proficiency. I make a point of this because, at intervals, I have read newspaper stories glorifying some of the more prominent of our conductors that suggested strongly that the conductor could do this. This is so absurd on the face of it that no very eloquent denial should be necessary. As a matter of fact, not merely is there no conductor to my knowledge who can play every instrument in the orchestra well (a conductor like Hans Richter who could play many instruments capably is a phenomenon!), but very frequently a conductor cannot even play his own instrument half so efficiently as the most ordinary musician in his ensemble. I was told, for example, of a Toscanini incident in which, at a rehearsal, the maestro was attempting to obtain a very difficult effect from the violoncellos. In disgust at the failure of the violoncellists to understand his explanations, Toscanini snatched the instrument from one of the men (it must be remembered that Toscanini was originally a violoncellist) and attempted to reproduce the effect he had just explained. The result was a performance so pathetically inferior to even the worst efforts of the violoncellists that the humor of the situation struck even Toscanini.

Accompanying this personal and intimate acquaintance with the technique of the various instruments of the orchestra, must come a thorough knowledge of the musical score. This may sound dangerously like a truism to the average music-lover; the truth, however, is that any number of orchestral performances in our everyday musical experience are robbed of all subtlety and penetration primarily because the conductor is not half so familiar with his music as he should be. A conductor should be so intimate with the music that he is performing that the slightest markings on the printed page are known to him. After all, a conductor who is not thoroughly acquainted with a work, so that every indication of the composer is familiar, is likely to pass over too many of the subtle requirements of the music, and too many of the nuances. It is, moreover, quite impossible to rehearse competently, if one cannot remove the eye from the printed page. This is equally true of performances. At the concert, the conductor who keeps his nose deeply buried in the score cannot expect to dominate his men so completely as the one who is liberated of score and can focus his entire attention upon the players.

This, it should be stated emphatically to avoid any misconceptions, does not imply that conducting from memory is an indispensable requirement. As a matter of fact, conducting from memory can become a very pernicious practise, as I shall point out in a later chapter. Many great conductors realize this and, although they know a work from one cover to the other with marvelous thoroughness, they prefer to keep the book in front of them at the concert because its presence has a reassuring effect upon them.

A keen ear is even more essential to the conductor than a retentive memory. The conductor must be sensitive to different sonorities and tone-colors and, even in climactic passages of great complexity, the ear of the conductor should be sufficiently acute to hear every part of the orchestra clearly, and to be able to recognize that every section is giving voice to the necessary quality and style required for proper balance. Moreover, the conductor must be sharp enough to detect the slightest defect in performance.

A slight change in the rhythmic figure, an almost imperceptible slur of a phrase, the slightest change of dynamics by any one section of performers should strike the conductor as forcefully as a hammer-blow. When we discuss Toscanini we shall see that this is one of his most powerful assets as a conductor—his ability to hear clearly every instrument in the orchestral maze as though it were a performance of a solo.

Almost as important to the conductor as a keen mind and a penetrating ear is versatility. The difference between the genuinely great and the second-rate conductor is very often precisely this ability of the former to play many styles and schools of music with equal effectiveness. The supremely great conductor is essentially a chameleon, changing with every work he conducts; it is only the conductor of lesser stature who is a specialist in one or two styles alone and who—in all other styles—twists the music to conform to his temperament. It is this, I feel strongly, which keeps Richard Strauss from the ranks of truly immortal conductors. In Mozart (who can ever forget his sparkling, magical rendition of *Cosí fan tutte* which, for many years has been the crowning artistic event of the summer festivals in Munich?) he stands with Toscanini and Muck and Nikisch. But in the works of other composers his baton loses its charm and exquisite perfection—and his Wagner, supposedly his second war-horse, is oversentimentalized and overrefined to give a curiously Mozartean conception of the Wagnerian music-drama.[1]

The great conductor can adapt his personality with pliancy so that he can perform a classic symphony of Haydn and Mozart, a romantic symphony of Schumann or Schubert, a tone-poem of Richard Strauss and an atonal piece by Schönberg with equal felicitousness, and in the explicit manner that these different composers require. In playing Mozart, the conductor must be able to retain the classic line, the clean orchestration, the exquisite grace and delicacy without oversentimentalization of melodic lines and overburdening the fragile sonorities. In romantic works, he must suddenly forget his restraint and poise and become glowingly effusive and poetical. And in the moderns, he must be able to give apt expression to the dynamic harmonic schemes of the rebels. I am not suggesting that the greatest conductors of our day can play everything equally well; even the greatest possess a fatal Achilles' heels. But their range is invariably plastic and can span many styles and different schools.

Another infallible sign of the great conduc-

[1] The writer recalls, particularly, a strangely distorted performance of *Tristan* which he heard in Munich under Strauss.

tor—one which has never been sufficiently stressed
by writers on this subject—is his ability to retain his
freshness and enthusiasm for a musical work even if
he has conducted it a lifetime; the great conductor
will never permit familiarity to make him less stringent and exacting in the preparation of a score. The
really great conductor will rehearse Beethoven's
Fifth Symphony or the *Pathétique* of Tschaikovsky
with as much zest, passion and attention to detail as
though it were an altogether new work. Too many
conductors, who lack the divine spark, are tempted
to become lax and disinterested in rehearsing a piece
of music they have performed hundreds of times—
and although in their early performances of these
compositions they revealed enormous talent and
imagination, innumerable repetitions have robbed
them of their enthusiasm with the result that their
performances tend to become somewhat humdrum.
This, to a great degree, is precisely the fault of
Artur Bodanzky, the distinguished conductor of
German opera at the Metropolitan Opera House.
Although originally Bodanzky's performances of
Wagner were distinguished by their vitality and
freshness, continual repetitions have stripped
Bodanzky of his former zest for the music with the
result that, after many years, each performance of
Wagner under Bodanzky became mere routine, leth-

argic and stereotyped. Mr. Bodanzky, I have always felt, is a much more talented conductor than his performances at the Metropolitan would lead us to believe; and those who recall his remarkable work with the Society of Friends of Music—burdened as he was by a very inadequate and tired orchestra—can vouch that, confronted with an unfamiliar work, Mr. Bodanzky often possesses a very potent and eloquent baton.

In conclusion, it should be added that a conductor should always have a very clear conception of his interpretation of each musical work, and should not be satisfied until his performances achieve a full realization of it. He should have a broad vision, the capacity of seeing a work as a whole and not as a sum of so many parts; too many conductors concentrate so forcefully upon details that they fail completely to present a work as a coherent unity. He should be able to impose such discipline upon his orchestra that he can bring it to a point of technical efficiency where he can play upon it as though it were an inanimate instrument. Finally, he should possess a vibrant, dominating personality which, with no effort, can command obedience and respect from a hundred men; he should, as Berlioz has so aptly written, have an inward fire to warm his men and a force of impulse to excite them.

3.

In analyzing the technique of conducting we learn that the designation of *tempo,* and coincidentally rhythm, is still—as it has been in the past—the most important function of the conductor. "When a conductor's *tempo* is wrong," Edvard Grieg once said, "everything else he does is wrong." It should not be assumed that designating the *tempo* and rhythm is quite so elementary a task as it may appear to the casual eye. In modern scores where the *tempo* changes incessantly, where complicated cross-rhythms and polyrhythms are frequent intruders, designating the *tempo* and the rhythm with clarity and firmness becomes very exacting work which requires a keen ear, an alert mind, a decisive baton, and a feeling for *tempo* and rhythm which is almost instinctive.

This instinctive feeling for *tempo* and rhythm can be one of the strongest tools in the technical equipment of the conductor. Time, after all, is something essentially intangible and relative; a profound faculty is required to divine precisely what a composer had in mind when he designated *Andante con moto* or *Allegretto.* To conductors like Toscanini, Weingartner or Muck, a feeling for the exact *tempo* and for precise rhythm is something so deeply ingrained that it is as much of a sense as hearing or seeing. To such conductors *Allegretto* in 2/4 time will always retain precisely the same pace irrespective of what composition they perform or when; time to these conductors is no longer something relative but absolute and certain, and each note in a rhythmic figure however complicated will be given its exact value.

A conductor with a meticulous sense for *tempo* and rhythm is the backbone of every great orchestral performance; the orchestra, under a distinct and infallible beat, can play with self-confidence and assurance, with decisiveness, clarity and accuracy. Such a conductor will not permit his beat to slacken unnecessarily in slow movements (even a conductor as great as Bruno Walter will frequently allow his beat to relent beyond the demands of the score in a lyrical passage), or to accelerate unconsciously in fast ones; always will a rigid balance be maintained. And in complex rhythmic passages there will never be slurring of notes or uneven time values, but the relationship between one note and the next will always be exquisitely maintained.

The great conductor will rarely take liberties with the *tempo* or rhythmic figure designated in the score, although, to be sure, a certain amount of elasticity will always be present; it is only the untalented conductor who will completely disregard the designation in the score and will twist the *tempo* into distorted contours and remould the rhythm in order to bring new effectiveness to a thrice-familiar symphony. For this reason, the great conductor is very sparing in his use of *tempo rubato*.[2] *Rubato* is a marvelously potent tool in the hand of the conductor to heighten effects in the score—but only if used with the utmost discretion. The conductors who know how to use it with discrimination, without twisting the performance of a musical work out of shape, are a handful in number. More often, conductors use *rubato* indiscriminately. Felix Weingartner devoted many pages in his monograph, *Über das Dirigiren,* to its abuse in the hands of third-rate conductors, pointing out how artificial effects through exaggerated *tempi* are the persistent ruin of the performances of so many conductors who had failed to learn that the *rubato* is dangerous as well as effective.

In considering *tempo,* it is not out of place to speak of baton technique, which is a much more significant phase of orchestral conducting than the layman suspects. Great performances are, not only the result of efficient manual manipulations at

---

[2] According to Bekker's Dictionary of *Music and Musicians, tempo rubato* is defined as: "Stolen, robbed—the deviation from strict time giving one note or phrase greater, and others less, duration than the signature calls for."

the concert; and many mediocre conductors are supremely efficient in their technique of the baton. But it is an element whose importance no significant conductor will underestimate. Baton technique should not merely be brought to a point of efficiency where it can outline *tempi* and clarify rhythms with the utmost of ease and lucidity; the great conductor likewise realizes that it can be utilized to heighten effects, etch in nuances and solidify balances while the performance is in progress. And it can have a powerful psychological effect on the men as they play. Elaborate gestures are not essential; as a matter of fact, the greatest conductors of the past and present have been most sparing in their movements. A beat can be given decisively with the slightest motions of the wrist; and, in giving cues for entrance, the long-experienced conductor will be most economical, enlisting them only for the more complex pages. But what is equally important is the fact that with slight suggestions of the hands, it is possible for the great conductor to get telling results during the performance. The electric incisiveness of Koussevitzky's stroke often instils a marvelous energy in his men, and they play with much greater vitality than they would under a less stinging beat; Stokowski and Felix von Weingartner often draw a sensuous *legato* with the beautiful sweep of the left hand; and those who have heard Karl Muck's performance of Beethoven's *Coriolanus Overture* speak of the tremendous opening he produced with his powerful sashweight beat in the first bars of the music. Musicians in modern symphony-orchestras will tell you that a conductor can often inspire and electrify them with his gestures, or else—if he is sloppy and inexperienced in his baton technique—will succeed only in obtaining from them lethargic playing.

Next in importance to *tempo,* comes balance. An orchestra is, after all, composed of many component parts. To blend these various parts into a marvelous tonal unity in which each part is given precisely the emphasis it requires to be fused harmoniously with all the other parts is a task which only a few conductors can achieve with consummate success. Balance is as much of a problem in so fragile a framework as a Haydn or a Mozart symphony, as it is in the grandiose tonal structures of Wagner, Mahler, Richard Strauss or Shostakowitch. In inferior performances, the brass and tympani invariably thunder the other parts of the orchestra out of existence in climactic passages. In great performances, however, there will always be found a vitreous transparency, a crystal-clear distinctness in which the subsidiary sections can be heard as clearly as the major ones, in which there is not one but many voices, each one clearly discernible. It was this that Toscanini was striving for when, at a rehearsal, he made his penetrating, and now-famous observation: "In *fortissimo* passages," he advised his men, "you should be able to hear the next man; in *pianissimo* you should almost be unable to hear yourself."

4.

I have thus far not spoken of the art of interpretation which, after all, is the ultimate goal of the conductor—the end for which technique is only the means. It is apparent that the great conductor must not only be a master of every phase of the technique of conducting, but he must possess an exquisite balance between emotion and intellect, he must be endowed with a deep poetry, a sensitivity to beauty and a cultural outlook that make it possible for him to penetrate deeply into the heart of a musical work and bring its inmost messages, and most latent emotions, to the surface.

As I have already suggested, interpretation of a musical work does not—as so many young conductors delude themselves into believing—consist in distortion of *tempo* and rhythm, caressing of the melodic line until it becomes cloying, exaggeration of dynamics, etc.—which curve a musical work into a shape altogether different from the original intentions of the composer. Interpretation, rather, consists in giving expression to the inner voices of the music, in making the work flow easily, freely and spontaneously, in endowing the melody with freshness, youth and a continuity of line and, finally, in performing a work with a broad understanding of its wholeness, and evolving each effect and nuance so that they do not obtrude from the general plan of the whole.

Interpreting a musical work, in short, does not mean that the conductor should bring to it a new body and face, but rather to give expression to the slightest intention of the composer, and to bring to life his most elusive dream. It was a very eminent musician—it may have been Vincent D'Indy—who once said that the supremely great conductor is the one who has succeeded in bringing out in his performance exactly what is on the printed page—that, no more and no less.

I

VON BÜLOW—HANS RICHTER—
MAHLER

1.

IN OCTOBER 1880, Hans von Bülow—one of the most distinguished piano virtuosos of his time —was appointed *Hofmusikintendant* by the Duke of Meiningen. It was in this post, which included the direction of the Meiningen Orchestra, that von Bülow virtually revolutionized the art of conducting. He was no novice at the stick: As early as 1864 he had been the principal conductor at the Royal Opera House in Munich where he gave distinguished performances of *Tristan und Isolde* and *Die Meistersinger*. But at Meiningen—where for five years he assumed sovereign command over the orchestra of fifty players—he succeeded in definitely establishing conducting as a complex and an important art.

When he entered upon his tenure in Meiningen, von Bülow possessed many firm convictions about the art of conducting. He believed, first of all, that a conductor should not lift a baton unless the work he is performing is indelibly engraved on his mind.

"A score should be in a conductor's head, not the conductor's head in the score," was one of the aphorisms he was fond of quoting and requoting. Aided by a prodigious memory, von Bülow studied each work minutely before conducting it, and was the first conductor to make a periodic practice of conducting without the aid of a score in front of him. Another equally rigid principle in von Bülow's personal conductorial philosophy was that the director of an orchestra should be a martinet, dominating tyrannically over his men and completely subjugating them to his will. Finally, it was his belief that in the interpretation of music a conductor should not be enslaved by the printed page but should permit his temperament and personality to shape the performance; that, far from adhering rigidly to the score, a conductor should take as much liberty with the music, in tempo, phrasing and dynamics, as is essential to give the work renewed effectiveness and a new lease upon life.

We are told by those who heard the Meiningen Orchestra perform under Hans von Bülow that this conductor accomplished something approaching a miracle with his organization. Accustomed to play lackadaisically and frequently incorrectly, this band underwent a complete metamorphosis under von Bülow's baton. His dictatorial mastery over his

HANS VON BÜLOW

men soon succeeded in bringing a mechanical efficiency to the orchestra which was without parallel at the time. And the careful preparation and study, as well as the enormous musicianship, with which von Bülow approached each of his performances brought to the music he directed new lustre and finer qualities. When, therefore, von Bülow and the Meiningen Orchestra toured throughout Germany, it created an unprecedented sensation among audiences who had never before so fully realized the importance of a conductor. Musicians marvelled at the complete dominance which von Bülow's baton exercised over the orchestra, now calling from it the most subtle effects, and now drawing tempestuous climaxes with a hand that never faltered; they commented endlessly on the technical efficiency of a musical machine that seemed to recognize no technical problems and which functioned smoothly, almost inevitably, under the firm and compelling beat of his direction; and they admired the new, bright face that von Bülow's interpretations brought to thrice-familiar classics.

Though von Bülow was a great artist, whose sincerity and genuineness were never doubted, he could also be spectacular in his conducting. His performances invariably wrenched effects from the music in his incessant attempt to emphasize his great individuality—effects that completely revolutionized the original message of the composer; in his valuable monograph, *Über das Dirigiren,* Felix Weingartner indicates some of the amazing liberties that von Bülow took with the *tempi* and phrasing of Beethoven's symphonies. His gestures were extravagantly elaborate, directed more at the audience than at the men. Circus-tricks, however, were also an indispensable element in his art. When he repeatedly had his orchestra perform several classic symphonies from memory,[1] he resorted to merely one of the many stunts in his copious repertoire. He never forgot that there was an audience behind his back. In a particularly effective passage he would frequently turn sharply around while conducting in order to notice his audience's approval. And, like a celebrated conductor of our day, he was irremediably addicted to making speeches before his performances —and very often it was not particularly clear what was the cause for the speech, nor what constituted its essential message. One example will suffice. In a concert in Hamburg which took place shortly after the death of Wilhelm I—a concert in which von

[1] In the Winter of 1934, Eugene Goossens revived the trick by having the Cincinnati Symphony Orchestra perform the Wagner *Meistersinger Overture* from memory. This fact was greatly publicized, without mention being made of the fact that, far from being a radical innovation, it was an almost everyday feat with the Meiningen Orchestra under von Bülow.

Bülow was to conduct Beethoven, and Brahms was to conduct his own music—von Bülow suddenly turned to his audience before beginning to conduct and inexplicably elaborated upon the genius of Felix Mendelssohn, comparing him to Wilhelm I; then, just as mysteriously and irrelevantly, heaping praise upon the genius of Johannes Brahms. "Mendelssohn is dead; the Emperor Wilhelm is dead"; von Bülow whined at the conclusion of his speech. "Bismarck lives; Brahms lives." And then, impetuously, he wheeled sharply around, and his baton descended for the opening bars of Beethoven's *Eighth Symphony*.

Volatile by temperament, unpredictable in his whims and moods, eccentric in his mannerisms, strongly addicted to exhibitionism, and profoundly gifted as a musician, Hans von Bülow was essentially a theatrical conductor of the twentieth century. His influence was far-reaching; he was the all-powerful force in establishing conducting as an art. But, it must be confessed, von Bülow has likewise been a pernicious influence. His method of tampering with the score has created something of a tradition among German conductors which persists until this very day. The frequent use among so many modern German conductors of *"Luftpausen"*—momentary pauses inserted into the texture of a composition to herald the approach of a significant passage—and much of the exaggeration and overstatement that appear in so many performances of classic symphonies can be traced directly to von Bülow. Felix Weingartner has told in his monograph on conducting of an occasion when he heard a performance of Beethoven's *Pastoral Symphony* in Germany in which the conductor inserted a *"Luftpause"* in the second movement breaking the entire continuity of the music. "After the performance," wrote Weingartner, "I tried to convince the conductor of the wrongness of his interpretation, pointing out to him that just as it would be impossible for a rippling brook suddenly to be made to stand still so it was unnatural to interrupt arbitrarily the flow of the music at this point. To my astonishment I got this answer: 'I really don't like it myself, but the people here are so accustomed to it from von Bülow that I must take it the same way.'" With many other conductors, it is not merely a case of yielding to the desires of the public or orchestra-men, but rather a firm conviction on their part that the tradition established by von Bülow in the performance of Beethoven or Brahms is the only true one, and must be adhered to rigidly.

2.

Although the art of conducting took seven-league strides under Hans von Bülow, it became integrated only with Hans Richter.

Hans Richter was Wagner's personal choice as the conductor of his music-dramas. Combining a phenomenal musicianship (it was said that Richter could play any number of orchestral instruments competently), an infallible ear, a retentive memory and a severe artistic integrity, Hans Richter appeared to Wagner as the Moses to lead his music-dramas out of the sterile desert of humdrum performances to which, until then, they had for the most part been subjected. After living with Wagner in Lucerne (1866) where, in the morning, he would copy the score of the *Meistersinger* and, in the afternoon, bring relaxation to the master by performing for him on the organ or piano, Richter served an all-important apprenticeship with the baton by conducting opera in Pesth from 1871 until 1875. His true stature, however, did not become fully apparent until 1876 when he was called upon to inaugurate the first Bayreuth festival.

Short, stubby, altogether unimpressive in appearance—wearing his inseparable skull-cap—Hans Richter did not altogether create a crushing impression at the first rehearsal in Bayreuth when he clambered up to his stand and, in a nervous voice, began to fire the first of his instructions at the men. But it was not long before the players realized forcefully that he was a personality with whom they had to reckon. The fact that he never referred to the printed page—and revealed a bewildering familiarity with every marking in the score—made the musicians look up and take notice of the little man in front of them. Moreover, there was no fumbling or groping as far as the conductor was concerned during the rehearsal. Richter knew precisely what effects he desired as though he had performed the work a lifetime, and knew how to explain himself clearly and succinctly to his men. When there was a doubt in the mind of a musician as how a phrase should be performed, Richter would often snatch the instrument from his hands and show him. This conductor seemed to know everything, seemed to be able to do everything in the realm of music.[2] And he was

[2] Franz Fridberg, a personal friend of Richter, has left us several amazing lines about Hans Richter as a music-student. "Was there no trombonist, Richter laid down his horn and seized the trombone; next time it would be the oboe, the bassoon, or the trumpet, and then he would pop up among the violins. I saw him once manipulating the contra-bass, and on the kettledrums he was unsurpassed. When we—the Conservatory Orchestra—under Hellmesberger's leading, once performed a mass in the Church of the Invalides, Richter sang. How he did sing! . . . I learned to know him on that day, moreover, as an excellent organist."

If this was true of a mere pupil, what then could one say about the mature musician?

HANS RICHTER

mercilessly despotic. The minutest phrases were repeated again and again before they satisfied him with the shape they finally assumed. To players formerly accustomed to listless, apathetic, uncertain direction, Hans Richter's minute fastidiousness to details was something of a revelation. And there were thirty-six rehearsals (a rehearsal consumed an entire day!) before this exacting conductor pronounced the *Ring des Niebelungen* ready for performance.

But what most aroused the musicians to wonder, at those early rehearsals in Bayreuth, was the manner in which—by some inexplicable magic of personality —Hans Richter elevated them to spheres of greatness which they had never before known. This droll, chubby fellow—who, at first sight, presented an almost ludicrous aspect when his beard and baton beat time together in rhythmic accompaniment—no longer seemed so comical when he was conducting. He was like a dynamo, and with his magnificent fire he converted the efforts of his musicians into electric energy. And when, in a particularly inspiring passage—the awakening of Brünnhilde by Siegfried's kiss, the dismissal of Brünnhilde from Valhalla or the cataclysmic music that accompanies Siegfried's bier—he would stand in front of them, his muscles tense and drawn, his eyes aflame as though they had been pierced by lightning, singing half-audibly the principal orchestral part, the musicians felt an altogether new inspiration infused into them. The men, at those initial performances at Bayreuth, repeatedly confessed that Richter's personality at those rehearsals had the effect of uplifting and intoxicating them as they played.

There could be little doubt that the high artistic success of that first Bayreuth festival was principally the result of Hans Richter's genius. "If Napoleon's presence with his troops was worth, as Wellington said, an army corps of 20,000 men, what is the value in an orchestra of this emperor of conductors?" asked a critic in the *London Daily Telegraph* (May 9, 1879). "We cannot appraise it, but we can feel the influence of Richter's supreme mastery; of his all-embracing *coup d'oeil,* of his perfect resource and, not less, the confidence with which he must infuse his followers. Hans Richter is a 'conductor' of verity, and we are glad to have him amongst us as an example."

Bayreuth was the inauguration not merely of a world-famous festival but also of a magnificent career for its conductor. In London, where took place the enormously successful "Richter concerts," the conductor emphatically established himself for his public as something of an idol. It was quite true—as many of his contemporaries commented—that in new music Hans Richter's baton was not very eloquent. He became bewilderingly self-conscious and pedantic—and it is told authoritatively that when he first conducted Brahms' *First Symphony,* Brahms himself viciously attacked the conductor for his stilted and humdrum *tempi.* But in familiar territories—Beethoven and Wagner particularly—Richter was an unquestionable monarch.

The fact that he conducted an entire historical series of orchestral concerts, "From Bach to Brahms," entirely from memory, first aroused the awe and admiration of the audiences. Richter's unostentatiousness in gesturing—he employed an incisive beat in which no movement of the arm was more elaborate than the pressing of the left hand against the heart in tender passages—his sincerity, integrity and humility further endeared him as a personality. His exquisitely refined performances in the classics (it was apparent even to the layman that under his baton the orchestra was completely transfigured, and played as though it were under some magic spell!) incited the wonder of all music-lovers.

Hans Richter became in London something of a legendary figure, and his name inspired myth and adulation. The conductor-idol was now an institution in musical life.

3.

It was with Gustav Mahler that the art of conducting was brought to the very threshold of our day. The last word in conductorial autocracy, Mahler was a vicious martinet with the baton. Supremely sure of himself, magnificently confident that his conception of the great musical works was the only true one—and burdened by a savage conscience that would never permit him to tolerate any compromises with his ideals—Mahler insisted upon being complete lord over his musical domain. He demanded full dictatorial powers wherever he raised his baton. When he was the conductor in Prague, he resigned peremptorily from a very profitable position—willing to accept unemployment and poverty—only because his commands were not followed out to the letter. Several years later, he resigned once again from a highly lucrative post in Vienna because Francis Joseph, the emperor, insisted that a favorite tenor of his—whom Mahler had pensioned because he was too old to fulfil his position satisfactorily—be reinstated. And Mahler could be as tyrannical with audiences as with his directors and musicians, and whenever their conduct disturbed the performance he would turn sharply around on the platform

GUSTAV MAHLER

and give them a thorough verbal lashing that was not soon to be forgotten.

Musicians who played under Mahler tell us that his magnetic eyes, his square jaw, his lashing tongue and his stinging beat instilled fear in the heart of everyone who sang or played under him. Paul Stefan, quoting J. B. Foerster, informs us that "his solo rehearsals with singers were almost dreaded. . . . With inexorable severity and the fiery zeal that always possessed him, he demanded the utmost exactitude in the rhythm of the music. . . ." And yet, though the singers and musicians feared him, and were terrified at his anger, they were at the same time exhilarated and inspired by his enormous idealism. There was no mistaking Mahler's glowing nympholepsy. When he first assumed the conductorship of the Budapest Opera, he came to the first rehearsal with the following plea on his lips: "Let us dedicate ourselves heart and soul to the proud task that is ours. Unwavering fulfilment of responsibilities by each individual and complete subjection of self to the common interest—let this be the motto we inscribe on our banner. Expect no favoritism from me. If I may pledge myself to one thing today it is this: I shall endeavor to be an example to you in zeal and devotion and duty." Conductors before Mahler, and after him, have made pretty

123

speeches on approaching a new assignment; but
none ever meant them more deeply than he. He
was always a flaming example to his performers of
zeal and devotion and duty; for every ounce of
energy he expected his musicians to expend, he contributed a pound. His men always realized this and,
for this reason, their fear of him was mingled with
enormous admiration and affection.

Mahler was a firm believer in accomplishing everything at the rehearsal, and leaving nothing to chance
at the performance. His rehearsals, therefore, were
undescribably exacting, and he worked his musicians
until they were limp with fatigue. At the concert,
he would permit the music to progress by itself,
whipped on by the fiery magnetism of his baton—as
he yielded to something of a delirium which made
him altogether oblivious to the artists in front of him
or the audience behind his back.

In discussing Mahler's many extraordinary qualities as a conductor, Paul Stefan informs us that he
"had an aim which only Wagner before him had
sought with such tenacity to attain: Distinctness.
The experience of many years had given him un-
erring knowledge of the capabilities of every instrument, of the possibilities of every score. Distinctness, for him, was an exact ratio of light and shade.
His *crescendi,* his storms, growing from bar to bar,

now taking breath for a moment, now crashing into *fortissimo;* his climaxes, obtained by the simplest means; his whispering *pianissimo;* his instinct for the needful alternation of tranquillity and agitation; his sense of sharpness of the melodic line; all these were elements which equally went to make up his power. Added to this were his outward attention to and inward hearing of details, hidden secondary parts and nuances which others hardly noticed in the score, and lastly a hypnotic power of will over all who had to hear and obey."

Perhaps the severest criticism that has been levelled at Mahler as conductor was the liberties which he, like his contemporary von Bülow, took with whatever work he performed. He not only remodelled orchestration when he sincerely felt that it was defective, but he also reconstructed an entire plan of a work so that it acquired a new personality and character than the ones conceived by the composer. He was viciously opposed to tradition. "There is no such thing as tradition," he once said, "only genius and stupidity." As a result, he persistently attempted to improve upon the work he was conducting, rather than follow in the footsteps of other conductors; and, it must be added, not always did he succeed. For this idiosyncrasy, Mahler suffered considerable abuse at the hands of contemporary critics.

However, even when the necessary subtractions are made, Mahler remains one of the geniuses of the baton. Even his most critical listener had to confess that in Mozart and Wagner he was supreme. Wherever he came to conduct, he left his unmistakable fingerprints—in the form of performances of electrifying quality. We are told by his contemporaries that even when he was compelled, during his career, to conduct orchestras of a third-rate quality, his genius ultimately transformed them, and he emerged with magnificent, unforgettable performances.

"There are no bad orchestras; there are only bad conductors." No one proved this more emphatically than Gustav Mahler himself.

II

"THE INCOMPARABLE NIKISCH"

1.

"HE IS the chosen one among the elect," Franz Liszt once wrote. He was speaking of Artur Nikisch—Nikisch, a name that was like a flame across the musical sky for more than three decades. Artur Nikisch, often called "the incomparable," who, at the height of his fame, was subject to such adulation that even his fingertips and the romantic crop of his hair were rhapsodized in poetry; who brought to music his hot Hungarian blood and made it boil with tempestuous emotions.

Considered by many, one of the supremely great conductors of his time, he was likewise one of the most fascinating personalities to step upon the concert-stage. When he stood in front of his orchestra he was a portrait of elegance. True, nature had handicapped him; he was short and solid and, therefore, not altogether impressive at first glance. But his grace and carriage and manner soon atoned for his physical shortcomings. His elegantly curved back, his soft poetical and romantic eyes, his majestic gestures were all subject for romanticizations. The delicately poised hands, encircled at the wrists by lace-cuffs that puffed somewhat foppishly from out the sleeves of his dinner coat, were world-famous, and frequently commented upon. The elegance of his baton! "The expressive suppleness of his stick," commented that celebrated English conductor, Adrian C. Boult, "has been an example to many conductors. It seemed part of himself, and appeared to grow out of his thumb as if made of flesh and blood." And his lambent readings of musicial masterpieces—splashed with the intense color of his personality—aroused the wildest enthusiasm.

As a child in Hungary (where he was born in 1855), Nikisch disclosed a most precocious bent for music. At the age of three he could evoke agreeable tunes from the piano, and at seven he could write from memory piano arrangements of well-known Rossini overtures. When he entered the Vienna Conservatory (he was then only a boy of eleven), he revealed so great an aptitude for his studies that he was soon placed in the highest class, to rub elbows and exchange lessons with students ten years his senior.

While studying at the Conservatory, Nikisch had the opportunity to play several times under the baton of Richard Wagner and to learn what fiery

ARTUR NIKISCH

zeal and conscientious art can accompany the baton.
His first contact with Wagner was at a concert of
the Vienna Conservatory Orchestra to which the
great composer had been invited as guest. After the
concert, three students of the orchestra were elected
to present the master with a goblet; and by one of
those inexplicable curiosities of Fate, all three boys
later became world-famous Wagnerian conductors
—Emil Paur, Anton Seidl, and Artur Nikisch. In
1872, Nikisch performed a second time under Wagner, this time at Bayreuth, in a performance of Beethoven's *Ninth Symphony* which commemorated the
laying of the cornerstone of the festival-theatre.

When Nikisch reached man's estate, he left the
Conservatory to become a member of the Vienna
Hofkapelle where for three years he received a rigorous and valuable training under such conductors as
Liszt and Brahms. Young and plastic, he was considerably influenced, no doubt, by the passionately
warm interpretations of Liszt and the romantic expressions of Brahms; and it is more than probable
that his future romantic outlook on musical masterpieces stems from this apprenticeship.

It was at this time that Felix Otto Dessoff, a conductor in Vienna, befriended Nikisch and became so
attracted by this young man's unmistakable musical
gifts that he wrote to Angelo Newmann (the impres-

sario, who devoted himself so passionately to the cause of Wagnerian music-drama) recommending the young musician in no uncertain terms. The result was that, in 1877, Nikisch came to the Leipzig Opera as chorus-master. Here, once again, his amazing talent won many devoted friends among those high in power; his incredible memory which seemed to remember every page of the Wagnerian scores, and his often penetrating suggestions to the conductors on matters of interpretation aroused considerable admiration and comment. It was decided, therefore, to give the young man an opportunity to prove his mettle, and with the written consent of Newmann—who, at the time, was away from Leipzig—Nikisch was assigned to conduct one performance of *Tannhaüser*.

The exhilaration that Nikisch must have experienced in seeing a life-long dream suddenly fulfilled was soon enough to be smothered. The orchestramen, humiliated that they were soon to be compelled to take orders from a boy of twenty-three, vigorously opposed the forthcoming performances and grumblingly announced that, should the management press the issue, they would all resign. Nikisch's great opportunity seemed to hang by a single hair when Angelo Newmann's instinctive diplomacy and tact came to the rescue. Informed of the precarious

situation at his opera-house, Newmann wired from
Vienna to the orchestra that if it would permit the
young man to rehearse merely the overture, it could
then decide whether it wished him to conduct the
remainder of the opera or not; and the decision would
be rigidly upheld by the management.

This seemed to be an equitable arrangement, and
the orchestra entered the rehearsal determined to
resign as a body if the management did not adhere
to the bargain. What followed at the first rehearsal
was the miracle which, every once in a while, performers of symphony-orchestras witness. Nikisch
brought a new quality and depth to the music; under
his magic baton, the work was suffused with a glow
and warmth, tenderness and magic which it now
seemed to possess for the first time. The rehearsal
continued for two hours, as the overture underwent
the microscopic dissection of a keen intellect and a
sensitive heart. Then the men could restrain themselves no longer. They rose and cheered Nikisch,
and some of the older men in the orchestra—who
had never before realized that this music possessed
such subtle voices—had tears in their eyes. The
former rebellion now seemed strangely absurd to
the orchestra-men; and when, that afternoon, they
came for a second rehearsal they were determined
to work their fingers to the bone for this new, be-

wildering conductor whose work bore so indisputably the mark of true genius.

Artur Nikisch's sensational debut came on February 11, 1878. His triumph with each succeeding appearance was so emphatic that, the following year, he supplanted Josef Sucher as principal conductor of the Leipzig Opera.

The reign of Artur Nikisch was soon to begin. It was not long before his elegant appearance, his instinctive flair for showmanship and his genius were to arouse the adoration of his public in Leipzig. When, in 1879, he performed Schumann's *Fourth Symphony* no less a critic than Clara Schumann became rhapsodic in her praise of Nikisch's art. "If only Robert could have heard your performance," she told the conductor. "He never realized that the work could sound this way!" When Nikisch rehearsed a Brahms symphony, revising certain aspects of the score which he felt required improvement, Brahms cried out: "Is it possible, did I really compose this?" Then, when Nikisch had completed his rehearsal, Brahms came to him, his face beaming, and clenched the conductor's hands in his own. "You do it all quite different, but you are right. It simply must be so!"

And Nikisch could be sensational not only with magnificent performances. He knew as well the value of showmanship. And so, at one time (1885) he conducted unfamiliar works by Liszt from memory, creating a sensation with this feat; and at another performance he suddenly interrupted a work to scold a lady in the front row for staring at him during the performance. He was meticulous about his personal appearance, and always fastidious that his movements should possess symmetry, poise and elegance. As a result, Nikisch aroused the imagination and inspired discussion as few conductors before him succeeded in doing. In a bewilderingly brief period, he was accepted by both the general public and the foremost musicians of the time as one of the great conductors of the period.

"The Leipzig Opera may well be proud of its gifted young Kapellmeister," wrote Tschaikovsky in his day-book, in 1887. "His conducting has nothing in common with the effective and, in its own way, inimitable manner of Hans von Bülow. In the same degree in which the latter is nervous, restless and effective through the eccentric methods he employs, Herr Nikisch is quiet, economical in regard to superfluous movement but extraordinarily commanding, mighty and thoroughly self-controlled. He does not merely direct, but yields to a mysterious spell. One hardly notices him, for he makes no effort to attract attention to himself, and yet, nevertheless, one feels that the orchestral body, like one instrument, is in the hands of a remarkable master, is thoroughly under his control, willing and submissive."

In 1889, Nikisch came to America for the first time, to conduct the Boston Symphony Orchestra. The technical efficiency of the orchestra so delighted him that, at the first rehearsal, he cried out: "All I have to do is to poetize!" And while he poetized with singular eloquence for the next four seasons, his full stature as an artist was not fully appreciated. The audiences who, at first, crowded the hall to hear his great performances soon cooled in their ardor, and then became uninterested. There followed numerous disagreements between conductor and management, petty feuds and dissensions over the artistic policy of the orchestra, hot clashes of temperament. Finally, Nikisch offered five thousand dollars to be released from his contract. He returned to Europe to accept the most important post towards which an orchestra leader of the 'Nineties could aspire. And it was in this position—as the conductor of the historic Leipzig Gewandhaus Orchestra which he held with unprecedented glory until the end of his life (1922)—that Nikisch attained his flaming reputation.

His reputation with the Gewandhaus soared and

swelled to such an extent during his first decade as its conductor that when Nikisch returned to America in 1912—in a nation-wide tour with the London Symphony Orchestra—it was no longer as an unappreciated artist that he was accepted but as the most glamorous conductor of the day. Newspapers spread his picture across the front-page, speaking of him as the "$1,000 a night conductor." Poems were dedicated to him in the press:

> *Have you heard of Artur Nikisch,*
> *Of his poise and manner slickish. . . .*

Legends were created about his phenomenal memory (Nikisch conducted his American concerts without a score), his profound musicianship (it was rumored that he had helped many of the important composers of the day in their most famous works!) and his impressive personality. He was stopped in the streets by sentimental admirers who would kiss his hand; and at the concerts he could not escape from the adulation of a mob that would embrace him. And critics, formerly so indifferent, were unable now to summon sufficient encomiums with which to describe his magnificent art.

Such adulation and appreciation were to dog Nikisch's footsteps wherever he raised his baton. Not only in Germany and America, but also in France,

England, Hungary and Austria he was accepted as one of the immortal conductors of the day, to be compared only to Karl Muck. That position he held until his death. And there are still many— remembering the warm pulse that throbbed in his performances—who feel that, at his best, he was truly "incomparable."

2.

It was Artur Nikisch's firm belief that music, far from being an intellectual pleasure, should stir the blood and quicken the heart-beat as wine does. A conductor, he felt strongly, must approach a musical work, not with classical aloofness, but with all the passion and romanticism that he can summon to his command. Thus Nikisch was at his greatest in performing Tschaikovsky and Liszt. During rehearsals he would vigorously stamp his foot upon the ground and cry out: "More fire, gentlemen, more blood!" And with his powerful eye and bold beat he would stir his men into an emotional intensity that would enable them to play with all the fire that was within them.

It is for this reason that—as critics pointed out more than once—the persistent use of *rubato,* and sentimentalizations of the melodic content of a work, were frequent with Nikisch. But, we are also informed, Nikisch had such an exquisite sense for form and design that he could reconstruct an entire work to conform to his romantic interpretations, and always did he maintain a marvelous balance among the various sections of a composition. In works that called for such romantic treatment, Nikisch was, no doubt, "incomparable." The music under him seemed to be infused with a new breath of life, seemed to possess an altogether new soul as many of the composers themselves have since testified.

Nikisch was a master in producing orchestral effects. Dramatic passages under his hands stung and lashed like a crackling whip. He could tear a *crescendo* from the throat of his orchestra that would burst upon the audience like a volcanic eruption. At other moments he could reduce the orchestra to a contemplative repose which never faltered under his fingers. His *pianissimo* possessed a sensitivity that never cracked under the strain of its fragility. His tone could sing with a pure, glowing warmth. Nikisch seemed able to cull every effect he desired from the orchestra with the slightest gesture and with the piercing expression of his eyes.

Moreover, Nikisch seemed to endow every work he conducted—even after a hundredth repetition—with youth and freshness and bright face. It was said that he never read a work twice alike. In giving a performance of a Beethoven or a Tschaikovsky symphony or a Wagner fragment, which he had played more times than he could count, he would restudy the work for new effects and new approaches, and thereby would invariably succeed in retaining a marvelous spontaneity and enthusiasm in his interpretation.

Always more interested in enthusiasm and freshness of performance than in technical perfection, Nikisch never was scrupulously thorough at the rehearsal. He would explain his conception of a work as a whole, would tersely explain his intentions to his men, and would then go through random passages of the score that, he felt, required special treatment. At the concerts he would complete his work. He could accomplish miracles with the most fragmentary rehearsals, because he required only a few explanations to impart his intentions to the men and because at the concert he could accomplish so much with facial expressions, with manual gestures and with the force of his personality. It gives us a peculiarly illuminating insight into the importance with which Nikisch regarded his work at the concert when we understand that one of his most effective methods was to exaggerate every effect of the score at the rehearsal and then, at the concert, to pare down his interpretation to the proper line and balance.

Great though Nikisch was, it cannot be said that he was without faults. His rigid conservatism deafened him to the most important tendencies in the music of his time, and his programs were too often reactionary and stereotyped; it was only his friendship with Liszt and Brahms and Tschaikovsky that brought their music to his concerts. Moreover, Nikisch's musical tastes, it must be confessed, were not of the purest. It was characteristic of his standards that he should have given such exaggerated importance to the music of Tschaikovsky throughout his entire career, and that he so persistently should perform such shoddy music as Weber's *Invitation to the Waltz,* and the Hungarian rhapsodies, the *Les Préludes* and the *Mephisto Waltz* of Liszt. Finally, Nikisch's fiery romantic temperament and hot romantic blood were strongly out of place in the classical works of Haydn and Mozart. In his own territory—and his own territory was by no means a limited one!—Nikisch was of Gargantuan stature, head and shoulders above the majority of the conductors of his time. It was only when he strayed to foreign pastures that Nikisch proved that even a conductor so great as he could have vital shortcomings.

139

3.

Much of Nikisch's enormous success in completely subjugating his men to the will of his smallest finger, arose from an instinctive tact which he possessed in his relationship with them. Feeling with conviction that he could derive the most felicitous results from the orchestra if it were sympathetic to him, Nikisch always treated his players with the utmost civility, and with a great consideration for their individuality. He could be the supreme diplomat. Never the disciplinarian nor the unreasonable school teacher, he had an uncanny ability in making the men believe that they were playing their own interpretations when they were, in truth, following out his intentions to the letter. If any of the men disagreed with him concerning his views on a certain phrase or a passage he would, far from losing his temper, gently turn to them and, confessing that there was much to be said for their opinion, would add: "But, gentlemen, listen just once more to my conception and you will see how much more effective it really is!"; and by his gentle but firm powers of persuasion he would always bring his men to his camp. Or else, he would tactfully revise their interpretations until, before long, they became synonymous with his own. However, in the performance of solo passages of sym-

140

phonies he always gave the player full liberty to express his own personality and, although ready with advice, he would never attempt to impose his own will severely upon the performer; on the contrary, he would put down his baton and listen to the solo performance with the eager attention of an admirer.

Nikisch was unusually considerate at the rehearsal. In difficult passages he was supremely patient with mistakes, and it was well known that he rarely lost his temper. When one of the players had an unusually difficult passage, he would never glance in his direction for fear of making him nervous. He was rarely angry, rarely temperamental, and never unreasonable. Seldom did he raise his voice. Only infrequently, in the heat of rehearsing, he would attempt to arouse his men by shouting his desires at them excitedly and nervously. But even at such moments, when the passage came to an end, he would once again assume his customary poise and explain to the men quietly and patiently how to improve upon their performance.

And Nikisch could be unusually appreciative of the efforts of his men. There were times when the orchestra played with unusual brilliance or beauty at the rehearsal. On such occasions, Nikisch would put down his baton and listen to the playing of the orchestra with rapt attention, his face beaming with

141

sunshine. We are told that there were times when, at the end of the performance, the tears would stream down his face. And more than once did he say to his orchestra: "You played it so beautifully, gentlemen! Please—please play it once again for me!"

Many of the players employed in Nikisch's orchestras have published articles in which they have described the enormous faculty of this conductor to inspire them with unprecedented enthusiasm for music. Truth to tell, the men adored Nikisch, and because of him they adored their work. It has been written by one of these musicians, that, at one time, while rehearsing Tschaikovsky's *Fifth Symphony* in London—after an unusually strenuous day in which many other compositions were rehearsed as well— Nikisch stopped for a moment in the midst of the symphony to inquire of the men if they would prefer a short respite of ten minutes for relaxation and a smoke. He had, however, so fascinated each one of them with his interpretation of the Tschaikovsky symphony, and had so infused them with enthusiasm and zest for their work that almost unanimously the orchestra entreated him not to give them the intermission.

Certainly, greater flattery than this knows no conductor.

III

KARL MUCK—AN AMERICAN TRAGEDY

1.

NOTHING can so forcefully illustrate how two opposing methods of conducting can bring equally distinguished results than a contrast of Artur Nikisch with his celebrated contemporary, Dr. Karl Muck. These two conductors who, between them, virtually dominated the field of orchestral conducting for more than two decades, were opposite poles in the conductorial cosmos. A glance at their respective faces will reveal what a chasm separated their personalities. The one possessed soft features, deep poetic eyes, gentle slope of cheekbones and lips of expressive suppleness; the other has tense muscles, eyes of penetrating sharpness, lips with hard corners, and an assertive chin that speaks power.

And as their faces, so their temperaments. Nikisch was the unashamed romanticist who throughout his entire life revealed an almost boyish effusiveness and sentiment, while Muck was always the stern and rigid classicist. Nikisch conducted with a baton through which poured the turbulence of his emotions, while Muck's readings are carefully guided by a penetratingly analytical mind. Nikisch was essentially the poet, and his music was warmed by his Hungarian blood; Muck is the scientist, whose dissecting mind guides all of his interpretations.

Their methods are equally at divergent points. Nikisch's attitude in his relationship with his men could never be adopted by an artist of Muck's temperament. He is essentially the Prussian in his autocratic dominance over his players, and in his demand for military discipline. The supreme master of every situation, he is disinterested in the men as human-beings but manipulates them as though they are automatons. It is said of Muck's rehearsals that they are like a battlefield in which he is general and in which every movement and act is strictly routinized. Certainly, the most stringent discipline is imposed by him, and he can be merciless in the face of disobedience. He has a stinging tongue, an acid sense of humor, a satire more pointed than the end of a needle. It is well-known, for example, how at one rehearsal in Bayreuth he turned his rump informally toward the tuba-players and exclaimed: *"Ich kann damit viel besser spielen!"* ("I can play with this much better!"). His criticisms are often

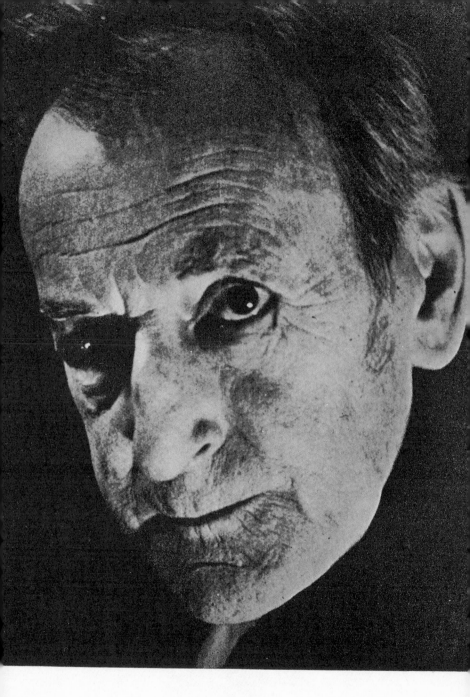

KARL MUCK.

scathing. His men at the rehearsal are always in fear of him, always on edge—and it is for this reason, possibly, that he has succeeded in getting so much out of them in concentration and effort.

Nikisch's method of resorting to superficial rehearsal, with the final work completed at the concert, has likewise been impossible with Muck. His mind is too meticulously scientific for so haphazard a procedure. Muck's rehearsals have worn a composition threadbare. Each phrase is placed under the magnifying glass of his profound musical scholarship, and before Muck brings his men to the concert platform each bar of music has been worked out carefully and deliberately so that, during the performance, he does nothing more than beat time.

As a conductor, Muck's outstanding trait has been his keen intellect, his well-disciplined and precise mind that has been reflected in each of his performances. Whenever he performs a work, he studies his score as a student might, examining, dissecting, analyzing. Unlike Nikisch, he cannot permit his emotions to guide him, but depends entirely upon his fine critical sense and his enormous intellectual background. His interpretations are carefully worked out from the score, and each effect evolved naturally and inevitably from the texture of the music. His conceptions are always coherent and balanced. And his cultural background has brought to his readings a richness and depth and maturity which are too often lacking in the performances of other conductors. When he performs Bach or Beethoven or Wagner, it is not merely tones that are given expression, but experiences and ideas.

It should not be assumed that, because his interpretations are so carefully studied and prepared, that Muck's performances are cerebral. His intellectual and emotional forces blend harmoniously, and he is capable of great sensitivity, refinement and beauty. Muck has within him a vital power that is uncontrollably dynamic. The music under his hand derives from it a brisk accentuation and a vital moving force which always make it electrically alive. A sense for rhythm that is meticulously perfect, an infallible ear, an exquisite feeling for form, an ability to impart his lessons crisply and lucidly, and a profound reverence for great art are other qualities which have brought him greatness.

A dynamo of energy, Muck is capable of enormous work, even though he is today an old man. He never seems to require mental relaxation or physical recess. From the moment rehearsals begin until they end, he devotes every ounce of effort that is within him, and demands the same from every player. In Bayreuth, in 1930, I attended Muck's

rehearsals of *Parsifal* and marveled at the enormous
energy that he possessed. From ten o'clock in the
morning until evening, he was indefatigable—a
nervous force persistently driving him on. And
then—while the orchestra-men emerged from the
theatre bent with exhaustion—he would remain on
the stage for conferences with the singers to review
with them their respective parts.

Perhaps the most characteristic attribute of Muck
as an artist has been his fierce honesty. His sincerity
and integrity can never be subject to question. For
this reason, his first law as a conductor has been a
strict allegiance to the score. He cannot, as Nikisch
too frequently did, mould the music to suit his whims,
and he can never permit himself the luxurious freedom of changing a single phrase or a rhythmic
figure of a musical work; always unswervingly true
to the composer, he feels forcefully that a conductor
is primarily an interpreter, and not an editor. For
this reason, too, he can never pander—as Nikisch did
more than once—to an audience. Muck has always
been the scrupulously sincere artist who, in the face
of his art, was oblivious of his public and could never
exploit it to glorify his own personality. As a result,
he utilizes the simplest possible gestures in his conducting, avoiding any suggestion of spectacle or
display; and occasionally, when he felt that his mar-

velously drilled orchestra did not require his beat, he would put down the baton and permit the men to perform without any guidance. Simplicity and unostentatiousness have always characterized his work; humility, his personality.

Where art was concerned, Muck has had a severe conscience which never permitted him to practise duplicity or hypocrisy. It was this savage honesty with himself and his art that brought Muck the major tragedy of his great career—the American tragedy.

2.

As we look back upon the War episode from the comfortable perspective of almost two decades and with a vision unblurred by the hysterics of a mob, we realize that it was we, and not Muck, who emerged from the incident in disgrace.

When Muck came to Boston in 1905, at the invitation of Henry Lee Higginson he had already acquired an enviable reputation with his baton. He was born in Darmstadt in 1859. Academic studies were, at first, his major interest, and having attended the Universities of Heidelburg and Leipzig he emerged with a doctorate degree. His initiation into music, as a profession, occurred in his twenty-first year as a concert-pianist. Solo performances, however, dissatisfied him, and he turned to conducting as a much richer medium for artistic self-expression. His early training was pursued in Salzburg, Brünn and then Prague. In 1889, his powerful performances of Wagner first aroused admiration in Russia, whither Muck had come with Angelo Newmann's itinerant Wagnerian company. It was not until 1892, however, that his true greatness was perceptible; in that year he was appointed Kapellmeister of the Royal Opera in Berlin, and his work was so distinguished that a nation-wide attention was focused upon him. From that time on his fame assumed gigantic stature, particularly at Covent Garden (1899) with his interpretations of the great Wagnerian music-dramas, and with the Philharmonic concerts of Vienna (1903) in the symphonic repertoire. When, therefore, he came to America for his first visit, in 1905, he trailed behind him a great and successful career, and he was welcomed in Boston at the time as one of the foremost batonists of the day.

In Boston he was to scale even greater heights during his two periods as principal conductor of the orchestra. His unrelenting discipline brought the orchestra to a technical assurance it had not known even with Wilhelm Gericke; and his genius as interpreter—as well as his alert experimentalism which placed upon his programs the foremost representatives of contemporary musical expression—made his concerts artistic events of first importance. It was well recognized by American music-audiences that, under Karl Muck, the Boston Symphony Orchestra had become the first orchestra in America, and possibly in the world; and their appreciation was commensurate with his importance. There was hardly a dissenting voice among American music-lovers in that choir which perpetually sang his praises.

But that was before the sombre days of 1914.

When Karl Muck came to America from the War Zone, in 1915, to fulfil his contractual obligations with the Boston Symphony Orchestra, he was met at the boat by a newspaper reporter who wished to interview him on the subject of the Belgian atrocities. With his customary honesty, Muck—far from attempting to equivocate—frankly told the reporters that he could not believe that his countrymen could be capable of such exaggerated bestialities. It was to be expected that the newspapers should spread Muck's words across the front pages. And when, a few days later, Muck conducted his first program, which—perhaps by coincidence, as Muck later asserted—was devoted entirely to the German classics, grumblers asserted that Muck was using the popularity of his personality and the genius of his baton to spread German propaganda in America;

that, as a matter of fact, Muck was in the employ of
the Kaiser to bring America to German support.

But, though implications were strong and insinu-
ations dark during the year that followed—hinting
at Muck's political associations with the Fatherland
—his position was tolerable only so long as America
remained a neutral country. When America officially entered the conflict, Muck suddenly found
himself in a difficult and trying situation—in the
very centre of a maelstrom. Accused long before
this of being a German agent, Muck discovered that
these formerly silly accusations and pointed fingers
could become painfully embarrassing. Newspapers,
through subtle innuendo, began to drip poison into
the minds of American patriots. They singled out
the fact that Muck was German by birth and, a very
intimate friend of the Kaiser to boot. The question
was not, at first, directly posed by the newspaper
stories, but it lurked all too obviously between-the-
lines: Were we to nurse an enemy in our very midst?

In vain did Muck attempt to answer the insinu-
ations published by the newspapers. It was true that
he was a German by birth but he proved that he was
a Swiss—and not a German—through naturaliza-
tion; how, then, could he be regarded as an enemy?
As for his friendship with the Kaiser, did not the
newspapers know well (and, at the time, publicize

the fact) that he had had serious altercations with the Kaiser which, finally, led him to resign from his important post as the director of the Royal Opera in Berlin? These arguments were brushed aside, and the newspapers—summoning their strength—hurled one stinging question at the somewhat bewildered conductor. Was it not true, they asked, that in his sympathies Muck was intensely pro-German? Muck, far too honest to dissemble explained that— although he could not be reasonably expected to hate the Germans who were his dearest friends, his relatives and his closest associates—he sincerely felt an artist was not a politician and could, in his behaviour and speech, maintain a strict neutrality. The editors, too bent upon destruction to follow the subtle line of his reasoning, seized upon this answer and hurled it, in a garbled form, across the country. Flaming headlines now announced the fact that Dr. Karl Muck, by his own confession, acknowledged the fact that his sympathies rested entirely with the Fatherland.

It required now the slightest spark to ignite the waiting dynamite. Shortly before a concert which the Boston Symphony Orchestra was scheduled to give in Providence, Rhode Island, on October 30, 1917, a demand was made by the citizens of Providence through telegrams and newspaper editorials

that Dr. Muck preface his concert with a performance of the *Star Spangled Banner*. "It is as good a
time as any," spoke the editorial of the *Providence
Journal*, "to put Prof. Muck to the test." Muck,
whose courage could be matched by his artistic
sincerity, refused vigorously to perform the national
anthem, maintaining that poor music had no place
upon the program of a serious symphony-concert,
even in time of war.

Then the storm broke about Muck's head with
thunder and lightning. Women's groups and patri-
otic societies joined as one to denounce Karl Muck
viciously for his unpatriotic stand, and to accuse him
openly for the first time of that, which until now they
had been expressing in whispers and deft suggestions—namely, that Karl Muck was a German agent
in America, supporting the German war with American money.[1]

[1] At this point two questions should be answered to clarify this
situation further. Why did not Muck, at this time, resign from his
post and escape into obscure confinement as Fritz Kreisler, for example, had done? The answer is today much more apparent than it
was fifteen years ago. From the moment America entered the War,
Muck pleaded with Higginson for permission to resign from the position. Major Higginson who, until the very end remained Muck's
staunch friend, convinced Muck that to resign at that time was a
weak gesture acknowledging both guilt and defeat; that Muck's
paramount duty as a great artist was to fight valiantly during those
catastrophic years to free art from the yoke of politics. As a matter
of fact, on November 4, 1917, Muck fiercely demanded that his resignation be accepted, but Higginson tore up the request.
A second question is not so easily answered, except by those who
can understand the conscience of a great artist. One can level criti-

THE MAN WITH THE BATON

When, on November 3, 1917—at the insistent
instigation of Henry Lee Higginson, who forcefully
realized the emergency—Muck conducted the *Star
Spangled Banner,* he showed his sharp teeth to the
audience. Not merely did he present his own arrangement of the anthem—using the Wagnerian chromatic accompaniment of the *Tannhäuser Overture*
as a counterpoint to the main melody (having the
doubly satiric effect of combining a German and an
American melody, but also of having the German
theme laugh in derision, in its downward chromatic
sweeps, at the American anthem)—but, when the
performance was over, he refused to acknowledge
the applause and cheers of an audience too blind to
realize that it had been laughed at. His refusal to
turn around and accept the applause of his audience
was the last straw; and from that time on Muck's
fate in America was sealed.

The storm was now to grow in intensity and fury,
and to gain rapid momentum with each passing day.

cism at Muck's lack of tact and grace in refusing to conduct the
Star Spangled Banner at a time when war hysteria was numbing the
reason of an entire nation. But to an artist of Muck's stature, his
conscience would not permit expediency to alter his artistic standards. For Muck to have conducted a work which he honestly felt to
be bad music would have reduced him in his own eyes to a charlatan.
One recalls in this connection that, not so long ago, Mr. Toscanini was
equally guilty of such lack of tact when—commanded by Italy's black
shirts to perform the Fascist hymn at a concert devoted to Martucci's
music—he vigorously refused.

On November 7, a mass meeting was called in Baltimore (after a concert, scheduled there by the Boston Symphony Orchestra, had been officially forbidden by the Police Commissioner) to denounce Karl Muck as an enemy of the American people. Governor Warfield of Maryland, stabbing his fist towards the galleries, cried out that no true American could remain satisfied until Muck had been "mobbed" to death; and he succeeded so admirably in arousing the fever of the audience that a gray-haired lady in the gallery forgot her poise sufficiently to exclaim towards the speaker, "Let's kill the bastard!" Shortly thereafter, the *Providence Journal* openly accused Muck in its editorials of acting as a paid-agent of the German government. And Ladies' societies consecrated to patriotism announced that henceforth a general boycott of the concerts of the Boston Symphony Orchestra would be in effect, and that anyone daring to enter Symphony Hall in Boston would be branded a traitor to his country.

By March of 1918, the antagonism to Muck had become so bitter and vitriolic that even Henry Lee Higginson was compelled to confess that discretion was now the better part of valor. It was announced that at the end of the season Muck would, finally, relinquish the baton. But a nation, once aroused, was not to be so easily silenced. It was no longer

satisfied with Muck's resignation but demanded
revenge in a form more palpable. On March 13, Dr.
Manning joined the now-nationwide conflict, using
his enormous energy and prestige to inflame American patriots against this dangerous enemy. And
perspective had, by this time, become so warped that
we even find a Detroit newspaper referring to Muck
as "the world's worst conductor."

In the last weeks of March, Karl Muck—who did
not permit the venom of a mob's hate to poison his
artistry—was working ten hours a day preparing
Bach's *St. Matthew's Passion* for the last concert of
the season. He was expending as much scrupulous
care in details and as much high inspiration as though
he were working under the most ideal conditions, as
though there were no war across the ocean nor an
angry mob outside of the concert-hall, as though the
only important consideration in the world at the time
was to play Bach as beautifully as possible. After
one of these intense all-day rehearsals—on March 25
—Muck was arrested at his home at nine o'clock in
the evening for being an "enemy alien." The newspapers implied with dark references that there rested
in their hands powerful evidence, which they could
not at the time disclose, but which definitely impli-
cated Muck as a political enemy. For a long time,
this "powerful evidence" remained a dark secret.

Finally, when the truth leaked out, it was learned that the only complaint that the Government had against Muck was the fact that he had not registered as an "enemy alien," as was required at the time by law of all Germans; and Muck had not registered because, being a Swiss citizen, he did not consider himself an enemy.

Pending a sentence from Washington, D. C., Karl Muck was confined in prison, and the event aroused wide jubilation and self-congratulations from one end of the country to the other. On April 5, the decision, finally, arrived from Washington. Karl Muck was found guilty of espionage by the Department of Justice, and was ordered interned for the remainder of the War in Fort Oglethorpe, Georgia. Justice had finally prevailed; one of the world's foremost artists was now "Prisoner 1337."

For fourteen months, Muck remained a political prisoner in Georgia. Then—silent forces having been at work—it was decided at Washington to deport him as expeditiously as possible. On August 12, 1919, Muck was hurried in secrecy and stealth aboard the *Frederic VIII*. He had arrived in America in glory, but he was to depart as a criminal. His bon-voyage had a fragrant odor, indeed! "Good riddance of Dr. Karl Muck" was the flower which the editorial page of the leading musical-magazine in

America contributed to the bouquet. And a second prominent musical journal was no less generous: "There is no room for any Dr. Mucks at the head of the Boston Symphony Orchestra or any other musical institution."

3.

There was no doubt that this American episode for a long time left a bitter taste with Muck. His friends have described how, for a long time, his spirit and health were crushed; how, as a matter of fact, he found it difficult to return to the baton. But, fortunately, when Muck returned to conducting—to assume the leadership of the Hamburg Symphony Orchestra and to give his prophetic readings of Wagner in Bayreuth—his greatness had lost none of its proportions, and he once again assumed a leading position over the conductors of the world.

That position he still maintains, even though his concerts have become few and far between. Herbert F. Peyser, the foreign musical correspondent of the *New York Times,* has commented that in the rare occasions when Muck today steps upon the concert-platform, he reveals a vision in his interpretations that is almost other-worldly, a conception that is heroic, and a mellow majesty and nobility which, long ago became closely identified with all of Muck's readings. Karl Muck is an old man, but when he raises his baton (the writer will always cherish the memory of his performances of *Parsifal* in Bayreuth) he has the strength and freshness and zest of youth.

IV

FELIX WEINGARTNER

1.

WHEN early in January, 1935, the Vienna State Opera House searched for a luminous name to succeed Clemens Krauss, who had resigned as its principal conductor and artistic director in order to assume a similar position in Nazi Berlin, it called upon Felix von Weingartner. Thus, in his seventy-second year, Weingartner relinquished his post of conductor in Basle, Switzerland, and returned to Vienna, there to end his magnificent career where, many years before, he had earned his greatest triumphs. More than a generation had done honor to his art, and—at the dusk of his life—he still found himself one of the great conductors of the world, and at the head of a great European musical institution.

Weingartner's rich career virtually spans the history of modern conducting and, together with Muck and Nikisch, he played an all-important rôle in giving it shape and direction. He was born in Zara, on the Dalmatian coast, in 1863, and as a student at the

160

FELIX WEINGARTNER

Leipzig Conservatory, he revealed unusual talents for conducting. At one of the student concerts, he directed from memory the Conservatory orchestra in a performance of Beethoven's *Second Symphony*— only to receive a vigorous verbal thrashing from his instructor, Karl Reinecke, who was a little peeved at finding a mere boy accomplishing what he had never been able to do at his concerts with the Leipzig Gewandhaus. However, though Weingartner failed to receive his deserved share of appreciation at the Conservatory, encouragement was not slow in coming. Completing his studies, he came to Weimar where he met and became a close friend of Franz Liszt. Liszt was to exert an enormous influence on the young man's artistic career. Recognizing Weingartner's all-too apparent talents for conducting, he urged him to turn to the stick as his profession—and he procured an opening for him as assistant to Hans von Bülow at Mannheim, perhaps the most desirable post a young conductor might reach for at the time.

His associations with Hans von Bülow were not particularly happy. The liberties that von Bülow took with whatever music he directed stung the young and sensitive musician who could not understand why masterpieces should be tampered with. When Weingartner took his turn with the baton he stubbornly refused to follow von Bülow's example.

At one time, he rehearsed Bizet's *Carmen* with attention to the most minute requests of the composer, and von Bülow—who stood nearby to listen to his assistant—viciously criticized Weingartner for adhering so rigidly to the score. But Weingartner was even then a musician with principle. He slammed his score and, rushing from the platform, muttered under his breath that unfortunately he had an artistic conscience, even if von Bülow did not. With that final thrust, their relationship came to a disagreeable end. Von Bülow frequently maintained afterwards that Weingartner was wasting his time with the baton, because he simply was no conductor!

Hans von Bülow never learned how far he had strayed from the truth. Although Weingartner was appointed conductor of the Royal Symphonic Concerts in Berlin in 1891, it was not until after von Bülow's death that his star began to rise. His reputation was slow in establishing itself. He was by no means a spectacular figure on the platform. His gestures were most simple and unpretentious; his platform mannerisms, at certain moments, approached the awkward. It required considerable intimacy for his audiences to realize what a pungent beat his baton possessed (a beat in which even the most complicated rhythms were enunciated with the utmost of clarity and firmness), and how eloquent the sweep of his left hand could be in a particularly moving passage. It likewise required a very close association with his performances for the public to recognize the remarkable purity, the cleanliness and correctness of all of Weingartner's performances.

It was with the Vienna Philharmonic Orchestra— to which organization Felix Weingartner had come in 1908—that his genius was unmistakably perceived. From that time on, his work with the celebrated orchestra, as well as his frequent visits to Paris and London, brought him a preeminent position among the conductors of the age. In London, as a matter of fact—where he has conducted the Royal Philharmonic Society so frequently that English music-audiences have begun to esteem him as one of their own—Weingartner has often been considered the *ne plus ultra* of symphonic interpreters, the logical successor to Artur Nikisch.

2.

Felix Weingartner is a classicist by temperament and training, and in classic literature his touch is at its firmest. Sensibility, restraint and a mature intellect bring his performances a very impressive nobility —and it has often been expressed that the majestic grandeur of his Beethoven has been equalled by no other conductor of our time, not even by Toscanini or Muck. Weingartner can maintain the classic line of a musical work with a hand that is always sure of itself, he can give voice to the most delicate harmonic schemes, and even the most fragile balances. His Mozart, therefore, can be as sensitively poignant as his Beethoven can be majestic. But perhaps the most significant quality of Weingartner's conducting is his unusual faculty for seeing a musical work as a whole; he has an instinctive feeling for architectural design. With each of his performances he creates a coherent conception in which, as Walter Pater has said of all great art, the end foresees the very beginning "and never loses sight of it, and in every part is conscious of all the rest, till the last sentence goes out, with undiminished vigor, to unfold and justify the first." This has always been an important trait of all supremely great conductors; and, like Nikisch, Muck and Toscanini, Weingartner possesses it to a very marked degree.

In his conducting, Weingartner has combined important characteristics of both Nikisch and Muck. Like Nikisch, he believes in inspiring friendship and affection among his orchestra-men. At rehearsals, he is always generous, warm and soft-spoken. He is not the dictator, nor the unreasonable school teacher. He convinces his men of the truth of his conceptions through the eloquence of his explanations, and not through stinging phrases and stern, commanding voice. He is sympathetic to the problems facing his men, and is largely instrumental in helping them solve them. And, though his rehearsals are intensive and thorough, he does not require very elaborate verbal explanations to transfer his ideas to the players. Performers under his baton have told us that his eyes have a very expressive quality which can explain his intentions to them with considerable clarity while they are performing. In this connection, the editor of *Musical Quarterly* has related an interesting anecdote: "Weingartner called upon one of the students to take the stick (in a 'lesson' on the first movement of a Brahms symphony). All went on swimmingly until the young man came to a stop. He tried again, with no better luck. Weingartner asked another student to conduct the passage. He, too, came to grief. Then Weingartner himself picked up the stick. But before raising it, he hesitated a moment, and then said: 'Gentlemen, I don't blame you. That is one of those places that I, myself, don't beat with the stick or hand. I conduct that with my eyes. Let's take the place again, and watch my eyes.' The players began the passage once more, at the danger point they watched Weingartner's eyes, and the result was perfection."

But Weingartner is more like Muck than Nikisch

in that his entire aim in his art is to translate the printed page into performance as accurately as he can; with the passing of years he has lost none of his youthful contempt and impatience with those conductors who boldly revise and change. Just as Wagner fought against the constraining formalism of Mendelssohn's conducting, so Weingartner— from the very dawn of his career until the present time—has bitterly rebelled against the overemphasis and false dramatics of the Wagnerian and the von Bülow school of conducting. Weingartner has felt strongly that it is the conductor's duty to efface his own personality when he is interpreting a masterpiece, that it is only the composer who must speak in the music. "The more your individuality disappears, finally to hide behind that created by the work," he has written in his autobiography, "nay, rather to become identical with it, the greater will your performance become."

And like Muck, Weingartner possesses a severe artistic conscience that recognizes no compromises and permits no concessions. This conscience has forced him throughout his entire career to remain religiously faithful to his art and to maintain it, at all times, on the highest and loftiest standards.

I

TOSCANINI

1.

IN 1886, an Italian opera-company headed by a
Brazilian conductor, Leopoldo di Miguez,
toured through South America in a series of popular
opera-performances. The conductor was not in very
great favor with either the orchestra or the singers,
and during the tour the company did everything in
its power to make his position uncomfortable. For a
long while, Miguez quietly tolerated the hostility of
his performers. Then, when the company came to
Rio de Janeiro, Miguez suddenly announced his
resignation, and in a statement published widely in
the local newspapers, fully explained how, having
until now suffered the antagonism of the entire
opera-company, it was impossible for him to continue.

The opera scheduled for the evening was *Aïda*
and, the advance sale having been particularly good,
there was a full house despite Miguez's sudden
resignation. An assistant conductor, a maestro
Superti, was hurriedly called upon as a substitute,

but no sooner did he make an appearance than a wave of hostility swept across the opera-house; from the first row of the parquet to the last row of the balcony, stamping of feet, hissing, loud and angry exclamations announced that the audience would not accept a substitute with docility. Behind the scenes, the director of the opera-company, pale and trembling, clenched his fists fiercely and muttered vile oaths under his breath. Obviously, the audience would not permit Superti to conduct; the commotion had not even as yet begun to subside. Where at this late hour could he find another conductor who might meet with the approval of the audience?

A few of the orchestra-men scrambled back-stage to bring the director a discreet suggestion. Among their number was a young, diffident 'cellist—Arturo Toscanini, by name—who had repeatedly proved to them that he knew the music of the operas remarkably well. He had, as a matter of fact, time and again performed his 'cello part from memory, and by his frequent comments revealed to his fellow musicians that he had very definite ideas about conducting. Why not call upon this young musician to direct *Aïda*? Futility and despair made the director receptive to any feasible plan. And so, in a few minutes, the lights in the house were once again lowered. A mere boy, wearing an evening suit far too

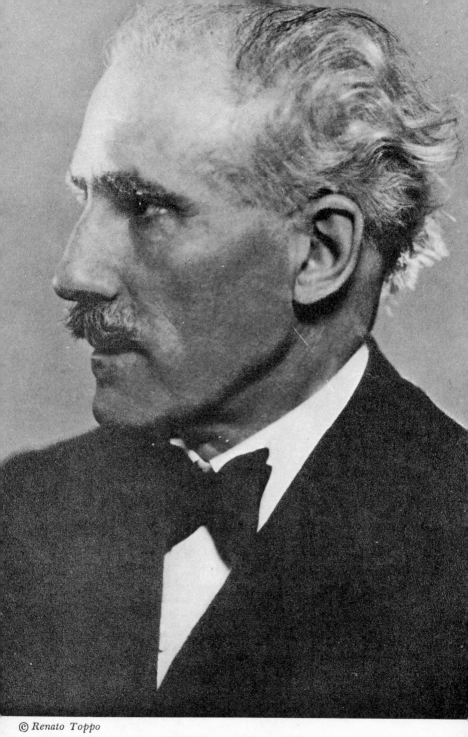

ARTURO TOSCANINI

large for him, nervously leaped upon the conductor's stand. The curiosity of the audience was aroused, and momentarily its bitter resentment had been pacified.

The young man rapped his stick sharply on the desk and then, without opening the score which rested idly on the stand in front of him for the entire length of the performance, he waved the baton through the air. The baton was like the saber of a Cossack, slashing over the heads of the orchestra-men, driving them to work fiercely, passionately. It seemed to emit with each sweep an electric current. The men, swept by forces they could not understand, played as they had probably never played before. The melodic lines acquired an altogether new exquisite contour; the rhythms became decisive and firm; the balance of the orchestra suddenly acquired new solidity and depth. Something about the conductor (was it the demonical gleam of his eyes which, never diverted to the score, was savagely pinned upon them, or was it the Herculean strength of his beat?) electrified them, and as they played they seemed as though they were possessed by a Spirit.

And an audience that had come expressly to jeer and hiss, remained to stand and cheer. It had never before heard an *Aïda* such as this, and the young conductor—directing the score from memory at a moment's notice—stirred its imagination. After that evening, Arturo Toscanini became the favored conductor of the itinerant opera-company. During the tour he was called upon to direct no less than eighteen operas—and to the speechless amazement of both audiences and musicians never once did he touch a score.

Thus brilliantly was the name of Arturo Toscanini introduced to the music-world. Upon his return to Italy, he continued to startle and electrify. Called upon to conduct opera in Turin, he proved once again that conducting came as naturally to him as speech to others; his ability to arouse enthusiasm and zest in the tired orchestra-men inspired wonder and awe among all musicians. He was to arouse even more amazed comment as his conductorial career progressed. In 1896, when he was appointed conductor of the orchestral concerts of the La Scala in Milan, he shattered the insularity of his countrymen by giving them a rigorous musical diet of German and Russian music, as well as a frequent taste of modernism. Three years later, as conductor at the La Scala Opera, he inaugurated his rigorous rehearsals, and his unapproachable high standard of performances, which made the La Scala Opera House the most important institution of its kind in the world.

Since that time, his career has persistently risen to greater glory. At the Metropolitan Opera House, from 1908 until 1915, his exquisitely perfect performances created sensations each time this little man sat in his conductor's seat. At the head of the New York Philharmonic Symphony Society—and as guest to the principal orchestras of the world—he has convinced even the most recalcitrant critic that as a symphony-conductor he has equalled his prodigious achievements in opera. Finally, in 1930, the greatest honor rested upon his shoulders: He was the first foreign conductor to be invited to direct Wagnerian opera at Bayreuth.

Today, with his seventieth birthday not far in the distance, he finds himself one of the glories of the modern musical world. There will not be many to doubt that, among the immortals of the baton the name of Arturo Toscanini must always be featured prominently. Discussion arises only when the relative position of Toscanini, among the great conductors of all-time, is posed. There are some who believe that in classic symphonies Felix von Weingartner had a vision far greater and a depth more profound than Toscanini; that in the music of the Romantics, Nikisch could be much more poetical. There are some who feel that in the temple of the Wagnerian music-drama, Toscanini must yield the altar to Karl Muck—and, having heard both of them in Bayreuth, I will not acquiesce so easily. However, there is no one, intimately familiar with Toscanini's performances, who can deny that in sheer versatility Toscanini is greater than any of his predecessors or contemporaries. A touch that can be so exquisite in Mozart, so heroic in Wagner, so poignantly lyrical in Verdi and Puccini, and so tremendously volcanic in the music of modern composers, is certainly unequalled in its scope and variety. There will be no one to doubt, too, that though Nikisch or Muck or Weingartner may have, in certain inspired performances, touched greater profundity and musical genuineness than Toscanini, neither one could ever boast of performances so meticulously perfect in every detail as those of the Italian maestro; among the conductors of the world, Toscanini is probably the greatest virtuoso that ever lived. Finally, there will be none to deny that in certain performances, Toscanini can outstrip the most inspired efforts of any conductor, as far as our fumbling memories can guide us. And when we hear his Mozart, his Verdi, his Wagner, his Vivaldi, we are tempted to say of him what a critic once wrote of de Pachmann: "He is, after all, the master of all in his field; for the way he plays some things, no one can play anything!"

2.

Once in discussing orchestral conductors with a veteran performer who had played under more batons than he could hope to remember, I heard a penetrating comment which, I feel, is singularly applicable to Toscanini. "Some conductors," this musician told me, "are uniquely gifted in mind. Others are especially endowed in ear. Still others, possess sensitive hearts. The supremely great conductor is the one who is equally strong in mind, ear and heart."

In discussing Toscanini's many fine qualities as conductor, endless paragraphs might be written about his magnificent rhythmic sense, his infallible instinct for dynamics and orchestral balance, his fine classicism, his deep and sensitive poetry, his ability to see a work "steadily and see it whole," his amazing capacity to penetrate into the very soul of a musical work and give it expression. Leopold Stokowski has neatly summed up Toscanini's strength when he wrote: "The first thing that struck me, was his compelling rhythm—so subtle and flexible and vibrant. His beat breaks every academic rule—yet it is always clear and eloquent. But it is between the beats that something almost magical happens: one can always tell when he has reached the half-beat or the three-quarter beat, even when he does not divide his

175

beats; and it is this certainty and clarity of beats which creates such a perfect ensemble when he conducts, so that the orchestra sounds like one giant instrument. . . . The melodic line, he moulds just as a sculptor moulds soft clay, the forms appearing under his fingers. His sense of harmonic balance is extraordinary—he draws into relief the notes in the harmony which have color and character and keeps in the background the notes which are of secondary importance; from this comes the unique quality of his harmony."

But, though these analyses of Toscanini's characteristics as conductor are very illuminating, we can understand the maestro's art much more intimately when we attempt to apply my friend's penetrating formula for the great conductor. Toscanini is that rare conductor who combines a great mind, a great ear and a great heart.

He has a profound knowledge of music—historical as well as technical—and he possesses a pungent critical faculty. He can put his finger upon a weakness of a score by merely glancing through it, and usually he knows the remedy. Once, a young American composer submitted a work to Toscanini who, merely passing his eye over the manuscript, pointed to a passage and inquired whether the composer should not have orchestrated it far differently. "You know," the composer told me afterwards, "when I had finished the composition of the work, I felt a keen dissatisfaction with that one passage, but did not know how to remedy the defect. And there, in a few moments, Toscanini had not only found the deficiency but had given me the precise remedy!"

Added to this enormous musical knowledge, is the fabulous musical memory, which has absorbed in its sponge-like tissues the bulk of symphonic and operatic literature. That during a conductorial career which spans four decades and in which Toscanini has performed a bewildering variety of works, classic as well as modern, he should never have resorted to the printed page in performance, and only rarely at rehearsals, is a phenomenon such as music history, I am sure, cannot parallel. There have been conductors before Toscanini—Hans von Bülow, for example, or Hans Richter—who have had amazing memories and who, therefore, conducted without the aid of a score. But even these conductors frequently leaned for support upon the printed page in unfamiliar old or new music, and certainly neither of these conductors could match Toscanini's amazing repertoire.

I have frequently read that Toscanini was compelled by necessity to develop his memory because, being myopic, he could never use a score unless he brought it up to his very nose. But this explanation is not altogether satisfactory. A memory like Toscanini's cannot be developed through necessity. It is well-known that in his student-days, Toscanini startled his teachers by playing his exercises on the violoncello without looking on the printed pages in front of him; and when one of his professors questioned Toscanini about his memory he convincingly proved his powers by taking pencil and paper and writing down the entire orchestral score of the **Prelude** to *Lohengrin.* Today, of course, his feats of memory are even more bewildering. He will receive a score of a new work on Friday morning and read it in bed as though it were a book; on the following Monday he will come to rehearsal knowing every note and every mark upon the page. At one rehearsal—it was of Ernest Schelling's *Impressions of An Artist's Life*—he amused both Mr. Schelling and the orchestra by repeatedly correcting the composer (who was playing the piano part with the music in front of him) in certain nuances which were definitely marked in the score. A famous anecdote is, in this connection, worth repeating. A doublebassoon player once came to Toscanini before a rehearsal and complained that his instrument was defective and that it could not play the note of E-flat. Toscanini held his head in his hands for

for several silent moments and then, patting the musician gently on the shoulder, said: "That's quite all right. The note of E-flat does not appear in your music today."

There are times when the fabulous Toscanini memory seems to falter, but invariably it emerges triumphant. At one time, while rehearsing a Vivaldi concerto, he stopped the orchestra and turned abruptly to the first violin section. "Can't you see that those four notes are marked *staccato?*" he cried out. The concert-master discreetly brought his music to the maestro and, pointing to the notes, showed him that there were no *staccato* notes in the passage. "But that's impossible!" Toscanini exclaimed. "It simply must be *staccato!*" An orchestral score was brought from the library, and after consultation it was found that this, too, did not have the debated *staccato* notes. "I can't understand it," Toscanini whined, almost to himself. "Those notes simply must be *staccato.* It can't be otherwise." It was quite true that Toscanini had not consulted the score for almost ten years. But was it possible that his memory was beginning to play pranks? The following day, Toscanini triumphantly brought a different score of the Vivaldi Concerto, published some fifty years earlier than the one used in the previous rehearsal, and considered much more authoritative.

"You see?" he exclaimed glowingly. "Didn't I tell you that those notes had to be played *staccato?*" Toscanini had been right; the score, published earlier, had the questionable notes marked *staccato.*

Equally incredible as his memory, although considerably less publicized, is Toscanini's ear, which is so hypersensitive that it can penetrate through the most complicated mazes of sound and unravel them. It has been said that Toscanini can tell when one of his violinists is bowing incorrectly. While this approaches the mythical, it is quite true that he can tell when one of his sixty violins is slurring an intricate passage. Nothing seems to escape his keen aural perception. When in a stirring climax one of the violinists accidentally, and faintly, struck a foreign string, Toscanini immediately detected it and waved a warning finger at the culprit. At another rehearsal, which I was fortunate in attending (the work in preparation was Respighi's *Pini di Roma*), the orchestra reached a thunderous *fortissimo* in the fourth movement. Toscanini stopped his orchestra angrily because he had heard—through this inextricable labyrinth of sound—that the flautist had not played his few notes with sufficient clarity and precision!

It is this ear that makes it possible for Toscanini to attain his marvelous balances: he knows precisely the quality that each section of the orchestra should attain, and even in the most complicated passages he can clearly hear if the various instruments are giving voice to the exact quality he seeks.

3.

We come now to a consideration of Toscanini as a personality; for, without a great personality, there can be no great artist.

Among the musicians of our day, Toscanini is probably the most modest in the face of the music he adores. He approaches music as a high priest approaches his religion, with self-effacement and unpretentiousness. Music to him is a ritual, something to be treated with awe and humility. It is for this reason that Toscanini is as scrupulous as Muck and Weingartner in adhering to the slightest intent of the composer; music, to him, is not for meddling. It is for this reason, too, that in his conducting he will resort only to the simplest gestures—a circular movement of the right hand, while the left is resting upon the hip or else, in tender passages, pressed against the heart.

It is this approach to music that makes Toscanini, in its presence, frequently so soft and sentimental. There was, for example, the occasion of Toscanini's performance of Puccini's *Turandot*. Puccini died before concluding the score and, although Franco Alfano (as Toscanini himself confessed) completed it admirably in the spirit of its creator, Toscanini refused to conduct, at the world's première of the work in Milan, any but the uncompleted version. And so, in the middle of a phrase, the work came abruptly to a halt and Toscanini, turning around to the audience with tears streaming down his pale face, announced: "Here—here—the maestro died!" This, as those who know Toscanini well, will attest, was not mere histrionics; it was the sincere gesture of one who loved the score and its composer. Music softens Toscanini from iron to clay; he has been known to weep like a schoolgirl at a tender passage from Wagner or Beethoven.

Too often, Toscanini is accused of display of temperament. But Toscanini's temperament is not sheer theatricalism but the product of a profound devotion to art. When he accepts applause as though it were some bitter medicine—fleeing from it, at the first opportunity, as though it were some plague—it is only because he honestly feels that applause diverts the tribute from the composer to the interpreter. There was the incident in Milan when Giovanni Zenatello was featured in Verdi's *Masked Ball* under Toscanini's baton. Toscanini had long before this announced that he would permit no encores when he conducted, feeling strongly that encores shattered the artistic unity of an opera. Zenatello, however, sang with unusual brilliance that evening and, at one point, the audience, forgetting completely the edict of the conductor, stormed and shouted for a repetition. For several tense minutes, Toscanini waited for the ovation to subside; then—maddened by the thought that the entire artistic conception of the work had been rudely broken by this obstreperous demand for an encore—he rushed out of the opera-house, running through the winter streets of Milan without hat and coat. As he ran he bleated poignantly to himself, like a sheep which had been stabbed in the heart. At home, he locked himself in his room and refused to see anyone. The following morning he suddenly left for Genoa, vowing never again to conduct in La Scala.

In the same fashion, when Toscanini refuses to play music he dislikes (as, for example, the *Fifth* and *Pathètique* Symphonies of Tschaikovsky), or will rudely refuse to shake the hand of a modern composer whose standards are not of the highest, it is only because he finds shallowness in the art he loves unforgivable. Moreover, Toscanini's famous tempers, as a result of mediocre performances, are not merely the products of temperament but rather spring from a fierce artistic integrity that will recognize no compromises and that will satisfy itself only with perfection in every detail. When, at such infrequent occasions, his terrible temper bursts and erupts like a volcano, it is not because he is a pampered and petted artist who has been offended, but because he is a sensitive genius who has seen the art he worships sullied and maltreated.

And yet I, for one, feel that the stories of Toscanini's volcanic anger have been greatly exaggerated. While it is quite true that, at certain times, hell knows no fury like Toscanini's—these occurrences are sufficiently infrequent to make me believe that these stories are enormously overemphasized. Toscanini can be—I know definitely—the most gentle and lovable human-being under the most trying and difficult circumstances, if his artistic conscience is at peace; even during long, arduous rehearsals his patience and equilibrium are admirable. He can rehearse, and he has rehearsed, phrases innumerable times before they are performed in the style he seeks. I have heard him rehearse a flute passage from Pizzetti's *Concerto dell' Estate* more than sixty times before the flautist could give expression to the subtle shadows that Toscanini found in this music—and not once during this period did Toscanini lose his temper. In Bayreuth, he must have rehearsed the half-dozen notes which the horn sounds at the conclusion of Act

I of *Tristan* for more than a half an hour—and each time the horn-player failed to give these notes the interpretation Toscanini sought, Toscanini would repeat the effect for which he was searching with the utmost of calmness and patience. He is, therefore, by no means the unreasonable tyrant.

There are times, however, when the celebrated Toscanini temper manifests itself. Once, during a rehearsal, his sharp ear caught a violinist attempting to slur over a very intricate passage in a Richard Strauss tone-poem—I believe it was *Ein Helden-leben*—and this conductor, who could be coolly patient with mistakes, flew into a rage in which the baton was split into pieces and music-stands were hurled demoniacally on the floor. Sloppiness is a thing which he cannot learn to accept patiently—sloppiness or indifference or apathy.

Toscanini can enjoy no happiness greater than having his orchestra perform beautifully. He will giggle like an adolescent, flushing with contagious delight, his eyes sparkling merrily because his men have just performed unusually well. But when this perfection is not attained, Toscanini is an altogether changed man. He becomes surly, cross, impatient. He reaches the depths of despond. When he is weaving and carving the final form of his music with his baton at the performance, a passage badly played strikes him as stingingly as a lash of the whip. I remember one concert when his orchestra played without its customary brilliance and eloquence. The music was that of Wagner, and Toscanini was so sharply stung by a mediocre performance of music he loved, that he behaved as though he had been poisoned. He rushed from the stage, stormed through the hall leading to his rest-room, and there punched with his fist at the wall of a wooden closet with such ferocity that it crashed into splinters.

And Toscanini can be as severe with himself as he is with his men. At one time he conducted Vincent D'Indy's *Istar* in which there is a page where there occurs an intricate change and interchange of rhythm. For one of the rare times in his career, Toscanini's memory proved false, and the maestro during the performance forgot to change the beat. There followed, for several moments, pandemonium until Toscanini could whip his men back into the correct *tempo*. At the end of the performance, Toscanini refused to take a bow, refused to turn and acknowledge the applause, but rushed to his rest room and there moaned softly in pain, holding his head in his hands. The intermission over, Toscanini returned to the stage, and before beginning the next number he whispered to his men: "Gentlemen—forgive me. The fault was entirely mine. Please, forgive me."

Anyone who knows Toscanini is familiar with the fact that no bodily pain can burn him so agonizingly as when his artistic standards are lowered. I remember seeing Toscanini in Bayreuth, in 1931, when, suddenly, he appeared for the first time to be a very old man. He had come to Bayreuth with flaming enthusiasm—remembering the conditions existing there the year before, which enabled him to attain performances of *Tristan* and *Tannhäuser* which were incomparably perfect—for here, he felt, he could procure the number of rehearsals and the type of artists necessary for the great performances of Wagner that he envisioned in his mind. But this year his dream betrayed him. He suddenly encountered petty politics, jealousies on the part of other Bayreuth conductors, picayune nationalistic feeling on the part of Germans (somewhat upset that an Italian had so victoriously invaded their intensely German shrine) which made it impossible for him to secure the cast he sought, or the number of rehearsals he deserved. No longer was Bayreuth to be the haven for his artistic ideals, but another setting for human pettiness. The fact that his performance of *Parsifal* (magnificent though it was!) did not reach the standards he had set for himself, almost broke his heart. He had become an old man overnight. For days he would eat little, say nothing, his face black and intense, his eyes soft and sad. He was bitterly unhappy and morbid. His artistic conscience was fiercely smitten.

This capricious temperament of Toscanini's—which brings him from intense happiness to despair—is nothing more than the result of his urgent need to express himself in music without blemish, and an impatience with scarred and wounded performances. His is a savage artistic conscience at whose hands he is entirely helpless. Everything about him can be explained by this insatiable hunger for perfection. His quarrels with managers, his volatile moods, his occasionally terrible temper, his tyranny at certain moments—all this comes from something deep within him which relentlessly demands the best expression of music that it is humanly possible to attain. When, for more than ten years—at one phase of his career—he refused to perform Beethoven's *Coriolanus Overture,* it was only because he despaired of translating the music he heard with his mind's ear to the orchestra; and he would not tolerate anything but the highest performances.

This, certainly, is not temperament; rather it is the guiding force of a sublime artist.

4.

But the real Toscanini is known only to those who have attended his rehearsals.

He stands in front of his men—twisting his baton nervously with his fingers—a handkerchief bandaged around his neck, the muscles of his face taut, his brilliant eyes flashing command. In front of him, one senses instantly that one is in contact with an electric current. As he stands there, demanding complete subjection, enormous concentration and effort from his men, he quietly explains his intentions —teaching through illustration and epigram—going over an effect again and again until it is clearly understood by the players. Toscanini's rehearsals— like those of Muck and Mahler before him—are characterized by minute and painstaking thoroughness. Toscanini does not, like so many other modern conductors, rehearse a symphony merely by going through some of the salient and more difficult passages and concentrating upon them, even though he is rehearsing a work like a Beethoven symphony which he has performed with the same orchestra time and again. He begins his rehearsal with the first note, and minutely dissects each passage until the end of the composition, fastidiously weaving the various parts into a coherent and inevitable whole. To Toscanini there are no unimportant passages in a musical work; no section is so negligible that it will not bear reviewing. As a matter of fact, Toscanini has said that the important passages of any symphony will usually take care of themselves, but it is the negligible section, or the supposedly unimportant passage, that demands painful rehearsal.

Usually, Toscanini tries to explain his conception of phrasing and color by singing the music at the top of his high-pitched, sharp, cracked voice. Sometimes he will hurl unrelated adjectives at the players, adjectives which are supposed to epitomize the mood of the score. He characterizes each sound. One chord is described by him as a "fist"; a staccato note is said to be "mischievous"; this phrase must depict hate, another lust. But when words and song and epigram fail him in his attempt to depict his subtle conceptions (and very frequently they do) Toscanini will then dance and posture and act—try almost any antic that occurs to him at the moment—in order to bring his meaning forcefully to the consciousness of the players.

To illustrate how a certain burlesque passage for trombones in Respighi's *Feste Romana* should sound, Toscanini kicked the air with his right foot, clenched his fists and emitted a deep, resonant groan

TOSCANINI DURING A REHEARSAL

that suggested the roar of an animal. In telling a clarinetist the quality he sought in a trill, he hunched his back, raised his hands and shook quivering fingers at him. The first subject of Beethoven's *Seventh Symphony,* first movement, should sound—he told his men—"like a mother, rocking her baby to sleep." And so, with folded arms, he swayed his body back and forth as he sang the theme softly. The opening measures of Mozart's *Jupiter Symphony* he described as "angry music"—and a black face gave the men a graphic description of what the music should convey in tone. And once, when words failed him completely in his effort to indicate a very delicate effect he sought in the first movement of Beethoven's *Ninth Symphony* (the tender passage for violins beginning with bar 197), he whipped his handkerchief from his pocket and dropped it in front of him. "Like this the music should sound," he remarked. "Like this handkerchief, falling down."

Very often Toscanini will secure the performance he seeks through instilling terror into the hearts of his men. He will break batons, and fling Italian invectives at the men to incite them to greater industry. He may fall on his knees, clench his hands in prayer, and cry out: *"Please,* gentlemen, *pianissimo!"* At one time, he was rehearsing a new work, and he had repeatedly explained the effect he desired in one of the passages. It was, however, difficult to attain, and the men seemed at a complete loss to reproduce it with their instruments. Finally, the maestro lost his temper and screamed in such violent Italian that the men paled under the torrent of his rage. Presently, exhausted by his emotion, he flung aside his baton, and took refuge in a remote corner of the stage, where he sat, his face buried in his hands, a pathetic picture of hopeless dejection. No one dared to say a word; two hundred eyes looked upon him with a deference that bordered upon awe. At last, Leo Schulz—at that time the first violoncellist of the New York Philharmonic—ventured to pick up the master's baton and offered it to him. Schulz did not say a word, but his eyes pleaded with the maestro to try them once again. Humbly, Toscanini returned to his podium and once again explained the effect he desired; and this time the orchestra handled the measures with such competence that the maestro's stormy face suddenly broke into smiles.

5.

Toscanini's art—like that of Muck and Weingartner—grows richer and more mellow as he grows older. Great artist that he is, Toscanini can never permit stagnation to set into his performances. He is always changing, always revising his conception of a masterwork, permitting it to grow and expand as he grows wiser with experience. Today, for example, his dynamics in Brahms (particularly in the last movement of the *Second Symphony*) and some of his *tempi* in the Beethoven symphonies are much different than they were several years ago, with the result that his conceptions of these works are today on a higher plane of greatness. He is perpetually restudying his performances so that they may never become routine, for he believes—as Gustav Mahler did before him—that "in every performance a work must be reborn."

With old age, many conductors are inclined to become a little eccentric in their interpretations. But as he grows older, Toscanini more and more demands that perfection in performance consist of adhering slavishly to the composer's demands. Once while attending a performance of Beethoven's *Fifth Symphony* in New York, performed by a celebrated confrère, he was so infuriated at the liberties which the conductor took with the music that he escaped from his box, muttering *"Vergogna, vergogna!"* ("Disgrace, disgrace!") under his breath. Occasionally, there may arise criticism that Toscanini has deviated from the exact letter of the score. Time and again conductors have quibbled with Toscanini over his *tempi*—the opening measures of Brahms' *First*

Symphony, or the second movement of *Schubert's C-Major Symphony* both of which he plays much faster than tradition would dictate. But invariably, when they return to their scores for verification, they discover much to their bewilderment that it is Toscanini, and not tradition, who is in the right. In Bayreuth in 1930, for example, there was considerable commotion among the "perfect Wagnerites" because it was felt that in the prelude to *Tannhäuser,* Toscanini took an altogether unorthodox *tempo.* Toscanini quietly summoned his critics to a piano and there, with the aid of a metronome, proved that his *tempo* was meticulously perfect, precisely the way Wagner had so carefully designated in the score. A series of inept conductors at Bayreuth had persistently tampered with Wagner's original intentions with the result that something of a tradition had been established—until Toscanini, with his penetrating insight and his infallible intelligence punctured the tradition completely.

6.

It is often said of Napoleon's soldiers that, wounded on the battlefield, they died blessing their general. No less remarkable a phenomenon to me is it that Toscanini's men—who are forced to work under him until they are exhausted mentally and

194

physically—would rather play under him than under less exacting conductors who make of rehearsals mere play. It was one of the violinists of the New York Philharmonic Orchestra who—several years ago when Toscanini was still the guiding genius of La Scala—confessed to me that, although Toscanini worked him to death, he would only too gladly go to Milan to play under him without remuneration if Toscanini permitted him to come. Toscanini may be the severest taskmaster that music knows, and working under him may tax the last ounce of energy that the musicians possess; but the musicians know his flaming sincerity, his simple modesty, his unaffected passion for great music, and his genius—and they worship him.

But what, probably, touches them most poignantly is this little man's crushing humility. One recalls in this connection a rehearsal of Beethoven's *Ninth Symphony* when Toscanini scrupulously, indefatigably laid bare the soul of the music for the men. With his keen explanations of how the many parts were blended into the whole, with his subtle shadows and colors which he painted into the performance, with his slashing beat that endowed the work with altogether new drama, he gave the musicians of the orchestra (who had played this symphony so frequently before this) an altogether new insight into the work. The men, overwhelmed by the realization that—through Toscanini's inexplicable magic—they had just been given an altogether new vision of a masterpiece, arose as one man at the end of the rehearsal, and cheered the conductor in front of them at the top of their lungs. The little man gestured wildly, desperately trying to arrest their enthusiasm. Finally, when their spontaneous cheering had subsided, he turned a pained face to his men, and tears were glistening in those brilliant eyes of his.

"Please—please—" he called out in a pathetic voice. "Don't do this to me. You see, gentlemen, it isn't me. It's Beethoven!"

II

STOKOWSKI

1.

THE first time that Leopold Stokowski appeared before a radio microphone, he immediately made his vibrant personality felt to his millions of listeners in a manner characteristically Stokowski. "We are eager to make the programs representative of the best music of all times and countries," he announced. "If you do not like such music, say so, and we won't play any more radio concerts. For I shall certainly never play popular music."

This is typically Stokowski. It is typically Stokowski in its sound musicianship—and there can be no doubt in the world that Stokowski is a musician to the very tips of his fingers. It is also typically Stokowski in that, with such words, a glamorous and picturesque personality—a super-showman who knows all the tricks of the theatrical trade—instantly makes itself felt. Stokowski is, among other things, essentially a dynamic personality who expresses that personality not only through his music but through everything he says and does. He is a flaming firebrand in American music. Whether he is on the air or on the concert-stage he radiates electricity and magnetism and charm. Everything about him has an indefinable Stokowski magic.

Early in his career, Stokowski heard Artur Nikisch perform, and this fascinating personality made an unforgettable impression on the young and plastic mind. It was probably Nikisch who first brought dreams of a conductorial career to Stokowski. Certainly, Stokowski has been vitally influenced by his eminent predecessor—not merely in his romantically passionate readings but also in his strivings for elegance in his personal appearance and in his leaning towards the dramatic gesture. Like Nikisch, Stokowski is that rare blend of genius and personality, musician and showman. Like Nikisch, Stokowski creates an unforgettable aesthetic picture as conductor. And like Nikisch, Stokowski has inspired the most exaggerated adulation and hysterical panegyrics not only for his art but also for his personality.

Certainly, Stokowski is the stuff of which public-idols are made. In appearance, his impressiveness is as indelible as Nikisch's was before him. Stokowski has a crown of gold hair which spreads over his head like an aureole. His features are clearly and sharply outlined—with a square jaw, an aquiline

LEOPOLD STOKOWSKI

nose and an assertive chin. A well-shaped body is clothed with meticulous perfection disclosing rhythmic outlines. When Pierre Monteux, the guest-conductor of the Philadelphia Orchestra, left the country several years ago in bitterness and anger because Philadelphia audiences had not responded favorably to his colorless personality, and commented with acerbity to the press that he would never again return to America because American music-audiences could appreciate only "tailor-models" for their conductors, it was no secret that he was speaking enviously of that baton Apollo who had preceded him in Philadelphia, and who held his audiences, at each performance, in the palm of his hand.

The Stokowski on the conductor's platform has equal fascination. From the moment he leaps from the wings of the stage, through his orchestra of men, to his platform—plunging into the first bar of music even before his feet land solidly upon the dais—he is a distinct personality, electric, magnetizing. There are innumerable trademarks to brand him apart from all other conductors. There are his conductorial gestures, the last words in grace, poise and elegance. His magnificent figure pulses and vibrates with the music as though it were a sensitive musical instrument. Graceful of body, lithe in all of his motions, Stokowski cuts a magnificent figure in front of the orchestra. There is his batonless hand; Stokowski conducts with the swaying motion of two open hands. There is that now-informal and good-natured, now despotic and ill-mannered attitude of the conductor towards his audience at every concert; the Philadelphia performances are marked by a very close bond between Stokowski and his public, even when he is most philippic. There is, too, that military precision of some of his manual gestures which clearly emphasizes that this man is a Napoleon over his performers—an iron will exerting power and dominance over a hundred and ten men.

And the final and most convincing trade-mark of all: there is the quality of music which Stokowski can draw from his orchestra—a sensuous tone from the strings, rich as honey; a magnificent timbre from the woodwinds of an undefiled purity; an orchestral tone fabric that is sometimes pure silk and sometimes a tonal tempest of volcanic power and intensity.

2.

A blend of personality and genius, a combination of great musician and electric showman—this is apparent in each of Stokowski's brilliant interpretations of the classics and the moderns; and it is apparent in each of his actions, and in every word of mouth. It was apparent during his entire musical career which has blazed from obscurity heavenward with the bewildering sweep of a meteor. Which of these two has been the more potent factor in making Stokowski a household word in Philadelphia, and the most idolized, perhaps the most envied, figure in all present-day American music? It is not easy to say.

In emphasizing the appeal of Stokowski's personality, I do not wish it to be suspected that I minimize his genius as conductor. Who can, after having heard so many of his rejuvenated interpretations? There have flowed more immortal interpretations under Stokowski's guiding fingers than under the hand of any other one man in our time, with the possible exceptions of Muck, Toscanini and Weingartner. And, although it is equally true that Stokowski is not without his grave faults as an artist, he most certainly is to be considered among the great conductors of our day, a conductor who has developed a symphonic organization which is one of the greatest orchestras in the world. This his genius has accomplished.

However, to become an almost legendary figure in music, to be spoken of everywhere with awe and reverence, to inspire obedience and terror in those with whom he comes into contact (be it player, manager or patron), to be literally worshipped by an audience for a period that spans two decades, to be always a fresh topic for discussion, controversy and conversation, to be front-page news with every move and every word—for this it is infinitely more essential to be an impressive personality than an outstanding musician. Stokowski, fortunately, is both. He, therefore, occupies today a position quite unique in American music.

Personality and genius, great showman and musician blend so inextricably with Stokowski that, to understand his art, one must know the man. It is not easy to paint here a coherent picture. He is a man of such strange contradictions and paradoxes that to attempt to analyze his personality may prove to be baffling. One may mention, for example, that, in spirit, he is a fiery modernist with eyes pinned to the future; how, then, reconcile this with the fact that he is, likewise, the devout believer in Oriental philosophy, religion and mysticism, and figuratively prostrates himself before a culture many thousand years old? One can point to the fact that Stokowski is inordinately fond of self-advertisement—he does not seem to neglect an opportunity to appear on the front page with a new radical idea or an astonishing thought. And yet, in mentioning this, one is immediately confronted with his unusual modesty and self-effacement in other directions. For years now he has refused permission to many publishers to have his work and personality glorified in book-form. And in his daily relationship with people he will never talk about himself or his work; question him about his art and his answers, likely as not, will prove to be Delphic. "I am of no importance," he will tell you in all sincerity. "It is great music, and great music alone, that is of importance. I am merely a channel for great art." Or else he will say—as he once wrote to me in a letter: "There is too much written about artists *themselves* and too little about art *itself*. I like to do my work and then go home and be quiet until the moment arrives for the next work. I am against placing stress upon the personal life of an artist; in my opinion the illumination should be put on the art." But, if actions speak louder than words, there is his incredible modesty concerning those magnificent orchestral transcriptions of the organ and piano music of Bach which, for so many years, he has featured on his programs. For years, critics and admirers have questioned him concerning this tasteful, and anonymous, arranger, and for years Stokowski has maintained a sphynx-like silence. It was only recently, and after much persuasion, that he confessed that it was he who was responsible for them. "It is Bach who is important," he explained concerning his long silence. "Why should I deflect the enthusiasms of the audience away from the beautiful music of Bach and towards me?"

Other contradictions in his make-up assert themselves with equal force. At one moment, he can be as hard as steel. In his relation with his orchestramen, for example, the human element is strangely absent. When he enters the rehearsal he rarely greets the players, even if it is the first rehearsal of the season; and when it is over he merely closes his score and walks off the stage without a word. At all times, Stokowski treats his orchestra with a hand of iron, dismissing players at the first sign of disobedience, lashing them persistently with the stinging whip of his comments. And yet, this martinet is capable of unusual softness at other times: There was the occasion when one of the less important musicians of his orchestra was laid up in hospital for seven months. Not only did Stokowski see to it that the musician was not deprived of his salary, but some mysterious benefactor paid for his private room, nurse and doctor during the entire period; and no one knew who the benefactor was—that is, no one except the hospital official who, each Saturday, received Stokowski's personal check. In the same way Stokowski can be at one time your best friend and at the very next moment—with very slight provocation—your bitterest enemy; members of the

Philadelphia Orchestra speak of the many times when Stokowski, away on a trip, would write the most affectionate letters to members of his orchestra, only to dismiss them the moment he returned from his vacation.

One can, however, point to certain very definite, and important traits in Stokowski's character which have vitally influenced his art. There is, first and foremost, his love for theatricalism. There can be no doubt that Stokowski, during his entire career, has always employed the most efficacious histrionics in presenting himself to the audiences, and has seemed to find particular delight in them. He is something of the born press-agent. His art has always been accompanied by the proper strategy to arouse the enthusiasm and curiosity of the public. He was one of the first conductors in America to make a periodic practice of conducting without a score at the concert; and, when conducting from memory no longer attracted attention to him, he dispensed with the baton. He has timed his entrances on the stage for the effect they will have on the audience, and he has assumed a Polish accent in his speech which mysteriously deserts him when he loses his temper. When he feels that the audiences are beginning to accept his programs too complacently, he will present a concert whose unorthodoxy will tear them from their smugness; and when he senses that he is being taken too much for granted he will either threaten a resignation or take a leave-of-absence.

He is a master of dramatic gestures. It was not an accident that one of his early years with the Philadelphia Orchestra was marked, two decades ago, by a performance of Mahler's *Eighth Symphony*—a work which called for double orchestra, triple chorus (not to speak of considerable bravery on the part of a conductor who knew that his audiences were ill-disposed to Mahler)—which he conducted entirely from memory. Nor was it a coincidence, I feel confident, that the electric news of his resignation from the Philadelphia Orchestra, in the winter of 1934, was announced in the newspapers at the same time that Stokowski was giving poignant performances of Bach's grandiose *B-minor Mass* in Philadelphia and New York. Perhaps there was no cause-and-effect in Toscanini's magnificent success as guest conductor of the New York Philharmonic in 1925-6 —which removed every other conductor to an obscure background—and Stokowski's sudden decision to take a year's leave of absence to study Indian and Japanese music. In any case, Stokowski was not away long enough to learn even the elements of Oriental music, but his absence was sufficiently prolonged to have him sorely missed. Incompetent guest-conductors, substituting for Stokowski, persistently reminded the Philadelphia audiences how truly indispensable he was to them. His return, therefore, was a magnificent triumph—and Stokowski remains, perhaps, the only conductor in America whose lustre has not been somewhat dimmed by Toscanini's prolonged brilliance.

This love for the dramatic touch, for the theatrical gesture, is as important in Stokowski's artistic as in his personal make-up.

Equally significant, is his keen intellect. A lover of great literature (Dostoyevsky means as much to him as Bach), a student of philosophy, a lover of every phase of culture, he possesses an intellectual hunger that is as insatiable as it is healthy. I do not agree with those writers on Stokowski who point to his innumerable experiments and innovations as symptoms of his love for exhibitionism; those who know Stokowski well realize how sincere he is at the moment he poses the new idea, and how it springs from his enormous and inexhaustible intellectual curiosity. When, in first approaching radio, he attempted to learn something about the science of transmission in order to improve the quality of orchestral broadcasting, and when, in recording, he spent many days in the laboratory—ever eager to gain an intimate knowledge of the means through which his music was to be brought to the great public —it was not merely for self-advertisement but out of a desire to enrich his knowledge. And it can be said —much to Stokowski's credit!—that not merely is his scientific knowledge far from superficial but that, with his blundering experiments and penetrating suggestions, he has accomplished much in improving the quality of broadcasting and recording orchestral music.

In the same way, he is mentally always keenly alive, always searching for new ways with which to further his musical art. His many experiments are the inevitable results. Several years ago, Stokowski decided to experiment with visual colors wedded to music. A series of hues were flashed upon the screen while the men performed Rimsky-Korsakoff's *Scheherezade*. The colors were intended to heighten the effectiveness of the music. At another time he announced that henceforth applause must be dispensed with at his concerts because the concert-hall, he felt, was really a temple of music. And at still another concert, he tried to dispense with light ("music," he said, "should be heard and not seen"), realizing that the audience was focusing too much attention upon the conductor, and too little upon the music. He has attempted to create a process to record the vocal and orchestral music of operas by electrical transmission and synchronizing this music with the histrionics of actors who look and act their parts—thereby freeing opera from so many of its present-day visual absurdities. He is always experimenting with the position of the instruments on the platform, in order to improve sonority, and with new instruments added to the present-day symphonic choir (the Thereminvox—ether music—was for a long time a permanent member of his organization). He has dispensed with the concertmaster, in order to give each of his violinists a sense of conductorial responsibility, and he tried to free all the violinists of the life-long tyranny of bowing-together. He has ventured to train some of his orchestra-men as conductors at the rehearsals, feeling that there does not exist sufficient opportunity for a potential conductor to disclose his latent talents. He is always experimenting with programs, and is inquisitive about every new direction towards which the musical art tends. He even hopes that Oriental systems will be included in our Western musical thought.

His innumerable ventures, in short, might fill many pages. He is always working in new directions, in unexplored fields, with the hope of finding new vistas for music. Of course, in most cases, his experiments have proved failures, and they were instantly discarded. Stokowski, after all, was groping blindly in dark corners; it was to be expected that he should frequently falter. But his intellectual alertness is something to be grateful for. Stagnation and smugness are impossible with a mind so restless and so keen as Stokowski's. He is always attuned to new times and conditions, always seeking new avenues through which musical expression may flow. In consequence, his concerts have always been—and, probably, always will be—vital and alive and important, always reflecting the vigorous and healthy mentality of their conductor. What matter if Stokowski's experiments do not reach successful realization in the majority of cases? What is more important to us is the fact that, as a result, with him—unlike so many other conductors—music is not a combination of dead tissue, but a throbbing, growing organism.

3.

Whence has this man come?

He was born, not (as so many believe) in Poland, but in London; the year was 1882. In his youth, he came to America after having served his apprenticeship as organist in his native city, and accepted a post at the St. Bartholomew's Church in New York.

LEOPOLD STOKOWSKI

Here, Stokowski distinguished himself as an excellent musician with a profound interpretative talent. His reputation as organist grew until it attracted towards him the roving eye of the managers of the recently reorganized Cincinnati Symphony Orchestra which was searching the musical horizon for a new conductor. Having alighted upon this dynamic organist, it realized that it had finally found the object of its search. In 1909, Stokowski was offered—and accepted—his first conductorial position.

It was to be expected that his first year as conductor should have passed without adding considerably to his reputation; he was still fumbling with a new artistic expression. As a matter of fact, some of the musicians who were in the Cincinnati orchestra in 1909 have since told us that, at the first rehearsal, Stokowski was so completely at a loss as to how to pursue his work that the concertmaster arose and explained to him minutely the processes through which a conductor goes during rehearsal. But Stokowski could learn quickly. In a surprisingly short time he had not merely mastered the elusive technique of transferring his conception of a musical work to his men, but he had also learned the art of "selling" himself as a personality to his audiences.

For Stokowski, the showman, had already begun to disclose himself as early as 1910. We find him, for example, launching upon an extensive Western tour with his orchestra (the idea, of course, was his) —especially in cities which had never before heard a symphony-concert—and instantly enlarging his prestige and fame throughout the entire country. We already find him instituting his informal relationship with his audience, making speeches to explain the music he was about to conduct, and inaugurating elections whereby the audiences could vote for special request programs. And in less agreeable moments, he resorted—even in those halcyon days— to sharp speeches. "Please," he once cried out when the audience, fumbling with the programs, was disturbing the music. (The year, mark! was not 1932 —when Stokowski made a similar speech in Carnegie Hall—but 1911!). "Please don't do that! We must have the proper atmosphere. . . . I do not want to scold you or appear disagreeable. . . . We work hard all week to give you this music, but I cannot do my best without your aid. I'll give you my best or I won't give you anything. It is for you to choose." We find him electrifying his audiences with the most rebellious modern-music of the day, even venturing upon an all-American program! It was, therefore, not very long before the Stokowski magic was beginning to have a potent effect not merely upon the audience but also upon the box-office—and not very long before he became, in Cincinnati, bathed in limelight.

And then, with the characteristic Stokowski touch, when he had firmly established himself in Cincinnati's musical life, Stokowski suddenly handed in his resignation. The reason, he explained, was the lack of cooperation between the players and himself. At the following rehearsal, the entire orchestra rose as one man, and a spokesman promised Stokowski that they would henceforth do everything in their power to please him, if only he would retract his resignation. "I would immediately withdraw my resignation," Stokowski told them, "if a single one of you were in danger of his position. But there are many conductors more capable than myself, and one of them will be brought here to continue the work of this orchestra. None of you is in any danger of losing his livelihood, so I am afraid that there is no necessity for me to retract my decision."

It may have been a coincidence (as Stokowski later emphasized) but this resignation from the Cincinnati Symphony Orchestra was made on March, 1912, and three months later, while touring through Europe, Stokowski suddenly announced that he had accepted the post of conductor with the Philadelphia Symphony orchestra at the-then generous salary of

$600 a performance, and full control of the artistic policies of the organization.

Thus, Stokowski was brought to the orchestra which he immortalized and which brought him, in turn, his world-wide fame. For more than two decades his name has become synonymous with that of his orchestra—and it is impossible to mention the Philadelphia Orchestra without, in turn, thinking of Stokowski. For two decades, Stokowski has been fiercely asserting his own will, refusing to bow to any decisions of managers or advice of patrons. When he suggested performing the grandiose Mahler *Eighth Symphony*, the management refused to permit a performance that would entail such expenditure; needless to say, the *Eighth Symphony* was performed—and surprisingly enough, there were no financial losses. When Stokowski demanded many more rehearsals than was customary, once again the management complained that the expense would be ruinous, and once again Stokowski had his own way. He has been having his own way ever since—performing the music he desires, having the type of musicians in his orchestra he prefers, listening to the advice and complaints of no one. The result has been the development of one of the most perfect orchestras in the world, and the establishment of its conductor as one of the most fascinating figures in all music.

A word should, perhaps, be spoken about the recent friction between the directors of the Philadelphia Orchestra and Stokowski which, in the winter of 1934, resulted in the startling resignation of the conductor from a post he held with such glory for more than twenty years. It was no secret that the directors and Stokowski had had very serious altercations, although I seriously doubt if the precise cause of Stokowski's resignation will ever be known. There are some who point to the fact that, in 1934, the orchestra had instituted a new policy of alternating symphony-concerts with opera (the latter under conductors other than Stokowski) with such success that much of the limelight was stolen from Stokowski; and Stokowski could not look with favor upon such a situation. There are some who recall that in 1926 one of Stokowski's fondest dreams was to reach realization—an extended tour of the orchestra throughout the principal cities of Europe—only to collapse at the last moment; Stokowski has not forgotten that dream. Still others speak of the fact that Stokowski's endless performances of modern musical works was a persistent source of irritation with the forces in power, who felt that the concerts would be even better attended if Stokowski leaned more heavily upon thrice-familiar music. In any case, an open break was inevitable. Stokowski is not the man for compromises; and the directors were becoming stubborn. Resignation was the next step with Stokowski. With Philadelphia rested the choice as to whom they preferred to guide the destinies of their orchestra—the directors or the conductor.

It is only too well known what the decision of Philadelphia has been. After full command of the policies of the orchestra, it was electrified, early in 1936, to learn that beginning with the 1936-1937 season, Stokowski would withdraw from conductorial activity—except for a few guest-appearances—to pass on his Philadelphia baton to Eugene Ormandy.

4.

It may come as a surprise to the swollen army of Stokowski worshippers that there exist any number of sincere musicians who raise a skeptical eyebrow each time they hear adulation and praise poured out so lavishly for Stokowski, and who do not hesitate to criticize him in no uncertain terms as a conductor. These disparaging criticisms invariably point a finger at Stokowski's performances of Beethoven— so often marred by exaggerations of dynamics and *tempi* to bring greater dramatic intensity to the music—to his overromanticized readings of Mozart, and to the general nervousness and hysteria of so many of his other performances.

It is, however, not difficult for a critic with balance and perspective to weigh the pros and cons of the argument and arrive at an equitable estimate of Stokowski as a conductor. Stokowski, it must be understood at once, is a conductor who is swept by his temperament, and by intuitive forces. He reacts to music sensitively, sincerely, passionately, much more with heart than with mind. He is essentially the poet. He does not, like so many other admirable conductors, first study a score minutely, put a microscope over each phrase and patiently dissect each effect—and then come to rehearsals with a clearly analyzed interpretation in his mind. He will, rather, read a score as one might a book, react to certain pages and moods emotionally, and then attempt to give expression to his personal feelings. He permits his heart and temperament to guide him in all of his interpretations. It is for this reason that Stokowski never completes his work, at rehearsals, but expects his men to follow his beat alertly at the concert as, by gestures, grimaces and the rhythmic pattern of his hands, he attempts to convey to them what he feels and precisely what effects he wishes them to produce.

This method of conducting yields, at different

times, admirable and deplorable results. At its best, it produces a spontaneity, freshness, emotional intensity, a vitality and moving power which more calculating conductors often fail to attain through the scientific method. And yet, this same method leads at times to very sorry consequences: unbalanced interpretations in which greater emphasis is placed upon details than upon the work as a whole; overstressed accentuations and effects, exaggerated emotionalizations and histrionics.

This, to a great degree, epitomizes the strength and weakness of Leopold Stokowski. His marvelous dramatic instinct, his Hellenic devotion to Beauty sweep him at times—in these personal, intuitive performances—to dazzling heights of greatness. I have heard him perform Bach (particularly in his own felicitous arrangements), the Brahms *First Symphony,* the Wagner *Liebesnacht* music from *Tristan,* and the *Charfreitagzauber* music from *Parsifal,* the *Fourth* and *Fifth* Symphonies of Sibelius, and music of Stravinsky, Ravel and Shostakowitch in a manner which place them proudly at the side of the great performances of the foremost conductors of all-time. Yet, his temperament is at a loss to cope with the exquisite classic line and harmonic fragility of Haydn and Mozart (it is for this reason that Stokowski almost never performs

Haydn, and chooses only the *G-minor* and the *Jupiter* Symphonies with which to represent Mozart on his programs), or to attain an organic whole out of a Beethoven symphony which is infinitely more than a mere sum of its parts. His temperament likewise will tempt him to caress melodic lines until they become cloying, to intensify dramatic climaxes out of proportion to the general design of a composition, to concentrate so keenly upon the general effect he is attempting to reproduce that he will often tolerate loose and unclean playing among the men.

These weaknesses—and I lament them strongly—will, I feel, ultimately exempt Stokowski from the Valhalla of the world's supremely great conductors. Versatile he most certainly is not; and, too often, his conception is not of the sublimest. As an artist, as a musician, as a personality his stature is considerably smaller than those of Karl Muck, Felix Weingartner or Arturo Toscanini. But, though I recognize Stokowski's faults, I feel that only a myopic vision will permit itself to be blurred by them and prevent it from perceiving his equally impressive virtues. As a force in our musical life, his importance cannot be overestimated. The twenty years he has conducted the Philadelphia orchestra have been important musically: Many of the modern works which today we so smugly accept as classics were first valiantly sponsored by Stokowski; the modern composer endowed with a new speech and an original message could always find a haven on Stokowski's programs, and always a sympathetic and understanding performance under his baton. And the distant past has received as flattering attention from Stokowski as the present: his all-Bach programs are aesthetic feasts; and he frequently reminds us that composers like Purcell, Vivaldi, Palestrina and Monteverde were creators of great importance.

Finally, as I have already mentioned, Stokowski is in certain works a rare and sensitive interpreter. There are times when Stokowski is moved by inspiration to performances of incomparable brilliance, depth, drama and beauty.

Stokowski may not be included in the realm of the greatest conductors of our age; but he should always be numbered among the great.

5.

Rehearsals under Stokowski are by no means the routine performances that they have been under Muck or Weingärtner. They are, as a matter of fact, so full of surprises that his men are at a loss to know what next to expect. Stokowski is convinced that the orchestra can understand a composition much better if it is in a psychological frame of mind to perform it. Hence he will bring a pagan icon to the rehearsals of Henry Eicheim's *Bali* and, burning incense in it, will place it in front of the orchestra while it reviews the work. Hence, too, Stokowski's numerous speeches on metaphysics or aesthetics or history or morality before opening the score of a work he is about to rehearse. The psychological preliminaries over, Stokowski will briefly and firmly explain how he wishes a musical work to be played, and will demand that the players follow him much more strictly than they do the printed page. Then —except with difficult works, or first performances —he will concentrate only upon certain essential details in the music. He will never rehearse frequently passages of a classic symphony, but will go over it once or twice. Then, through his gestures, he will attempt to inflame the players with enthusiasm and zest.

There are certain conductors, like Sir Thomas Beecham or Walter Damrosch, who attempt to put their men into the proper frame of mind by instilling joviality and humor into rehearsals. Humor and levity, however, have little place in Stokowski's rehearsals, except in very rare instances when he is in a particularly jovial mood; and even then his levity is as ephemeral as lightning, and he will sud-

denly return to his severity and despotism, and will
even harshly upbraid the men for having laughed a
moment before at his witticism. He is a very hard
taskmaster, and very severe. It is said that at one
unsatisfactory rehearsal, several years ago, Stokowski calmly took out his pocket-watch and told the
orchestra that whoever was unable to play within the
next ten minutes the disputed passage in the manner
he had just explained, would be dismissed at the end
of the season; and Stokowski, as his men know too
well, is not given to making idle threats. His comments, at rehearsals, can often cut into the players'
sensibilities as sharply as a knife. At one time, dis-
pleased with the manner in which the concertmaster
of the orchestra performed, he said curtly: "Gentlemen! Will the first violins please play together?
And will the virtuosos of the orchestra kindly con-
descend to join them?" And at another rehearsal,
he flung this criticism at the wood-wind-players:
"This is not a sty, gentlemen! You are squealing
like pigs!"

On performing a new work, Stokowski—at the
first rehearsal—will sit in the back of the auditorium,
and have an assistant conductor direct the music
from beginning to end, as he makes profuse notes.
An intricate lighting system links his seat with the
assistant conductor's desk, and when Stokowski

wishes a passage to be replayed he signals to the conductor to stop. With his ideas on the new work clear in his mind, Stokowski will come to the platform and begin to shape his interpretation. Often, after hearing a work, Stokowski will decide that he will not perform it. For he has often said that he finds it impossible to perform a piece of music—irrespective of how excellent it is—if he does not feel it intimately with his heart and emotions.

6.

During his twenty or more years with the Philadelphia Orchestra, his orchestral transcriptions of the music of Bach have played such an important rôle on his programs that, I feel, no study of Stokowski can be complete without considering them.

Few tasks are so thankless as that of transcription. If a transcriber succeeds in making a work sound effective in a new dress, the praise invariably returns to the composer; if the transcriber fails, the blame is inevitably his own. Transcribing is, therefore, a monumental labor of love, bringing with it no rewards except the satisfaction of having done a worthwhile job well. It is for this reason that Stokowski has never received half the praise he deserves in a field where he has proved himself to be unusually important.

He is, in many respects, the ideal transcriber. He brings to his task a profound love for the music of Bach, so profound that nothing in the world would tempt him to tamper with the original conception of the master. He served his musical apprenticeship on the organ—and how better can one know the music of Bach intimately than through the organ? He has a prodigious knowledge of orchestration and instrumentation at his beck and call. Finally, he succeeds in completely submerging his own personality in his work, never leaving on the music betraying fingerprints. As a result, when one hears, for example, Respighi's arrangements of Bach, one hears half-Respighi and half-Bach; but in the case of Stokowski, one hears Bach and Bach alone.

Stokowski's transcriptions are extraordinary, not only because he has succeeded in bringing new richness to great music through the medium of a symphony-orchestra, but also because, in this new garb, the music is still true in every respect to the spirit of Bach. When Stokowski transcribes from the organ, he has always tried to retain something of the organ-quality of the music. In the case of the chorale, *Wir Glauben* one can almost hear the stops of the organ. In the celebrated *Toccata and Fugue in D minor,* Stokowski imitated the swell of sound of the organ with such fidelity that there are moments when it seems as though a supreme organist is now performing, except for the brilliance of color and clarity of the sonority. Finally, there is always the utmost simplicity in Stokowski's arrangements. What Bach tried to say on the original instruments, Stokowski has attempted to repeat as unpretentiously as he can with the orchestra. Much of the effectiveness of these transcriptions stems from the fact that they follow their original so closely.

And yet, there will be few to deny that Stokowski has added something vital to his transcriptions. He has taken some of the greatest music of the world, and then increased its effectiveness by the most adroit use of instrumentation. The superb close to the *Passacaglia in C-minor* was always a thrilling experience on the organ; but it is never so stunning as when Stokowski conducts it in his own arrangement. The piano *Prelude in E-flat minor* is a gem when played well; and yet, under Stokowski's fingers it seems to have acquired an altogether new poignancy that is heartbreaking. The inner voices that course and ebb through the "little" *Fugue in G-minor* are brought out with a marvelous, often breath-taking, effect in Stokowski's resplendent orchestration. And if, at times (as in the arrangement of the violin *Chaconne*) Stokowski yields to overdramatization and emotional hysterics, or (as in the *Siciliano*) he makes an orchestral arrangement of a piece of music which sounds infinitely more effective in its original, these are the exceptions in his usually successful attempt to bring new life to old masterpieces.

At his best, Stokowski has brought out the hidden color, the latent wealth, the inherent greatness of each Bach work he has transcribed. Under his arrangements, this music has not only been rejuvenated—so to speak—but its life has been prolonged, one feels, as long as the symphony-orchestra remains the greatest voice for musical expression.

III

KOUSSEVITZKY

1.

THE years following the World War found the Boston Symphony Orchestra in a pitiable plight. Under the ineffectual leadership of Henri Rabaud (1918-1920) the orchestra could not maintain its former supreme standards of excellence, and its deterioration became strikingly noticeable. With Pierre Monteux (1920-1924) the decline became even more alarming. Not merely had some of the ablest musicians of the orchestra been lured to New York and Philadelphia by handsome salaries, but with the failure of a general strike to establish a union in the orchestra more than twenty of the most competent musicians, including the concertmaster, resigned peremptorily. The orchestra, therefore, became a shoddy skeleton of its former self—and Pierre Monteux, who is a much finer musician and interpreter than he is a drillmaster and technician, was altogether incapable of concealing the yawning gaps in the orchestra's texture. Moreover, in contrast to the performances Karl Muck had given but a few years before, the concerts under Monteux seemed particularly uninspiring and prosaic. As a result, the concerts lost their appeal and importance, and the attendance dwindled terrifyingly. Obviously, a drastic reform was necessary to save this formerly great orchestra from complete disorganization and collapse.

And the first movement in this drastic reform came in 1924 when Serge Koussevitzky was appointed the permanent conductor.

Long before Koussevitzky came to America, his name had been encircled by a halo of glamor. From the distance of three thousand miles, his figure had been looming greater and greater, in the years before and after the War, until it seemed to fill the entire musical horizon. His rise in Russia as one of its greatest conductors, his further triumphs in Paris and London, particularly as an apostle of modern Russian music, had already become something of a legend to be repeated from mouth to mouth wherever music-lovers gathered. Here, then, seemed to be the personality who could lift the Boston Symphony Orchestra from its stagnancy and decay. And in his hands full power was entrusted to bring about a metamorphosis.

The moment Koussevitzky came to Boston, he made it emphatically apparent that he had every

SERGE KOUSSEVITZKY

intention of exerting his power. Almost within one season, the body and face of the orchestra changed unrecognizably. The older players were pensioned; those of the newer arrivals who could not approach the standards imposed by Koussevitzky were ruthlessly dismissed. And every corner of the country was carefully sifted for the best orchestral material that could be purchased. With the symphony-orchestra completely reconstructed, Koussevitzky then instituted his innumerable, painstaking rehearsals to thrash this new orchestra into discipline and efficiency.

Nor did his reforms end here. Koussevitzky's mission was not merely to create a great symphonic organization but also to restore the one-time glory to the Boston Symphony Orchestra, and once again to make its name synonymous with the highest ideals of the musical art. Henceforth, the programs in Boston were not to pander to public tastes, but were to be electric in their experimentalism. Koussevitzky banished the weekly "star soloist" from his programs (these soloists had become an integral part of the Boston Symphony concerts with Rabaud and Monteux, in an attempt to lure audiences into the symphony-hall) and in his place Koussevitzky enthroned the modern composers. Finally, Koussevitzky once again restored enchantment and fascination to conducting. In the eyes of the Boston audiences, both Rabaud and Monteux had been unimpressive personalities. But with Koussevitzky's flair for showmanship, with his suave mannerisms and dictatorial air, the baton once again acquired an electric appeal for the music public, and the conductor's podium once again became enveloped in glamor.

Thus, for the first time since 1918, a successor worthy to hold the stick of Karl Muck had been found. And with its cutting, piercing beat it restored, at last, the greatness that the Boston Symphony Orchestra had once enjoyed.

2.

When Serge Koussevitzky was a boy in Russia (he was born in Tver, in 1874) he would often, in play, simulate being a leader of a symphony-orchestra. He would line up rows of empty chairs in the parlor, and in front of these he would place a music-stand and the open score of his favorite symphony. Then he would go through the formalities. Entering the parlor stiffly, he would majestically bow to the empty seats and then, rapping his stick sharply on his stand, would give the imaginary orchestra the signal to begin. Suddenly he would begin to gesture wildly, and would sing the different parts of the orchestral score at the top of his voice.

This ambition to become a conductor, which made its presence felt so strongly from the earliest years, drew Koussevitzky magnetically to the baton. We are told that, even as a child of seven, he found an opportunity to direct a small orchestra in an orchestral work of his own composition. Later, as a student in Berlin, one of his first accomplishments was to organize a student-orchestra which could explore, under his guidance, the music of Beethoven and Wagner. In those student days his leisure hours were spent in the symphony-hall, particularly at the concerts of Artur Nikisch, where he not only smudged the pages of his scores with notations of Nikisch's interpretations, but he also made a mental picture of Nikisch's gestures and movements so that he might be able to reproduce them in his own conducting.

As a graduate from the Royal High School of Music in Berlin and the Philharmonic School of Music in Moscow, and as a double-bass performer of very obvious talent, the guiding force in Koussevitzky's life was still this indestructible desire to become a conductor. His happiest hours were spent with nose buried in symphony-scores, and with baton in hand carefully beating the rhythm of the music. When he acquired a prestige with his double-bass which encircled half the globe, he revealed no hesitancy or vacillation in exchanging his world-famous double-bass for a baton when the first opportunity presented itself.

His ambition to become an orchestra-leader was to materialize in an unexpected fashion. In 1905 (by this time he had concertized with enormous success in Germany, England, and France where he was generally conceded to be the Fritz Kreisler or the Pablo Casals of his instrument), he married the daughter of one of the wealthiest merchants in Russia. On the eve of the wedding, the merchant approached his prospective son-in-law and, with a smile of satisfaction beaming upon his face, inquired what the young man wished as a wedding-gift from his father-in-law. Money? A palatial home? A conservatory of music, perhaps? Koussevitzky had not forgotten his dream. With the simplicity of one who knew precisely what he wanted, he answered that his greatest wish was nothing more or less than a complete symphony-orchestra, to do with as he wished. The smile of satisfaction was erased from the merchant's face, and a look of incredulity and bewilderment supplanted it. A symphony-orchestra? But the young musician insisted that there was nothing else his heart desired more than this. As a result, several months after his prolonged honeymoon in Germany, young Koussevitzky gathered the foremost musicians of Russia to Moscow for the purpose of founding a symphony-orchestra. After careful selection and discrimination, Koussevitzky engaged eighty-five men, and, in 1907, the first of the Koussevitzky concerts took place in Moscow.

Now that Koussevitzky held in his hands the toy which, for so many years he had possessed only in imagination, he had no intention of utilizing it merely for self-amusement. He realized that it could be a powerful means for the spreading of great music among his fellow-countrymen. Thus, he was to introduce into his concerts his amazing initiative and resource from the very first. Composers whose music was rarely heard in Russia were introduced on his programs, and even such modern Russian composers as Skryabin and Stravinsky were first to find performance in Russia under Koussevitzky. Moreover, Koussevitzky introduced a series of Festivals, each devoted to one composer, which became annually the major artistic event in Russia; his Festivals devoted to Bach, Beethoven, Tschaikovsky, Rimsky-Korsakoff etc. were striking innovations for musical Russia, and they brought to their conductor great prestige.

But Koussevitzky's greatest artistic achievement with his orchestra was the extensive tours through the small towns of the Volga which he undertook in

1910. He had, for a long time, nursed the dream of bringing the glories of symphonic music to those hamlets and secluded villages of Russia where the art of music was virtually a stranger. And so, chartering a special steamer, he traveled with his men down the Volga, visiting obscure towns, and bringing Beethoven, Brahms, Wagner and Tschaikovsky to peasants with hard, cracked faces who, momentarily, deserted their shovels, to listen to these strange, magnificent sounds. At one town, Koussevitzky's symphony-orchestra was such a curiosity that—we are told by his biographer, Arthur Lourié —a delegate of merchants came to the conductor to request him to place the harp in the very front of the orchestra because some of them had seen the instrument unloaded from the boat and were eager to know how it was played!

Koussevitzky traveled more than twenty-three hundred miles with his orchestra, at a personal expense of more than a hundred thousand dollars, to preach his gospel of beauty. And it was to have a vital effect. Koussevitzky informs us that though, at first, peasants and merchants came to his concerts in niggardly handfuls, and only out of curiosity, they were soon to swarm in hundreds out of a sincere adoration for the music he had brought them. In this fashion, the name of Koussevitzky became, along the banks of the Volga, encased in legend; it represented a humanitarian and a musician who—like some mythological Volga Boatman—brought with him, wherever he came, new worlds of beauty.

These exploits brought enormous fame to Koussevitzky, and when he returned to Moscow he was recognized as one of the foremost conductors in Russia. His fame became so great that, as early as 1916, he received offers to come to America. Koussevitzky, however, was to remain in Europe eight years longer. When the Revolution broke out in Russia, his preeminent position among contemporary Russian conductors was recognized by the Soviet Union, and he was appointed the director of the Russian State Orchestras. This position he held until 1920, and relinquished it only because interference from the State Department made it impossible for him to pursue his work with his customary fervor and devotion. He, therefore, went to Paris, there to establish the *Concerts Koussevitzky* of world-fame.

Formerly preaching the gospel of European music to Russian audiences, Koussevitzky was now to enter a new phase in his career—spreading the propaganda for contemporary Russian music to European music-lovers. And under his flaming performances, the music of Skryabin, Moussorgsky, Stravinsky, Rimsky-Korsakoff and Miaskovsky acquired great vogue in important European cities.

But the richest phase of Koussevitzky's career with the baton stems from 1924, when he came to Boston. Here, more than ever before, he asserted himself as a distinct personality, a musical force of great power, and a prophet of modern music.

3.

Serge Koussevitzky's years with the Boston Symphony Orchestra have undeniably placed him among the great conductors of our time. In his many performances during his American career, Koussevitzky has revealed a rich imagination, a refined poetry, a youthful freshness and a power that have brought new horizons to many of the works he has performed.

As a conductor, Koussevitzky's instinct for building dramatic effects, for color, for correct phrasing, for expressive dynamics has aroused considerable comment and admiration. But other characteristics of Koussevitzky's art are of equal importance. His meticulous sense for rhythm is extraordinarily precise, and he is endowed with an unusual ability to cull sonorities of great richness from the brasses and a wonderfully singing tone from the strings. A marvelous technician with the orchestra, Koussevitzky knows its resources as few conductors do, and knows how to exploit these resources to best advantage. A complete command over his men—whom he has drilled to a point where he can receive, almost as a reflex-action, any response he seeks—gives all of his performances a technical sureness which has never been known to falter. He is not a mere metronome, and he has often expressed his contempt for those conductors who do no more than beat time at the concert. Koussevitzky expresses his individuality with each movement of his hand and body, and often induces his orchestra through this means to rise to heights of great inspiration in its playing.

Like Stokowski, Koussevitzky conducts more with emotion than with intellect. He responds to music intuitively and, in his interpretations, attempts to give expression to his feelings and emotions experience while first hearing the score. His method of preparing a new composition for performance is to have a competent sight-reader perform the work for him on the piano several times from beginning to end.[1] Koussevitzky will listen attentively, and as he listens his interpretation acquires body and shape

[1] Two or three years ago, a ridiculous but widely circulated rumor hinted that it was this assisting pianist, and not Dr. Koussevitzky, who was responsible for the high standard of performances of the Boston Symphony Orchestra. These rumors went to the absurd extremes of suggesting that Koussevitzky could not even read a score—an amazing accusation about one who, at one time, was the world's greatest double-bass virtuoso!

in his mind. He has an enormous faculty for perceiving the design, and the inherent messages, of even the most complicated works at a single hearing; he has been known to listen to a new composition while reading a book, and then criticizing it with penetration and acumen. In the same fashion, hearing the pianist perform a new piece of music, he will know precisely how it should sound in performance. At the rehearsal, there is no groping or stumbling where the conductor is concerned. Methodical as a business man, Koussevitzky's rehearsals are strictly routinized. He knows clearly and precisely every effect he seeks, and he explains his desires firmly and tersely, without dramatics or hysterics.

While Koussevitzky at his best is a singularly inspired and inspiring conductor—and while he is at his best more frequently than not—he swings from greatness to mediocrity and from mediocrity to greatness with the amazing consistency of a pendulum. Regular attendance at the concerts of the Boston Symphony Orchestra is often like a ride upon some spiritual scenic railway which, now, lifts the listener heavenwards and then, suddenly, sinks him to depths. Not only is Koussevitzky capable of a stunning performance of one work, and a lethargic reading of another, at the same concert, but very often he will play one and the same work brilliantly upon one occasion and then, a few weeks or months later, will give it the affected and pompous reading of a third-rate German bandmaster.

The truth is that, being essentially a romanticist and poet, Koussevitzky is not capable of performing a work with enthusiasm and inspiration unless he feels a very close and sensitive affinity with it. Certain works hold no fascination for him, and when he attempts to perform these he is discouragingly pedestrian and all too obviously insincere. Also, there are times when, for one reason or another, he is unable to respond emotionally even to a favorite work of his, and at such times his baton mysteriously loses its sting and driving power. Yet, shortly thereafter, his enthusiasm will return and the greatness of his conception will be restored to the musical work.

When the flame burns hot within him, his Beethoven can be grandiose, his Mendelssohn angelic, his Brahms profound, his Tschaikovsky poignant. But his temperament and his talents respond most effectively to the brilliant scoring, the dynamic rhythms and the pungent harmonic schemes of the modern composers. He is, probably, at his best in giving expression to the excitable, hyperthyroid utterances of modernists. Mr. Ernest Newman has commented, with his customary penetration, that one of the outstanding qualities of Koussevitzky as a conductor is his ability, even in works of the greatest excitability, to retain in his fingers the reins of the performance. "The more the artist is on fire, the cooler have to be the head and hand that direct the fire. Koussevitzky has the central ice in an extraordinary degree. I believe that it would be hardly possible to raise some works to higher pitch of nervous incandescence than he does; but the nervousness never gets out of hand. It is Koussevitzky's servant, not master. The excitement is always perfectly under control; one great plastic line runs round and through the work." It is, probably, for this reason that in the music of Berlioz, Skryabin, Sibelius, Ravel, Koussevitzky speaks with his baton a language which only a handful of conductors have been known to equal.

IV

A GROUP OF DISTINGUISHED GUESTS

1.

THE guest-conductor vogue, which often makes it imperative to bring as many as five different conductors a season to one and the same orchestra, has reached its greatest importance within recent date. Before 1920, a variety of batons was not an indispensible feature of the concert-platform, and there were many seasons in which one conductor was deemed sufficient to carry an orchestra through an entire year of concerts. A new personality upon the conductor's platform was, at that time, a rare event.

Today, however, batons change hands at our symphony concerts all too frequently. One cannot lament too strongly an innovation which not only has brought to the symphony-hall something of the appeal of a vaudeville-show but which also, truth to tell, is injurious both to the orchestra and the conductor. Great orchestras can never be the product of multiple personalities; an orchestra, after all, is not a chameleon that can instantly change its colors

241

to conform plastically to the temperament of every new conductor—and, inevitably, its performances must suffer. I, personally, do not believe that that marvelous instrument that was the Philadelphia Symphony Orchestra several years ago when Leopold Stokowski had been virtually its only conductor for more than a decade is so perfect today, with guest-conductors dividing among themselves half of each season. And, likewise, I believe that the unique technical strength of the Boston Symphony Orchestra lies in the fact that few intruders have been permitted to trespass upon Mr. Koussevitzky's territory since 1924.

Of course, a conductor like Toscanini is sufficiently great to make the New York Philharmonic his personal instrument after a few appearances. But other conductors—and they include such eminent artists as Bruno Walter, Erich Kleiber and Otto Klemperer—are unable to produce the results from the Philharmonic that would most certainly have been theirs were this orchestra their own for an entire season. It is too much to expect from a great orchestra that it maintain constantly an enormously high standard if, after having learned to adapt itself to the temperament and desires of one conductor, it is suddenly thrust in front of new leaders with new demands, whims and methods. It is also, perhaps, too much to expect that conductors—compelled to make an impression with a few appearances, instead of in an entire season—should not yield to sensationalism.

It was Willem Mengelberg who first established the fad of the guest-conductor as something of a permanent institution, particularly in New York. In 1921, fresh from a triumphant career in Holland where he had brought the Concertgebow Orchestra to world-prominence particularly as a result of his festivals devoted to the music of Beethoven, Mahler and Richard Strauss, Mengelberg arrived in New York to direct a few guest performances of, and to inject new interest into, Artur Bodanzky's newly-organized New Symphony Orchestra. From the very first concerts he conducted, Mengelberg created such a volcanic impression that almost immediately the new style in our musical life was inaugurated. Henceforth the two major orchestras in New York —the Philharmonic and the New York Symphony Society—were to vie with one another in bringing to their audiences as guests other leading European conductors who might inflame the imagination of the public as hotly as Mengelberg had succeeded in doing; and other important symphony-orchestras in America were to follow suit.

2.

No conductor ever made a début under conditions more auspicious than those existing in New York at the time of Mengelberg's first arrival. In 1921, the New York music-audience had for several years been fed upon an unsavory diet of symphonic-music; it had accustomed itself to the often lackadaisical, often careless and always uninspiring performances of Josef Stransky with the Philharmonic Orchestra, Walter Damrosch of the New York Symphony Society and, to a less degree, Artur Bodanzky with the New Symphony Orchestra. And so, when Mengelberg first rapped his stick upon the stand, he succeeded in reviving the concertgoing audience from its musical stupor. Audiences suddenly discovered that new blood was coursing into the veins of thrice-familiar music, revivifying them as though the conductor had succeeded in breathing an altogether new breath of life into their nostrils. The public, hearing their beloved Tschaikovsky and Beethoven symphonies, and the tone-poems of Richard Strauss, suddenly acquiring a new brisk vitality, a vernal freshness, a power and grandeur they never seemed to possess before under the somnolent readings of Stransky and Damrosch, drank the music gluttonously. For the first time in many years, it realized the

WILLEM MENGELBERG

importance of a great conductor to a musical work.

The result was that Mengelberg was repaid with idolatry such as few conductors have known in New York. Perhaps, as one writer was to comment at this time, the scenes that followed each of Mengelberg's concerts with the New Symphony Orchestra were disgraceful episodes for a temple devoted to great art. Mengelberg permitted himself to be kissed and caressed and pampered as though he were a cinema star. At any rate, one should not condemn too severely a reaction so spontaneous and sincere as that which Mengelberg's art inspired among his New York audiences.

Mengelberg's reign in New York was not destined to remain permanent, but it was a long one, and during its first few years was particularly brilliant. The concert-hall bulged with audiences who suddenly found a new, revived interest in symphonic-music as a result of this conductor's rejuvenating performances; and it echoed with the cheers of appreciation each time Mengelberg completed the performance of a major symphonic work. Mengelberg definitely became the man of the hour in New York's musical life.

And Mengelberg could inspire affection and admiration in his orchestra-men as well as in his audience. His was a personality full of magnetic power and genius, which could arouse the players as few conductors in their experience had succeeded in doing. At the rehearsal, Mengelberg could be majestically imperious and, at the same time, unusually soft and considerate. He knew his desires, and firmly demanded that they be carried out. But he did not believe in scolding; every mistake was gently pointed out, corrected and forgiven. Quoting from the valuable biography on Mengelberg by Mrs. Edna Richolson Sollitt: "Mengelberg can be severe; it is even terrible to watch him in a rare moment of anger, when he maintains a silence that is absolutely thunderous. But there is always dignity, always reason and control to the fore, and he never indulges in nerves, hysteria and temper. And never does a rehearsal finish in anger, or a player leave his presence with a weight of pain or injustice in his heart."

Mrs. Sollitt gives us a further picture of Mengelberg at the rehearsal which is particularly illuminating in giving us insight into his personality. "Mengelberg uses a specially designed stand for rehearsing, with side pieces and a narrow seat across the back. Theoretically, he rests his arms often on the sides and sits at ease while working. Actually, this seldom happens; he is too interested. When strenuously reminded of long strains to come, and urged with more than usual vehemence to save himself a little, he begins by sitting still, sometimes for several minutes, and using a trifle less energy in his beat. But comes a passage full of interest—and, for him, what passage is not?—and up he springs as if electrified, which indeed he is. . . . Never lived a man who better loved a bit of fun. Not long ago, at the end of an hour's repolishing of an overture already intimately familiar to the players, and after allowing them to play the last section through, Mengelberg led with full vigor up to the final chords, before he laid down his baton and maliciously awaited results. Anything more comic than the bewildered sheep-like confusion which followed would be hard to imagine and the rehearsal ended in gales of laughter." [1]

Mengelberg's influence upon symphonic- music in America, during this period, was enormously far-reaching and has never, I feel, been sufficiently stressed or appreciated. In a short while, he created a standard for performances so incomparably higher than what had preceded him that it soon became necessary for such conductors as Josef Stransky and Walter Damrosch, in New York, to withdraw from the scene and confess that their day was over; and, as a direct result, a higher type of conductor was

[1] *Mengelberg and the Symphonic Epoch* by Edna R. Sollitt: Ives Washburn, Inc., Publishers, New York.

demanded by every major symphony-orchestra in the country. Mengelberg, moreover, was an important factor in bringing about the mergers of the New Symphony Orchestra (and, several years later, the New York Symphony Society) with the new York Philharmonic, thereby considerably solidifying the formerly fragile structure of the latter organization. Then, as the conductor of the New Philharmonic Symphony Society, he brought about such a metamorphosis in its technique and artistic attainments that, when he finally yielded his baton to Toscanini, it had already become one of the major symphonic bodies in the world.

Unfortunately, New York audiences were not to remain faithful to their god. The reasons for this are multiple. No doubt, the most important was the fact that Mengelberg had arrived in New York at a time when the city was impoverished of great conductors, and so he could instantly assume a regal position; but, a few years after his arrival, he was to know the competition of such world-renowned personalities as Furtwängler and Toscanini. It was inevitable, therefore, that the enormous admiration which the public bore for Mengelberg should now be divided.

But this explanation, important though it is, does not tell the entire story. For Mengelberg, at his best, is one of the foremost conductors of our time, whose performances need not go hiding in shame in the face of those of other conductors. I have heard performances by Mengelberg—particularly when he was directing his own Concertgebow Orchestra— which assured me beyond a question of a doubt of Mengelberg's superlative qualities as a conductor. Certainly, in sheer conductorial technique there is no other conductor, with the possible exception of Karl Muck, who can match adroitness and skill with Mengelberg. The Concertgebow Orchestra, for example, is by no means an excellent orchestra; one would hesitate even to mention it in the same breath with some of America's second-rate symphonic-bodies. Yet, under Mengelberg's discipline its pliancy and flexibility are extraordinary. It responds to the slightest desires of its conductor's stick and gestures with sensitivity; it produces the most subtle effects and nuances that clearly prove that it is controlled by the hand of a master. Moreover, it was primarily Mengelberg's consummate technique that, in a short time, converted the New York Philharmonic from a mediocre orchestra to one of the greatest in the world. But Mengelberg is more than a great technician. In the ability to give voice to sonorities of full-bodied richness and grandeur, he has few equals; not even Toscanini could take a symphonic organization with obvious deficiencies and endow it with such depth, strength and resilience as Mengelberg has done time and again. Finally, in each of his interpretations, there is a coherent conception, a marvelously constructed design in which each pattern is an inextricable part of the whole. The music always speaks for itself, guided by a fresh emotion and a keen intellect.

Why, then, did a conductor of such unquestionable attainments ultimately lose his enormous prestige in New York? The answer, I am afraid, is that after a few seasons in New York, Mengelberg degenerated artistically from his high peaks of excellence—and so noticeably that the audiences were soon to find very little artistic satisfaction in his concerts.

It is not very difficult to understand why Mengelberg's art suffered a sudden decline in New York. For one thing, when Mengelberg sensed that his audiences, once so idolatrous, were dividing their adulation between him and other conductors, it affected his performances acutely. He, who until now had been such a solid and artistically inviolate conductor, began to resort to the most exaggerated interpretations in a futile and pathetic gesture to recapture a lost glory.

Equally important in bringing about the dusk of

Mengelberg's greatness in New York was the insistence on the part of both public and manager, after the first three seasons, that Mengelberg change his programs more frequently. Mengelberg has always been a very slow worker in preparing his concerts, and he requires long and frequent rehearsals to attain his ultimate results. Irremediably garrulous, he cannot rehearse ten bars of music without delivering a sermon on the import of the music, and the difference between good and bad playing. He is eager to have his men understand all the implications of the music they are performing, as well as his own reactions to it. Then, painfully meticulous about details, Mengelberg brings a symphony to shape piece by piece; his method is one of comprehensive thoroughness. Given all the rehearsals he requires, Mengelberg's method will bring his performances a perfection which few conductors can emulate. During the early seasons in New York, Mengelberg solved the problem of the comparatively few rehearsals allotted to him by performing only one program an entire week. But when he was compelled to instil added variety, by changing his programs over the week-end, four rehearsals proved to be sorely inadequate for his needs, and he was at a loss to cope with the situation. He was, therefore, driven to hurried preparations and, consequently, inadequate performances. And it was not long thereafter before New York audiences—which can be very discerning—began to discover a radical change in Mengelberg's performances and turned with both their enthusiasms and appreciations to other conductors.

Mengelberg, of course, realized forcefully that he had seen the termination of his magnificent reign in New York, and the realization embittered him. I recall one rehearsal particularly, when for one of the few times in his life Mengelberg uncontrollably lost his temper. This was in the Winter of 1930. Toscanini had become an idol in New York, and in another week he was to return for another season of concerts. During the rehearsal I have in mind, the men were unusually apathetic to Mengelberg's commands and were, for one reason or another, especially slow in following his instructions. Finally, Mengelberg split his baton into pieces and cried out: "That's all right, gentlemen! You don't have to pay any attention to me, you know! Toscanini will be here next week, and you can spare all of your effort for *him!*" Then, without another word, he stormed off the stage.

And this, I believe, was one of the last rehearsals that Mengelberg held in this country.

3.

The immediate result of Mengelberg's great success in 1921 was, as I have already mentioned, a spirited rivalry between the Philharmonic and the New York Symphony Society to bring Europe's foremost conductors as guests to New York. From 1922 until its demise, the New York Symphony Society presented such outstanding visitors as Albert Coates, Bruno Walter, Vladimir Golschmann, Otto Klemperer, Enrique Fernández Arbós, Fritz Busch, Clemens Krauss and Oskar Fried. The New York Philharmonic was no less energetic. Since the time of Mengelberg, it has brought to this country Wilhelm Furtwängler, Willem van Hoogstraten, Fritz Reiner, Toscanini, Sir Thomas Beecham, Molinari, Issai Dobrowen and Erich Kleiber.

Not all of these conductors were of gargantuan stature, to be sure; and many of them had merely ephemeral appeal at best. Albert Coates, for example, Willem van Hoogstraten and Fritz Reiner. Intimate acquaintance with the work of Coates, Hoogstraten and Reiner disclosed a lack of personality and character in their interpretations. Van Hoogstraten, therefore, turned to the less exacting requirements of summer concerts in New York and winter-seasons in Portland. Albert Coates, after his first few appearances, gave humdrum performances and, as a result, could never enjoy here the prominence that has since been his in London and Russia. And it was not until Fritz Reiner passed from the symphony-hall of Cincinnati to the opera-house in Philadelphia—where his fine instinct for accompaniment was to make his performances so memorable—that he succeeded in rising above the shoulders of mediocrity.

It is not difficult to balance tersely the strength and weakness, and to estimate the relative importance, of many of the other conductors to whom New York audiences played hosts in Carnegie Hall. Issai Dobrowen, though not of the first rank of conductors, exhibited much talent at his concerts. His stick has variety and taste, and it has recently brought a quiet distinction to the symphony season in San Francisco. Both Bernardino Molinari and Enrique Fernández Arbós revealed an orthodox technique and a serene approach to classical literature. Molinari, one of the principal symphonic-conductors of present-day Italy, and Arbós, the conductor of the Madrid Symphony Orchestra, revealed their greatest strength in the works of their native composers. Molinari—in the music of older Italian composers—and Arbós—in the compositions of Spain—had a particularly vital beat and fresh

CLEMENS KRAUSS

approach; away from this music both of these conductors proved to be in possession of dignity and intelligence, although not outstanding distinction.

Clemens Krauss, whose performances of *Der Rosenkavalier* of Richard Strauss has become a classic of interpretation in Vienna and Salzburg, proved disappointing in the symphonic-repertoire. His loose readings disclosed a lack of penetration or inherent comprehension of the works he conducted, and too frequently were the finer and deeper qualities of the music absent. His recent positions as director of the Vienna State Opera, and more recently of the Berlin State Opera, would tend to suggest that Krauss' strength lay in the opera-house rather than in the symphony-hall. But the writer who has attended many of Krauss' performances in Vienna and Salzburg failed to find very much subtlety or grace in Krauss' readings of the Mozart operas; and only in *Der Rosenkavalier* does he seem to possess a close affinity with the gorgeous orchestral effects of Richard Strauss. However, Clemens Krauss has, I am afraid, seen the termination of his successful career. To turn from Vienna—where he enjoyed a far greater prominence than he deserved —to Berlin, was a monstrous tactical error. In Berlin, he has met antagonism because his performances never succeeding in measuring up to the stature of those of his predecessor, Erich Kleiber. Austria is now definitely closed to him. And outside of Austria, Krauss has never succeeded in arousing very much admiration.

Eugene Goossens, from London, proved to be a scholarly and impressive musician, although his avoidance of sensationalism and self-advertisement made it difficult for him to acquire a very extensive following. Clear, finely carved performances are always to be expected from his conducting—and, occasionally, in the works of certain contemporary composers he approaches brilliance. His success in New York, although not overwhelming, was sufficiently marked to earn for him, in 1931, a permanent position with the Cincinnati Symphony Orchestra.

Much more romantic in temperament than Goossens—and much less objective in his approach—was Vladimir Golschmann, one of the younger French conductors. In 1919, he founded the *Concerts Golschmann* in Paris which were so significant in bringing the most important work of the young French composers to the attention of the music-world, and were directed with such keen intelligence, that they attracted towards him the roving eye of the directors of the New York Symphony Society, alert for new conductorial importations. Fiery and dramatic (one might suggest that he is, at times, over-dramatic to the point of arriving at artificiality) Golschmann is always warm and individual in his performances. Today, as the conductor of the St. Louis Symphony Orchestra, Golschmann has instituted a very vital repertoire.

Oskar Fried, one of the older modern German conductors, and Fritz Busch, one of the younger, both came to this country with enormous prestige behind them—the former, for his work as founder and director of the Berlin Symphony Orchestra, and the latter for his career with the Dresden Opera. However, their performances with the New York Symphony Orchestra were too academic to stir very great enthusiasm. Schooled in the German tradition of von Bülow, they brought with them the often formulistic and stilted readings of the traditional German Kapellmeister who knows his score thoroughly but who has very little either in personality or in insight to contribute to it.

Sir Thomas Beecham—he of the corybantic gestures—was disconcertingly uneven in his many concerts in New York. Coming to America with a reputation that for two decades had been soaring and expanding first in London and then throughout Europe, Beecham brought with him many high expectations. At times, these were more than fulfilled:

Sir Thomas could rise as an interpreter to heights which only few conductors of our time could touch; his *Don Quixote* of Strauss, his Delius and his Handel were the creations of a fine intellect, a sensitive emotion and a profound interpretative instinct. And yet, in many other performances—his Mozart, for example, in which he is reputed to be in his element—Sir Thomas could be innocently ingenuous, guilty of sentimentalization, overrefinement and lack of a coherent viewpoint. Sir Thomas Beecham is, without question, a musician of great attainment, a conductor who must always be ranked high, and a musical force in England whose indefatigable efforts on behalf of "opera for the masses" have been of inestimable significance. But his strangely frequent fluctuations from greatness to mediocrity must inevitably keep him, I feel, from the ranks of truly great conductors.

4.

Both Otto Klemperer and Bruno Walter were first introduced to America by the New York Symphony Society several seasons before they became important elements in our musical scheme—Walter coming in 1922, and Klemperer following him three years later. While both conductors gave performances which, at periodic intervals, possessed unusual

258

strength, and disclosed conceptions of great magnitude, their true stature was not apparent at the time. The reason for this was, to a great degree, the strong undercurrent of antagonism towards German conductors that existed at the time in Dr. Damrosch's orchestra, which made it particularly difficult for these men to draw the necessary response from the players and, thereby, attain consistently impressive performances. Bruno Walter, I understand, found it so difficult to maintain discipline that, in spite of himself, he was compelled to tolerate readings whose standards were lower than those to which he had been accustomed. And Klemperer's awkward mannerisms, as well as his peculiar dress (he rehearsed, wearing a frayed green sweater!) were not particularly conducive to inspiring great respect from inimical players. I attended rehearsals of Klemperer in which I found the conductor pleading with his men to follow his intentions, as though he were a schoolboy begging a picayune favor!

Notwithstanding this enormous obstacle, both Klemperer and Bruno Walter occasionally brought dignity and vitality to their readings which were immediately perceived by critics and the more discerning music-lovers. During their last concerts with the New York Symphony Society, they performed in half-empty halls, but their appeal to a small coterie of sincere musicians was a very great one. When Walter returned, in 1932, to become one of the permanent conductors of the New York Philharmonic, to be followed by Otto Klemperer who assumed the directorship of the Los Angeles Philharmonic and who gave guest-performances with the New York Philharmonic and the Philadelphia orchestras, this exclusive coterie of admirers had grown in size until it included the bulk of the music-public. Today, the American music-audience joins Europe in recognizing both Klemperer and Bruno Walter as two leading orchestral conductors of our time.

Bruno Walter was born in Berlin in 1876; Otto Klemperer in Breslau, in 1885. Both of these conductors were befriended in their youth—and encouraged, and given direction in their art—by Gustav Mahler, whom they worshipped as a personality and as artist. It was Mahler who first turned Bruno Walter seriously to conducting, when Walter was still a student at the Stern Conservatory in Berlin; and it was Mahler who gave Otto Klemperer his first important conductorial assignment, in Hamburg in 1909. World-prominence first came both to Walter and Klemperer in the opera-house. In 1922, Klemperer became the musical director of the Opera House in Wiesebaden, and in 1925 Bruno Walter—

BRUNO WALTER

who had previously enjoyed a rising fame in Munich
—came to the head of the Berlin Charlottenburg
Opera. Here, with their incandescent and revital-
ized recreations of classic German operas, and their
healthy experiments with new operatic expressions,
Klemperer and Walter brought great prestige both
to their opera-houses and to themselves. Bruno
Walter earned further glory subsequently with his
symphonic performances with the Leipzig Gewandhaus Orchestra, and his ebullient readings of Mozart
at the annual Salzburg festivals.

Both Bruno Walter and Otto Klemperer were
nurtured and raised upon the traditions of conducting created by Hans von Bülow—and their strength
and weakness as conductors are to a great degree
those of the school they represent. They are true
Germans in their solid musicianship, their enormous
knowledge of the musical repertoire, and their sincerely artistic approach—and here lies their great
power. But, like their predecessor Hans von Bülow,
both Walter and Klemperer look upon a musical
masterpiece as a plastic organism which the conductor can shape at his own discretion. Liberty with
tempi, with a preponderance of *rubato,* exaggeration
of dynamics, reconstruction of the melodic phrase
are occasional intruders into the performances of
both Klemperer and Walter.

It is true that there are times when the unusual interpretative gifts of these conductors bring new qualities to a musical work which, momentarily, makes the listener grateful that the score has undergone reconstruction. But more often overemphasis or understatement puts a musical work "sadly out of joint." On the one hand, for example, Klemperer's heavy hand will bring to the music he conducts a harsh brusqueness which will exaggerate the importance of the double-basses, brasses and tympani in the orchestra. and touch a work with the fat fingers of vulgarity; on the other hand, Bruno Walter's sensitivity will attempt to bring such an exquisite delicacy to certain works that it is impossible to hear his *pianissimo* passages, and frequently the sonorities lack a spine. On the one hand, Klemperer will attempt to bring pace and movement to a work by disregarding a *fermata,* or increasing his beat enormously; on the other hand, Walter will try to underline a particularly moving passage for strings by slackening the *tempo* to a snail-like gait.

Such defect in the art of Walter and Klemperer should not be disregarded in any evaluation of their work. However, after these faults are acknowledged and recognized, they become negligible in the face of the towering virtues of these two conductors: their ability to feel the heart-beat of most works they conduct and to retain it in the performances; their tremendous vitality and strength; the heroic outlines of their conception and the inextinguishable flame of their imagination.

In the case of Bruno Walter, I have always felt that his great powers as a conductor rested not in symphonic literature but in operatic music, particularly in the works of Mozart, Gluck and Weber. Away from the limelight of attention which is focused on symphony-conductors, and secluded in the more obscure depths of the opera-pit, Walter loses that flair for personal exhibitionism and that proclivity for self-exploitation in his interpretations that blemish his symphonic readings so frequently. His performances of Mozart's *Abduction from the Seraglio* and *Don Giovanni,* and Gluck's *Iphigenia in Aulis* are neat cases in point. Not merely refinement but restraint characterizes his performances of these works. His orchestra assumes the fragile quality of a chamber music ensemble without collapsing under the strain. The melodic line is permitted strength of character. And in his exquisite accompaniments to the arias, Walter permits the fine inner voices of the orchestration to assert themselves. When Bruno Walter conducts the operatic music of Gluck, Mozart, Donizetti and Weber, he belongs to a race of great interpreters—a distinction which is only infrequently his when he directs symphonic-music.

Like Otto Klemperer, Erich Kleiber is essentially at his greatest when he conducts the works of modern composers. In 1923, Kleiber was appointed general music director of the Berlin State Opera, one of the most significant musical posts in Europe. Here, while Kleiber always brought a fresh viewpoint to whatever opera he undertook to perform, he proved sensational in the music of the modernists. A driving rhythmic force, an ability to paint a coat of many striking colors with orchestral sonority, and a healthy vigor made him uniquely suited for the expression of younger rebellious voices. Introducing to the world Alban Berg's *Wozzeck,* Krenek's *Leben des Orestes,* Weinberger's *Schwanda,* his sympathetic understanding of the score, the lambency of his readings, and the intoxicating enthusiasm of his baton were important factors in bringing these works an immediate recognition. He can be authoritative and revealing in the classics as well—and his true interpretative gifts in the music of Brahms, Schubert and Mendelssohn, etc., have never been so fully appreciated in America as they deserved.

There will be very little controversy, I am sure, when I assign the preeminent place among modern German conductors to Wilhelm Furtwängler, one of the most uniquely gifted interpreters of our time. An exquisite balance between subjectivity and objectivity is achieved by Furtwängler in all of his performances, in which—though the composers desires are adhered to—the striking personality of the conductor is strongly assertive. This personality is essentially a poetical one; in shaping a melody, in building a climax, in purifying sonorities and giving color and depth to a musical message, Furtwängler's expression is poignantly lyrical, flushed with emotion and tenderness.

Those who attended his New York début with the Philharmonic on January 3, 1925 will probably never forget the impression he made. A program that included Richard Strauss' *Don Juan,* the *Concerto for Violoncello and Orchestra* by Haydn (with Pablo Casals as soloist) and the Brahms *First Symphony* possessed sufficient elasticity to reveal the tremendous scope of this conductor's genius. When he first stepped on the platform he seemed hardly to possess those qualities necessary for a conductor to create a profound impression in New York. Physically, he was most unimpressive; a malicious German critic had compared Furtwängler's appearance to that of a stalk of asparagus! His gestures were awkward, and the stiffly angular motions of his body were not pleasant to watch. Furtwängler's rousing triumph, therefore, was entirely a musical one. The electric current that shot through Strauss' poem, igniting the coruscant tone-colors with added glow, the angelic simplicity of the Haydn in which the orchestra suddenly became as fragile as precious chinaware, and the magnificently grandiose majesty and sublimity of the Brahms symphony—an interpretation built upon gargantuan outlines—will probably never be forgotten. Here was a bewildering versatility that could touch many styles with equal magic! Here, a conductor who could remain true to the printed page and yet cull from the music such hidden voices and colors that it seemed to be entirely reborn.

Technically, there are few batonists who can match Furtwängler's scope and grasp. His knowledge of the orchestra is consummate. He knows each instrument intimately and, when a technical problem arises in performance, he frequently is able to teach his players how to perform their part. The entire orchestra is supple clay in his hands; he has a marvelous capacity for shaping it at will with the slightest movements of his fingers. I recall several rehearsals of Tschaikovsky's *Fifth Symphony* and Dvorak's *From the New World Symphony* when Furtwängler, through the most economical means— the slight change of accentuation, a deft change of

WILHELM FURTWANGLER

color, a new method of phrasing—almost miraculously converted an ordinary performance into one of exquisite poetry. Finally, his knowledge of the musical repertoire is prodigious, to be matched only by Toscanini's; he rarely refers to a printed page in performance because every mark is familiar to him.

Like most supremely great conductors, Furtwängler not only received his maturity in the opera-house but is equally potent both in symphonic and operatic music. He can be as penetratingly profound and as genuinely poetical conducting a Wagnerian music-drama as in a Beethoven or Brahms symphony—as this writer who heard Furtwängler perform *Tristan und Isolde* in Bayreuth and *Die Walküre* in Paris, can testify.

He was born in Berlin in 1886, and in 1915 succeeded Artur Bodanzky as the opera-director in Mannheim. From that time on his star rose steadily. As the conductor of the *Wiener Tonkünstler Orchestra,* in 1919, and as the successor of Richard Strauss as director of symphony concerts of the Berlin State Opera (1920-1922) he rose to such peaks of artistic greatness that, when Nikisch died in 1922, Furtwängler was esteemed the only conductor worthy of assuming Nikisch's all-important symphonic-posts with the Gewandhaus Orchestra in Leipzig and the Berlin Philharmonic. To walk in

Nikisch's footsteps was not an enviable assignment for a young conductor. But Furtwängler was supremely confident in his strength, and achieved this feat with such dignity that his right to succeed Nikisch as the first conductor of Germany could no longer be questioned even by the most recalcitrant critic. Furtwängler remained the first conductor of Germany except for a brief period, beginning with December 1934, when he was temporarily banished by the Hitler government to that musical Siberia to which the Nazis have relegated all great musicians who failed to conform to Aryan standards.

The position of Furtwängler in the Nazi government deserves some clarification—particularly in view of the furor that was inspired in New York when the Philharmonic Symphony Society announced that it had engaged this German conductor to succeed Toscanini as the musical director of the orchestra. At the beginning of the Nazi regime, Furtwängler was, it is true, opposed to the wholesale dismissal of great Jewish musicians (particularly Klemperer from Wiesebaden, and Bruno Walter from Leipzig and Berlin), and the stigma placed upon all original expression among the younger composers; and he fought so savagely to prevent German music from descending completely to pedestrian standards that, at the end of 1934, the officials decided to give their rebel son a severe chastizing.

It was this friction between Furtwängler and the German *Kulturkammer* that inspired the New York Philharmonic to bring Furtwängler back to America, now that Toscanini had officially announced his retirement. However, there came to light considerable evidence that, when Furtwängler was restored to the good graces of the Nazi government in the Spring of 1935, he enthusiastically embraced the Nazi artistic policy as well. His complete rehabilitation became an established fact early in 1936 with the announcement of the *Kulturkammer* that Furtwängler was engaged as artistic director of the Bayreuth Festival of 1936, and was also again to be musical director of the Berlin State Opera the following winter.

In view of this evidence, many leading musicians in America felt strongly that, in accepting Furtwängler as the conductor of the New York Philharmonic, they would be doing honor to the leading musical representative of a government which has ruthlessly degraded the musical art. A bitter opposition to his appointment resulted, so bitter that, finally, Furtwängler decided to withdraw from this scene of battle. He cabled the offices of the Philharmonic that he could no longer accept the appointment of conductor.

V

THE DAWN OF THE GODS

IT IS not unlikely that when the musical historian of the future discusses the development of symphonic music in America, he will find the season of 1936-1937 a convenient line of demarcation. The recent symphony year has brought to our orchestral life a completely new character and personality. Simultaneously, in front of several of America's principal orchestras new figures appeared on the conductor's platform. What is particularly significant, however, and what sharply distinguishes the past season from all others is the fact that none of these figures boasted of unusually luminous European reputations; all of them were comparatively young in age and experience and some have even received their principal apprenticeship in this country.

In New York, in the place of Arturo Toscanini there was to be found not another world-famous personality, but a young and newly-discovered conductor from England, John Barbirolli. Philadelphia, for the first time in almost thirty years, played

EUGENE ORMANDY

host to a permanent conductor other than the electric and glamorous Stokowski; and the permanent conductor was not a veteran from the most celebrated European orchestras, but a comparative novice with the stick, Eugene Ormandy. Eugene Ormandy's position in Minneapolis passed on to other young blood, principally Leon Barzin, conductor of the New York orchestra of non-professional musicians, the National Orchestral Association. In Rochester, still another young conductor assumed his first permanent position, José Iturbi, the famous pianist.

When, early in 1936, it was announced that John Barbirolli had been engaged for a ten-week period with the New York Philharmonic Symphony Society—on the platform vacated by the incomparable Toscanini—the news was received with incredulity and bewilderment. True, Barbirolli's career as a conductor had been eventful and luminous, even though it had spanned only a few years; in a bewilderingly short time he had established his reputation in England. Since 1925, he served as a guest of leading London orchestras, was the founder of a chamber orchestra, and the permanent conductor of the Scottish Orchestra.

Barbirolli's success during his ten weeks in New York has been so well publicized that it would be repetitious to discuss it here. On the basis of this success, the directors of the New York Philharmonic decided to take a brave step. They appointed Barbirolli the artistic director of their orchestra for the next three years. This appointment has inevitably inspired bitter dissension and debate.

It is quite true that Barbirolli revealed, from time to time, that he was not as yet an integrated artist; his performances of the classic were too frequently episodic. But it is equally true that he revealed an enormous zest and enthusiasm which have brought to his readings a vigor and robustness frequently absent from the performances of older and wiser batonists. He poured the uncontrolled energy of his youth into his direction, succeeding at all times in making the music strikingly effective. His programs, moreover, were always interesting—fearlessly exploring deserted corners of old music, and featuring a healthy percentage of new works. His concerts, therefore—whatever their artistic faults may be—were alive.

2.

An even more meteoric career than that of John Barbirolli has been enjoyed by the new conductor of the Philadelphia Symphony Orchestra. Eight years ago, Eugene Ormandy was an obscure violinist of a motion-picture house orchestra, the Capitol

Renato Toppo

JOHN BARBIROLLI

Theater in New York. Today he is conductor of one of the greatest orchestras in the world.

Ormandy's first opportunity to conduct took place in the Capitol Theater where the permanent conductor, Erno Rapee, was suddenly taken ill. A substitute was not available, and one of the musicians suggested to Roxy—then the manager—that the violinist, Ormandy, be given a chance at the baton. To the amazement of the men he began to conduct the work—it was Tschaikovsky's *Fourth Symphony* —from memory; their amazement was intensified when they saw with what authority and understanding Ormandy conducted the work.

Ormandy's second great opportunity came in 1930. By this time, he had given several performances over the radio (on the Columbia Broadcasting System), and in summer concerts in New York and Philadelphia; and in his performances he was recognized as an agreeable and talented musician. In 1930, Toscanini was scheduled to direct a few special concerts with the Philadelphia Symphony Orchestra. Neuritis withdrew the great conductor from his assignment at the last moment, necessitating a hurriedly selected substitute. Ormandy was chosen because no other conductor would accept the job of substituting for Toscanini. Even Ormandy's best friends counseled him not to take the engagement. Ormandy, however, was self-assured and confident, giving a performance of such dignity and taste that he was retained for two weeks. Shortly after this, Ormandy was chosen as permanent conductor of the Minneapolis Symphony Orchestra.

His work with the Minneapolis orchestra attracted nation-wide attention. He took a second-rate symphonic body and elevated it to an eminent position. He instituted a repertoire of enormous range and variety in which his performances were always imaginative, careful and effective. It was so well publicized that when Leopold Stokowski decided to retire as conductor of the Philadelphia Orchestra, it was the young conductor from Minneapolis who had been chosen in his stead.

3.

José Iturbi came to his conductorial post in Rochester, New York, by way of Mexico City. In 1933, when Iturbi was on an extensive concert-tour as pianist in Mexico, he was asked to give a guest performance as conductor with the Mexico City Symphony Orchestra. He proved to be so adaptable to the baton, and gave performances of such striking quality, that he was immediately engaged for eleven more performances. In August of 1933, he was

Hillary G. Bailey

JOSÉ ITURBI

invited to conduct the New York Philharmonic in a week of summer concerts at the Lewisohn Stadium.

I recall vividly Iturbi's first rehearsals with the Philharmonic that summer because it was the most amazing exhibition which I, personally, ever saw an inexperienced conductor give. I, as well as many other musicians, had regarded Iturbi's recent conversion from the piano to the baton in Mexico with considerable skepticism. Iturbi was a great pianist, it was true; but conducting was something else again. Too many other great virtuosos had proved themselves to be helplessly inarticulate when they exchanged their instrument for a baton.

But during the first fifteen minutes of his rehearsals, I became convinced that Iturbi was a born conductor. The fact that he rehearsed the entire program from memory and revealed a fabulous knowledge of the scores, was not what impressed me most forcibly, even though I knew that the number of conductors who could *rehearse* from memory can be counted on the fingers of one hand. I was considerably more impressed by Iturbi's clear insight into the music he was rehearsing, and in his facility to transfer his slightest desires to his men without fumbling. I marked his ability to electrify his men and to draw from them immediate and enthusiastic responses, how it was impossible for them to slip into lethargy under the relentless drive of his incisive beat. I also noticed his faculty to see a work in its entirety even while working slavishly over the slightest details, retaining at all times the architecture of the whole while shaping the outlines of a melodic phrase or etching a rhythmic pattern.

Each time he performed a symphony anew, he remedied the defects of a previous reading and etched in new effects and qualities. Likewise, in each performance, he disclosed a growing mastery over the orchestra. Only recently, he directed Wagner's *Siegfried Death Music*, a work which he did not have the time nor the opportunity to rehearse. Yet his baton technique had become so supple and his control over his orchestra so consummate that he was able to shape an interpretation of unforgettable drama and poignancy during the performance itself.

4.

Both Hans Lange and Leon Barzin are familiar to us by virtue of their periodic orchestral performances in New York. They are conductors who know restraint, self-effacement and good taste, and they are both superb program builders. Technical flaws? To be sure—principally the result of a lack of sufficient experience. Also an inability to sweep their performances from the musicianly and the competent to high heavens of eloquence. But they can make their orchestra play with zest and precision at all times, occasionally drawing from the strings and wind majestic lines of melodic beauty.

During the past season, both Hans Lange and Leon Barzin received their most important conductorial assignments. Lange, for the first time in his career, had more than ten consecutive weeks of concerts at his disposal in Chicago. And Barzin came to the head of a major symphonic-body for the first time in his career. Their work in Chicago and Minneapolis respectively elicited such unanimous praise from the critics, it is perhaps not exaggerated enthusiasm to say that the careers of these two conductors have only begun.

Two young conductors have emerged after apprenticeship with Leopold Stokowski on the Philadelphia Orchestra. Artur Rodzinski—after his initial performances as Stokowski's assistant in Philadelphia, and as conductor of the Los Angeles Symphony Orchestra—went to Cleveland where he has been a rejuvenating influence. Instituting a very alive repertoire—which included the world-première of that amazing Soviet opera of Shostakowitch, *Lady Macbeth of Mzenzk*—Rodzinski proved that an electric baton was in his hand. In the Spring of 1937, Rodzinski served as a guest-conductor of the New York Philharmonic, receiving praise for many of his vital interpretations.

Sylvan Levin handles the orchestra well, and is able to make it express his desires with pliancy surprising for one so inexperienced. From his radio appearances, it was apparent that he exerted authority in his performances—even though one was also conscious of the great, perhaps damaging, influence of Stokowski in the younger man's occasional overbrilliant and overdressed readings. However, now that Levin has been a conductor of his own orchestra—the York (Pennsylvania) Symphony—his individuality is becoming increasingly apparent.

For so many years now familiar names and faces have dominated symphony-halls of America, that music-audiences have begun to nurse a rapidly growing fear that when these great names withdraw from our music scene our splendid era of symphony performances will pass to oblivion. Where the future of conducting is concerned, however, there should be no pessimism. The field is not barren, but fertile; we have only to cultivate it for it to yield fruit. The passing of Toscanini or Stokowski, or any of the other great figures, need not fill us with despair. For, in all probability, we are not witnessing the dusk, but rather the dawn of the gods.

VI

BATON EXHIBITIONISM

1.

WE SHOULD not conclude our discussion of conducting and conductors without commenting upon some of the abuses that are sometimes exercised. It has been said—with disconcerting justification, I am afraid—that there exists no group of musicians more addicted to vain exhibitionism and self-glorification at the expense of an art they are supposed to exalt than the conductors of symphony-orchestras. While there have always existed a few conductors who look upon their work as a high artistic mission in which the performance of music to the best of their abilities is the only possible consideration (need I mention the names of Toscanini, Mahler, Muck or Weingartner as examples?), the lamentable truth remains that, excluding a select and negligible handful, the orchestra conductor, of all musicians, is the most likely to exploit music in every possible manner in his attempt to glorify himself as an individual. He has become more and more the show-man and less the artist.

THE MAN WITH THE BATON

As early as 1912, the astute Henry E. Krehbiel lamented the-then slowly growing tendency on the part of the conductor to accord himself a greater importance than the music he performed. "In the highest form of the instrumental art, (except chamber music where, thank God! there is still a bit of holy ground!) as in the hybrid form of the opera which lives chiefly on affectation and fad, it is the singer and not the song that challenges the attention from the multitude. We used to have *prima donna* in New York whose names on a program insured financial success for the performance. . . . For *prima donna*. . . . read 'the conductor,' and a parallel is established in orchestral art which is even more humiliating than that pervading our opera-houses."

Today, of course, it can be said unequivocally that many conductors (once again permitting exceptions) place greater emphasis upon the externals of their art than upon artistic essentials. No longer is the conductor of Jullien's type a phenomenal rarity. With the majority of orchestral conductors today circus showmanship dominates orchestral conducting.

Conductors often resort to the most ludicrous, and pathetic, means with which to attract notice. Rumor has it that one of the foremost conductors in America today uses rouge and lip-stick before each performance. This is, no doubt, an exaggeration; but it is well known that one of the popular conductors wears a corset at every appearance so that he may present an elegant figure as he conducts, that another conductor changes his suit of clothing during the intermission, and that many other conductors rehearse their gestures before a mirror to insure their aesthetic impressiveness at the concert. As a very convincing example of flagrant exhibitionism in the modern conductor, I might point to Leopold Stokowski (my authority is the magazine, *Time*) who, before conducting the opera *Wozzeck* at the Metropolitan Opera House, conferred with the electricians to learn if it was possible to direct the electric light upon his hands in such a way that they would be reflected upon the ceiling during the performance!

These, of course, are merely picayune examples,—and should not be taken too seriously—of the superfluous methods adopted by some conductors to gain the admiration of their audiences. There are other, and far more important, examples; and it is these examples that reveal with discouraging force that competent performances of music is one of the least important features of the conductorial *prima-donna* act.

If a violinist or a pianist stepped upon the platform and attempted to gain the enthusiasm of his

281

audience through the blatant and spectacular methods generally employed by the orchestra-conductor during his routine, he would be dismissed with derision and contempt. The music-audiences, however, are strangely tolerant where the conductor is concerned, and readily succumb to the pompous self-advertisement, side show gymnastics and Barnum showmanship which he employs to impress them.

2.

Probably the most important weapon that the conductor possesses in attracting the admiration of the public is his stick. Gesturing has, for the most part, ceased to be merely the useful function of outlining rhythm and *tempo* for the benefit of the orchestra-men, and etching in nuance, but has, instead, become with many of our modern conductors something of a performance in itself, to be carefully studied beforehand for its possible effect upon the audience. A few months ago, I stumbled across a news item which prettily illustrates my point. "Paul Paray, talented and temperamental orchestra director of the Colonne concerts in Paris"—so runs a United Press dispatch—"switches batons in midsymphonic stream. In a recent rendition of César Franck's *Variations Symphoniques,* Monsieur Paray changed sticks with such lightning rapidity as to leave his audiences marveling at the apparent sleight-of-hand movements." The audiences, we are told further, throng the concert-hall in order to see this "talented" Monsieur Paray go through his necromantic monkeyshines.

While most conductors do not go to quite such extremes to entertain their public with their batons, they employ equally superfluous dramatics. It was Adrian Boult who admirably commented that a conductor, in his direction, should appeal to the eyes of his orchestra and to the ears of his audience. Too many conductors are infinitely more interested in appealing merely to the eyes of their audience. They resort to absurd corybantic gesturing which may fascinate the audience but which succeeds, more often than not, simply in confusing the orchestra. As I have already explained in an earlier chapter, the baton in the hands of an expert conductor is an all-important weapon. But I have also pointed out that the greatest conductors proved long ago that a slight and incisive motion of the wrist can serve the purpose admirably. When Artur Nikisch gave courses in the art of conducting, he would tie the left hand of the student behind the back and would insist that the right hand utilize only the most sparing motions. And the greatest conductors of yesterday and today have utilized the most economical gesturing. Artur Nikisch himself used a slight upward and downward beat which was almost imperceptible beyond the fifth row of the parquet. Toscanini uses a circular movement of the arm which is humdrum in its rigidity. Karl Muck and Felix Weingartner use a broad movement of the baton which, to the unschooled eye, might almost seem to lack any definite rhythmic pattern. Without exception, these great conductors never resorted to any motion of the head and body to impress their men; only the slightest suggestions were necessary for them to draw the necessary effects and nuances from the orchestra. Conductors of lesser stature, however, lead audiences and themselves to believe that their orgiastic posturing inspire the men to scale formerly inaccessible heights of inspiration.

Gesturing in recent years has passed, with many conductors, completely out of the realm of simplicity and has become a circus-show put on entirely for the benefit of the audiences. As Basil Maine has written: "By the majority of concert-goers the conductor is admired as much for chorography as for his musicianship." Sir Thomas Beecham hurls his fist at the orchestra with passionate abandon, and curves and rotates his body during the progress of a musical work until it resembles a demoniac dance. As a matter of fact we find an English critic—Mr. Edward

Crankshaw in the *Bookman*—yielding to ecstasy over Sir Thomas's antics by describing him as a "dancer," and adding that "to me he looks like Petrushka." Wilhelm Furtwängler sways his lithe body backward, in a tender passage, and lifts his face to the sky as though in supplication to the Muses. Sir Henry J. Wood utilizes such extravagant motions of the hands that critics have referred to him as "the windmill conductor." Such gestures, entirely superfluous to the performance, are examples of what usually takes place upon the conductor's podium during the concert. These conductors would have us believe that these movements are necessary to inspire and intoxicate the men; but elaborateness of gesture is not necessarily an effective gesture. Any orchestra-man will tell you that these extravagant movements are surprisingly absent when, at the rehearsal, there is no admiring audience to lavish adulation behind the conductor's back.

3.

Another equally important trick in the repertoire of the irregular orchestral conductor is the rather recent universal fad of conducting entire programs without the aid of a printed score—a fad which cannot be deplored too strongly. Conducting without a score is by no means a present-day phenomenon, as we have already frequently observed. Mahler, Nikisch, Richter, von Bülow all conducted familiar works without resorting to the printed page, long before it became a style. But that this was not an everyday event is proved by the fact that always, in the past, it caused exclamations of wonder. When Hans von Bülow heard Richard Strauss direct, what first attracted him to the younger musician was the fact that he conducted his own work from memory; and when Artur Nikisch conducted the *Faust* and *Dante* overtures of Liszt in Leipzig without a score in front of him, the evening was something of a sensation. Today, however, a conductor feels disgraced before the eyes of his public if he does not perform at least the classics from memory. And at least one important manager has refused to engage any guest-conductors for his orchestra who cannot accomplish this feat—little realizing that conducting without a score is primarily a trick, and in most instances not even a very good one.

With some conductors—Toscanini, for example, or Furtwängler—whose phenomenal memories make the support of a printed score quite unnecessary, or in the case of conductors who have directed a work so often that it is indelibly engraved upon their minds, conducting scoreless is a spontaneous and entirely unaffected gesture. In such instances, it is quite wise for the conductor to dispense with the music, for then he can concentrate entirely upon his men. But when this practice becomes a fetish, to be used indiscriminately for works old and new, familiar and unfamiliar, it becomes exceedingly dangerous. As Felix Weingartner has pointed out, "a good performance from the score has value; a bad one from memory has none." The truth is that most of the conductors who today appear week-in and week-out on platforms without the customary music-stand in front of them are only vaguely familiar with all the markings of the score. For them to attempt to direct their men without the support of the music is a very stupid and futile gesture. Inaccurate performances, innumerable omissions of subtle nuances and effects designated on the printed page but which elude the memory of the conductor are the inevitable results of this form of conductorial exhibitionism. Something of the casual way with which conductors regard the printed page can be suggested by quoting a remark overheard at a rehearsal of a very celebrated guest-conductor to the New York Philharmonic, who insisted upon rehearsing the music from memory. "Oboes—clarinets—bassoons," he called out impatiently. "Which one of you has the main theme here?"

Sloppiness and inaccuracies have become more

and more frequent intruders into orchestral performances since this fad has gained wide recognition among conductors in America. I remember hearing Bruno Walter conduct a passage from Richard Strauss' *Schlagobers* in four-quarter time when the score clearly designated five-quarter, confusing the players to such an extent that the entire section of the work was completely distorted in performance; and this accident would have been impossible if Walter were referring to a score during the performance. I also recall a performance of Stravinsky's *Sacre du Printemps* by Koussevitzky in which the conductor suffered a lapse of memory with the result that he was compelled to push his baton feebly for several minutes, during which time the balance of the orchestra collapsed into confusion, until he could bring back to mind the exact notation of the score. Such obvious ineptitude of conducting is, to be sure, not an everyday affair with conductors of the stature of Bruno Walter and Serge Koussevitzky. But what has become habitual among conductors who rely entirely upon their memories is the persistent disregard of subtle indications in the music for slight, but all-important, accentuations, syncopations, *rubatos* etc. Too often the artistic touches which the composer so deftly sprinkles over his scores are

288

omitted by the conductor, exerting his memory to recall all of the notes.

The severest sufferer of this fad—if we exclude the audiences and the composition—is the young conductor who directs from memory because he feels that he must keep abreast of the times. In the process of recreating a work of art, there are so many details upon which a young conductor must focus his attention that it is regrettable for him to divert so much of his time, energy and effort to a task so exacting as committing complicated orchestral scores to memory. The mere mechanics of memorizing concert-length programs will prove to be so enormous that, in spite of himself, the young conductor will be apt to neglect the much more important job of studying scores for their artistic content. Besides, it stands to reason that at the concert proper the more attention the young conductor devotes to recalling to mind the notes of the work he is directing, the less concentration can he expend upon the fine points of interpretation and recreation as the music pours from under his baton.

4.

To my mind, the most pernicious practice employed by some conductors in further self-glorification is the ever-increasing vogue for giving individual readings of classic works, upon which are smudged and smeared the fingerprints of the conductors through whose hands this music passes. There is only sensationalism and exaggeration in the performances of many of these conductors. Even artists of such unquestionable integrity as Artur Nikisch and Gustav Mahler frequently yielded to the temptation of changing the music they performed, and permitted their temperaments to twist the musical ideas of the masters into new shapes. Both Nikisch and Mahler, however, were artists of enormous stature so that there were many times when they actually succeeded in improving upon a masterwork. But when lesser conductors permit themselves the same freedom, the result is often artistically disastrous.

Some of the more obvious pitfalls into which such conductors fall, when they attempt to "recreate" a work of art, are exaggeration and overstatement, or understatement. *Crescendo* passages are magnified so that they resemble the blurred swell of an organ tone, in which clarity, clean playing and solid sonority are all sacrificed for the general kinaesthetic effect which massive sounds can produce. Rapid passages are greatly accelerated to a breath-taking pace, especially in climaxes, in the attempt of the conductor to sweep an audience off its feet by the sheer power of motion. Or, on the other hand, *pianissimo* is played so that it is impossible to hear it beyond the third row of the parquet, and *cantabile* passages are fondled until they become cloying.

There are few conductors, with the exception of four or five artists of first importance, who do not yield to these, and many other similar, temptations. We have already commented upon the fact that conductors like Otto Klemperer and, to a lesser degree, Erich Kleiber, place unusual emphasis on the brass, tympani and double-bass so that the music may sound more crushingly effective; these conductors mistake vulgarity and roughness of performance for red-blooded vigor. Bruno Walter persistently inserts *luftpausen* into the composition, to heighten its climactic moments. Leopold Stokowski will frequently permit false dramatics to creep into the music he conducts, and Sir Thomas Beecham will go to ridiculous extremes, at occasions, to accentuate the contrasts of light and shade.

Some conductors, however, go to even more radical extremes. Willem Mengelberg deleted an entire section of Tschaikovsky's *Fifth Symphony* in an attempt to improve the work; and Bruno Walter changed the *tempo* of the opening of the last movement of Tschaikovsky's *Fourth Symphony* until it resembled a burlesque of itself. Stokowski has given an altogether different *tempo* to the last movements of Schubert's *C-Major Symphony* than the one designated in the score, adopting a lighter and slower beat than was intended by the composer and thereby completely changing the conception of the work; on the other hand, he has exaggerated climaxes of Beethoven's *Pastorale Symphony* and the *Leonore Overture no. 3* until they yielded to hysterics. I have heard Otto Klemperer perform Beethoven symphonies in which he sublimely disregarded suspensions and rests, and in which he allotted greater importance to the accompanying sections than to the main themes.

Audiences may come to the symphony-concert for hero-worship; and they may derive pleasure from the circus spectacles which conductors offer with their music. But when such liberties are taken by conductors with musical masterpieces, when conductors so brazenly exploit art for the sake of self-advertisement, it is time that their admirers recognized the red light of danger flashing across our musical horizon.

OTTO KLEMPERER

BIOGRAPHICAL GUIDE

A SHORT BIOGRAPHICAL GUIDE TO CONDUCTORS OF YESTERDAY AND TODAY

ABENDROTH, HERMANN, born, Frankfort, January 19, 1883. He received his early apprenticeship as conductor directing the Orchester-Verein in Munich (1903), and a series of orchestral concerts in Lübeck (1905). In 1914, he succeeded Fritz Steinbach as leader of the Gűrzenich concerts at Cologne, and it was here that he received his European reputation as a prominent interpreter of symphonic music. In 1922, he directed a successful music festival in Niedderhein. Since that time he has conducted symphony concerts in Berlin, and has assumed the position of director of the *Konzert-Gesellschaft* and the *Musikalischen Gesellschaft* in Cologne.

ALBRECHT, KARL, born, Posen, 1807; died, Gatchina, 1863. After acquiring a reputation as a violinist, Albrecht came to Russia where he became conductor of the St. Petersburg Opera (1838). In 1842, he led the first performance of Glinka's *Russlan und Ludmilla*. In 1845, he was appointed conductor of the Philharmonic concerts in St. Petersburg.

ANSERMET, ERNEST, born, Vevey, Switzerland, November 11, 1883, one of the most significant of contemporary Swiss conductors. In 1912 he was appointed conductor at the Montreux Kursaal, and from 1915 until 1918 he officiated as the successor of Stavenhagen in a series of subscription concerts. He first came to prominence as a conductor of the Diaghilev Russian Ballet, touring England, Italy, Spain, North and South America. His name is intimately associated with that of Igor Stravinsky for whose works his baton has been a faithful protagonist. He has been a guest-conductor of leading symphony-organizations, particularly in London and Liverpool.

ARBÓS, ENRIQUE FERNÁNDEZ, born, Madrid, December 25, 1863, considered by many the foremost of contemporary Spanish conductors. After serving as concertmaster of the Berlin Philharmonic Orchestra (1883) and of the Glasgow Symphony Orchestra (1889) he returned to his native country to become conductor of the Madrid Symphony Orchestra (1904), which position he has held with unique honor. He has been a welcome guest-conductor of the leading orchestras in Europe, and during the past two decades has visited America several times as a guest of the New York Symphony Orchestra and the Boston Symphony Orchestra. (See page 254).

BAMBOSCHECK, GIUSEPPE, born, Trieste, 1890. He began his career by conducting symphony concerts in his seventeenth year. His official début as an operatic conductor was made at the Teatro Fenico in Trieste in 1908. Since that time he has associated himself almost exclusively with operatic music. From 1916 until 1929 he was the musical secretary and a conductor of the Metropolitan Opera House, New

York. After 1929 he devoted himself to radio work and movietone productions.

BARBIROLLI, JOHN. (See page 353).

BARLOW, HOWARD, born, Plain City, Ohio, May 1, 1892. He made his official début as conductor at the Macdowell Colony Festival of the National Federation Music Clubs, in July of 1919. He has associated himself most intimately with radio work, conducting the frequent symphony broadcasts of the Columbia Broadcasting System with great popularity. He has also served acceptably elsewhere as guest-conductor.

BARRÈRE, GEORGES, born, Bordeaux, October 31, 1876, esteemed one of the foremost of contemporary flautists. For seven years he distinguished himself as solo flautist of the Colonne concerts in Paris, and subsequently as first flautist of the New York Symphony Society and the New York Philharmonic. In 1914 he founded the Barrère Little Symphony Orchestra which under his intelligent direction has since been giving concerts of unfamiliar old and new music for small orchestras.

BARZIN, LEON, born, Brussels, 1900. For a long period, he was a violist of leading orchestras. In 1929, he accepted the associate conductorship of the American Orchestral Association of New York, and in 1930 he was appointed permanent conductor of the National Orchestral Association. In 1936, he was selected as one of the conductors of the Minneapolis Symphony Orchestra. (See also page 277).

BEECHAM, SIR THOMAS, born, Liverpool, April 29, 1879, one of the major batonists of present-day England. After founding the New Symphony Orchestra in London, which he conducted for two years (1906–1908), he came to prominence by forming the Beecham Symphony Orchestra. For a few years he directed opera at Covent Garden and Drury Lane. From 1916–1919 he was principal conductor of the Royal Philharmonic in London, and since 1919 he has been artistic director of the London Symphony Orchestra and Covent Garden. He has been one of the major forces to bring the music of Delius to recognition in England, organizing a special Delius Festival in October of 1929. He has been equally vigorous in his attempt to establish opera as a popular entertainment for the English masses. His frequent guest-appearances with the foremost orchestras of America and Europe have established his reputation throughout the entire world of music. (See pages 257-8).

BENEDICT, SIR JULIUS, born, Stuttgart, November 27, 1804; died, London, June 5, 1885. His early musical studies were pursued in Weimar, principally under Hummel. On his nineteenth birthday, upon the personal recommendation of Karl Maria von Weber, he was appointed conductor of the Kärnthnerthor Theatre in Vienna, holding the position for two years. From Vienna, he went to Naples to hold the post of principal conductor at the San Carlo. During the last twenty years of his life, he conducted operatic performances and symphonic concerts in England— opera, at Drury Lane, and symphony concerts with the Liverpool Philharmonic.

BENNETT, SIR WILLIAM STERNDALE, born, Sheffield, April 13, 1816; died, London, February 1, 1875. His professional début was launched in Leipzig in 1837 when he conducted his own *Naiades Overture* with the Gewandhaus Orchestra. For ten years (1856– 1866) he was principal conductor of the Royal Phil- harmonic in London, when he attained an international reputation as a conductor of symphonic music. In 1849 he founded the London Bach Society, and in 1858 he directed the Leeds Music Festival with great distinction. In the later years of his life he devoted his energy principally to composition and pedagogy.

BERGMANN, CARL, born, Ebersbach, Saxony, 1821; died, New York, August 16, 1876. His first important conductorial position came in 1850 when he was ap- pointed director of the itinerant Germania Society Orchestra. Here he made a marked impression, and upon its dissolution in 1854 he was engaged as one of the conductors of the New York Philharmonic Orches- tra. From 1866 to 1876 he was the sole conductor of the New York Philharmonic. He was also director of the Handel and Haydn Society in Boston (1852– 1854), the Arion Society in New York, and was responsible for the first performance of Wagner's *Tannhäuser* in New York (1859). (See page 52).

BERLIOZ, HECTOR LOUIS, born, Grenoble, December 11, 1803; died, Paris, March 8, 1869, world-famous French composer who likewise distinguished himself with the baton. After several successful engagements as conductor in Paris and Brussels (1842) he toured Germany, Austria and Russia, from 1843 to 1846, conducting concerts devoted primarily to his own music. In 1852 and 1855 he was engaged as director of the New Philharmonic in England where he proved his unquestioned talent in the interpretation of classical symphonic music. (See pages 84-85).

BLACK, FRANK, born, Philadelphia, November 28, 1894. He made his début with baton at the Century Theatre in New York in 1916. During the next few years he was employed as director of the New Fox Theatre in Philadelphia, and as musical director of the Brunswick Phonograph Company. He has become closely identified with the radio, and as the musical director of the National Broadcasting Company he frequently conducts programs of classical and modern symphonic music.

BLECH, LEO, born, Aix-la-Chapelle, April 21, 1871. In 1893 he assumed the post of director of opera in Aix-la-Chapelle, and six years later he was appointed Kapellmeister of the German Landestheater in Prague. A similar post became his at the Berlin State Opera in 1906, where his conductorial talent—particularly in the music of Mozart and Wagner—attracted so much attention and praise that he was offered the position of General Musikdirektor in 1913. It was in this capacity that he established himself as one of Germany's significant operatic conductors. In 1925, he made a short visit to the United States as conductor of the Wagnerian Opera Company.

BODANZKY, ARTUR, born, Vienna, December 16, 1887. Died November 23, 1939. He first conducted for Gustav Mahler at the Imperial Opera in Vienna (1904). After gaining a greater sureness with his stick and a maturer outlook upon his art in the principal opera-houses in Europe—particularly in Mannheim where he spent several successful years—Bodanzky came to London in 1914 to direct the first performance of *Parsifal* to be given in England, at the Covent Garden. His success with this performance was so great that, in 1915, Bodanzky was engaged as principal conductor of German opera at the Metropolitan Opera House, New York, where he was to enjoy his greatest conductorial triumphs. For more than ten years, Artur Bodanzky conducted the Society of Friends of Music in New York, which he founded in 1916, and in 1919 was founder and conductor of the short-lived New Symphony Orchestra.

BOULT, SIR ADRIAN CEDRIC, born, Chester, April 8, 1889. After receiving a valuable training under Artur Nikisch, he made his début at Covent Garden in 1914. In 1918 he first attracted notice as conductor of several concerts of the Royal Philharmonic in London. Since that time he has been enormously active with the baton, and has acquired a wide English reputation. In 1920, he conducted concerts of the British Symphony Orchestra, the Sunday concerts of the London Symphony Orchestra, and several performances of the Diaghilev Ballet. Since 1923, he has conducted the Birmingham Orchestra and the London Bach Choir. He has been an important guest to the foremost orchestras in Europe.

BRICO, ANTONIA, well-known woman conductor. Her studies in conducting were pursued under Dr. Karl Muck, and at the State Academy of Music in Berlin, where she was the only American—man or woman—

to have been admitted to the conducting classes. She made her world début as conductor in 1930, when she directed a concert of the Berlin Philharmonic. Returning to America, Antonia Brico conducted a symphony-concert at the Hollywood Bowl. Since that time, she has led the Musicians Symphony Orchestra, at the Metropolitan Opera House, the New York Civic Orchestra, and has given guest performances with the Detroit and Buffalo Symphony Orchestras. In 1934, she founded the New York Women's Symphony Orchestra, and has since been its permanent conductor.

BÜLOW, HANS VON. (See pages 111-116).

BUSCH, FRITZ, born, Siegen, Westphalia, March 13, 1890. In 1909, he was given his first important conductorial assignment at the Riga Opera where he served as chorusmaster. For several years after that he divided his time between conducting operatic and symphonic music in Bad Pyrmont and Aachen. In 1918 he was appointed operatic director at Stuttgart, and four years later he was offered the position that has brought him an international prominence—conductor at the Dresden Opera. He has been a guest of principal European orchestras, and for a short while a visitor to America as a conductor of the New York Symphony Orchestra. (See page 257).

BUSSER, HENRI PAUL, born, Toulouse, January 16, 1872. His early musical career was devoted to the playing of the organ at leading Paris churches. After a short period as chorus-director at the Opéra Comique, he was offered an important position as a conductor of the Opéra (1902) which he has since occupied with quiet distinction.

CAMERON, BASIL, born, Reading, August 18, 1885. He received his first opportunity to conduct in 1912 when he was offered the post of music-director of the orchestra at Torquay. The following Spring he gained praise and attention by a Wagner festival which he conducted in London. In 1923, Cameron divided his conductorial activities between Harrogate and Hastings, where his fame as orchestral conductor increased rapidly—particularly with his annual festivals which he conducted in each city. He has since conducted the Royal Philharmonic in London, the Czech National Orchestra in Prague, and the San Francisco and Seattle Symphony Orchestras in America.

CAMPANINI, CLEOFANTE, born, Parma, September 1, 1860; died, New York, September 19, 1919. His début as operatic conductor was made in Parma in 1883 in a performance of *Carmen*, and was sufficiently striking to bring him a post as assistant conductor at the Metropolitan Opera House the following year, where he gave the first American performance of Verdi's *Othello* (1894). After making extensive tours as operatic conductor in Spain, Portugal and South America, he returned to New York to direct at the Manhattan Opera House (1906–1909). In 1910, he went to Chicago to become principal conductor of the newly formed Chicago Opera House, and from 1913 until his death he was its artistic director.

CASALS, PABLO, born, Tarragona, December 29, 1876,

the most distinguished contemporary virtuoso on the violoncello. In 1919, he founded and directed the Barcelona Orchestra which has been a vital factor in spreading the appreciation of great symphonic music among the masses in Spain. His enormous musicianship and conductorial talent have brought the Barcelona Orchestra to the front rank of modern European symphonic organizations. Caşals has been a guest conductor in New York and London.

CASELLA, ALFREDO, born, Turin, July 25, 1883, eminent contemporary Italian composer who is equally prominent as conductor. In 1912, he conducted a series of popular concerts at the Trocadero in Paris which first brought him prominence with the baton. Since that time his conductorial assignments have brought him to Paris, Berlin, London, Vienna, Moscow, Italy, the Netherlands, New York where he particularly distinguished himself in his performance of old Italian music and in the works of the foremost contemporaries.

CHAVEZ, CARLOS, born, Mexico City, 1899, one of Mexico's most original modern composers and conductors. Early in 1936, he was guest-conductor to the Philadelphia and Boston Symphony Orchestras. He was one of the conductors of the New York Philharmonic Symphony Society during its 1936-1937 season.

CHEVILLARD, CAMILLE, born, Paris, October 14, 1859; died, Paris, May 30, 1923. In 1866, he became assistant to his father-in-law, Lamoureux, at the Lamoureux concerts. After this valuable apprenticeship he became the principal conductor of the orchestra, in 1897, upon his father-in-law's death. In 1887, he assisted at the first Paris performance of *Lohengrin.* (See page 50).

COATES, ALBERT, born, Petrograd, April 23, 1882. His early experience was procured conducting opera in Elberfeld, Dresden and Mannheim. In 1911 he was appointed chief conductor of the Petrograd Opera, and three years later he turned to the performance of symphonic music by assuming the direction of the London Philharmonic. He came to America in 1921 to conduct several guest performances with the New York Symphony Society, and two years later he assumed the direction of the Symphony Orchestra in Rochester. He has since toured extensively throughout Europe and America, performing in the principal symphony-halls and opera-houses. (See page 253).

COLLINGWOOD, LAWRENCE, born, London, March 14, 1887. His early experience as a conductor was procured in Russia, at the St. Petersburg Opera, as assistant to Albert Coates. In London, he has gained prominence by virtue of his operatic performances at the 'Old Vic.'

COLONNE, EDOUARD (originally named Judas), born, Bordeaux, July 23, 1838; died, Paris, March 28, 1910. In 1860 he assumed leadership of the Orchestra of the Paris Conservatory, where for more than a decade his authoritative performances gained widespread attention. In 1873, he founded the *Concert National* which later became the nationally famous *Concerts du Châtelet*. He further increased his prestige in Paris by performances at the Exposition (1878) and at the Opéra (1892). He was a frequent

THE MAN WITH THE BATON

guest of orchestras throughout Europe, conducting in England from 1896 until 1908, and giving successful performances in Strassburg, Lisbon and Russia. In 1905 he introduced his baton to New York. See pages 48-49).

COOPER, EMIL, born, Odessa, December 20, 1879. He began conducting in his seventeenth year, when the orchestra of the Odessa Exhibition was entrusted to him. He created a favorable impression so emphatically that he was appointed conductor of the Castellano Company, a well-known Italian operatic troupe. His career became more and more luminous as he filled the posts of principal conductor at the City Theatre in Kiev (1900), at the Moscow Opera House in Zinuria (1906) and, finally, at the Grand Imperial Opera House in Moscow. During the Revolution, Cooper founded the Philharmonic Orchestra of Leningrad, and several years later he toured the world as guest conductor of leading opera-houses and symphonic organizations.

COPPOLA, PIERO, born, Milan, 1888. After directing several performances at the La Scala in Milan, and at other leading opera-houses in Italy, he came to Brussels (1912) to direct performances at the Théâtre de la Monnaie. He came to prominence by introducing Puccini's *Girl of the Golden West* in Florence and Brussels. He came to London in 1914, and has since that time served as artistic director of His Master's Voice Co. in England.

CORTOT, ALFRED, born, Nijon, Switzerland, September 26, 1877, world-famous concert-pianist who is like-

306

wise distinguished with the baton. His early experience as a conductor came with the music-dramas of Wagner, first by assisting at Bayreuth, and then by conducting performances of the more famous music-dramas at Paris from 1902 to 1904. In 1903 he founded a concert society whose function it was to give performances of outstanding choral works. One year later, he directed the orchestral concerts at the *Société Nationale*. More recently, he has conducted the orchestra of the Ecole Normale in Paris.

COSTA, MICHAEL. (See pages 82-83).

COWEN, SIR FREDERIC HYMEN, born, Kingston, Jamaica, January 29, 1852; died, England, 1935. In 1877 he succeeded Sir Arthur Sullivan as conductor of the London Philharmonic, and for many years (from 1877 to 1892, and from 1900 to 1907) he enjoyed a distinguished career as the director of this orchestra. His conductorial career likewise included eighteen successful years with the Liverpool Philharmonic (1896–1914) and three years with the Hallé Orchestra at Manchester.

DAMROSCH, LEOPOLD, born, Posen, Prussia, October 22, 1832; died, New York, February 15, 1885. His conductorial career began in Germany where in 1859 he conducted the Breslau Philharmonic concerts and, in 1862, he founded the Breslau Orchesterverein. He came to New York in 1871 as conductor of the Arion Society, and from that time on was closely identified with musical life in this country. He founded the Oratorio Society of New York in 1873, and the New York Symphony Society five years later. In 1884, he was appointed director of German opera at the Metropolitan Opera House, New York.

DAMROSCH, WALTER. (See pages 60-67).

DEFAUW, DESIRE, born, Ghent, September 5, 1885. After a long period as a member of the Allied String Quartet, which he founded, he turned to conducting. He is the director of the symphony concerts given at the Théâtre de la Monnaie in Brussels, the most important orchestral concerts given in that city.

DE LAMARTER, ERIC, born, Lansing, Michigan, 1880. In 1911 he assumed the conductorship of the Chicago Musical Art Society. Seven years later he became the conductor of the Chicago Symphony Orchestra for one season. More recently, he has attracted notice with a series of summer concerts with the Chicago Symphony Orchestra in Chicago.

DE SABATA, VICTOR, born, Trieste, April 10, 1892. After several successful guest-appearances at the Monte Carlo Opera, he was called to direct the symphony-concerts at the La Scala in Milan. There followed appearances as conductor of orchestral music in principal cities in Italy. He came to America in 1927 as guest-conductor of the Cincinnati Symphony Orchestra, and in the same year gave the world première of Respighi's *Church Windows* in Milan.

DESSOFF, FELIX OTTO, born, Leipzig, January 14, 1835; died, Frankfort, October 28, 1891. After conducting for several years in theatres of small German towns, he was appointed conductor of the Court Opera in Vienna and director of the Philharmonic concerts. In 1875 he received an appointment as Kapellmeister at

Karlsruhe. From 1881 until his death he was first
conductor of opera at Frankfort, where his performances enjoyed a national prominence.

DESSOFF, MARGUERITE, born, Vienna, June 11, 1894.
As founder and leader of the Dessoff'sche Frauenchor
Frankfurter Madrigal - Vereinigung and Bachge-
meinde, in Frankfort, she first attracted notice as a
choral conductor of talent. Coming to America, she
became chorus director at the Institute of Musical Art
in New York. She has given frequent concerts directing the Adesdi Chorus and the A Capella Singers of
New York.

DOBROWEN, ISSAI, born, Nijni Novgorod, 1894. He
began a distinguished conductorial career in 1919
when he accepted the direction of the Grand Theatre
in Moscow. In 1922, he came to Dresden, and for
several years was prominent as a, conductor of the
Russian repertoire at the Opera House. He has been
a guest-conductor of leading symphony orchestras,
including the New York Philharmonic, and in 1933
he became principal conductor of the San Francisco
Symphony Orchestra. (See page 254).

DOHNANYI, ERNST VON, born, Pressburg, July 22, 1877.
His musical career was launched with a series of successful European and American tours as concert-
pianist (1897–1901). Since 1924, he has been a
principal conductor of the Budapest Philharmonic.
He served for a brief period as conductor of the short-
lived State Symphony Orchestra in New York.

ELMENDORFF, KARL VON. During the past few years
he has been one of the principal conductors at the

annual Bayreuth Festival. He is esteemed one of the most prominent Wagnerian conductors in Germany.

FIEDLER, ARTHUR, born, Boston, December 17, 1894. In 1925, he organized the Boston Sinfonietta, the first orchestra of its kind in the United States. His name is primarily associated with the annual series of Pop concerts given in Boston by the Boston Symphony Orchestra, which he began directing in 1930. He has also conducted the Cecilia Society, the Boston Male choir, the Macdowell Club orchestra, and the series of orchestral concerts on the Boston Esplanade which he himself organized.

FIEDLER, AUGUST MAX, born, Zittau, December 31, 1859. In 1904, he conducted the Hamburg Philharmonic with sufficient success to earn him a permanent appointment as conductor of the Boston Symphony Orchestra (1908–1912). He returned to Germany to become one of its more prominent symphony-conductors, directing the Essen Orchestra in 1916, and serving as guest-conductor of principal German orchestras since that time.

FITELBERG, GREGORY, born, Dinaburg, October 18, 1879. After a long and valuable apprenticeship as an orchestra-player, he was called upon to direct the Warsaw Philharmonic, which he did with such competence that he was retained as principal conductor from 1907 to 1911. In 1912 he accepted a post as conductor of the Imperial Opera in Vienna, and several years after that he introduced his baton to Russia.

More recently he has conducted symphony concerts in Warsaw and Berlin.

FRIED, OSKAR, born, Berlin, August 10, 1871. For six years—from 1904 to 1910—he conducted the *Stern Gesangsverein* in Berlin. In 1910, he turned his energies towards symphonic music, distinguishing himself by his intelligent performances of new and unfamiliar music. In 1925, he was appointed conductor of the Berlin Symphony Orchestra, and since that time he has given guest performances with the Berlin Philharmonic, at the Deutsches Opera House, as well as in Russia, the Scandinavian countries and the United States. (See page 257).

FURTWÄNGLER, WILHELM. (See pages 264-269).

GABRILOWITSCH, OSSIP, born, St. Petersburg, February 7, 1878, world-famous concert-pianist who has acquired a great reputation as conductor. In 1907, he led a series of orchestral concerts in New York which proved that his musical talent could express itself forcefully with the baton. When the Detroit Symphony Orchestra was founded in 1918, Gabrilowitsch was appointed conductor. He has since held this position with growing prestige, and has succeeded in establishing the orchestra as one of the more important symphonic organizations in America. He has also given successful guest-performances with the New York Philharmonic and the Philadelphia Symphony Orchestra.

GANZ, RUDOLPH, born, Zürich, February 24, 1877. After a successful career as concert-pianist, he was appointed conductor of the St. Louis Symphony Orchestra, a position he held for six years. Since that time he has given guest performances at the Lewisohn Stadium, New York, at the Hollywood Bowl, and with orchestras in San Francisco, Denver and Los Angeles. Since 1929, he has been the director of the Chicago Musical College.

GAUBERT, PHILIPPE, born, Cahors, July 4, 1879. After several successful seasons as one of the conductors of the Conservatory concerts in Paris, he was appointed first conductor to succeed Messager, in 1919. In 1920, he was appointed first conductor of the Paris Opéra, holding the position with esteem until the present time.

GERICKE, WILHELM, born, Graz, Styria, April 18, 1845; died, Vienna, November 1925. After serving a valuable apprenticeship under Hans Richter at the Vienna Opera (1874), he assumed the direction of the concerts of the *Gesellschaft der Musikfreunde*. From 1884 to 1889, and from 1898 to 1906 he held his most important conductorial post—with the Boston Symphony Orchestra, which he brought to a high degree of technical efficiency. (See page 58).

GIRARD, NARCISSE, born, Nantes, January 27, 1797; died, Paris, January 16, 1860. For nine years (1837–1846) he was one of the principal conductors of the Opéra Comique, where his work proved to be of such merit that he was soon thereafter appointed a conductor of the Opéra. Ten years later, he became general music director of that institution. He likewise distinguished himself as a conductor of

EUGENE GOOSSENS

symphonic-music, directing the Conservatory concerts from 1847 with great success.

GODFREY, SIR DAN, born, London, 1868. He made his début as conductor with the London Military Band in 1890, and has since that time become one of the living authorities on band music. In 1893, he was appointed conductor of the Bournemouth Municipal Orchestra. In recent years, he has distinguished himself as a guest-conductor of leading London orchestras.

GOLSCHMANN, VLADIMIR, born, Paris, December 16, 1893. He first came to the attention of the music world in 1919, with a series of *Concerts Golschmann* which he organized in Paris, introducing many now-prominent young French composers for the first time. In 1924, he came to New York as guest-conductor of the New York Symphony Society, and since that time has assumed the leadership of the St. Louis Symphony Orchestra. (See pages 256-257).

GOOSSENS, EUGENE, born, London, May 26, 1893. After assisting Sir Thomas Beecham as conductor of the Queen's Hall Orchestra, he made his official début by directing Stanford's opera *The Critic*. In 1921, he founded his own orchestra and gave six concerts devoted principally to new and unfamiliar music. He disclosed such unmistakable talent with these concerts that his conductorial career was instantly established. In 1922, he brought his baton to Covent Garden; in 1926, he directed several performances of the Diaghilev Ballet. Shortly thereafter, he was invited as a guest for several performances with the New

York Symphony Society. He was appointed permanent conductor of the Cincinnati Symphony Orchestra
in 1931. (See page 256).

Gossec, François Joseph, born, Vergnies, Belgian
Heinault, January 17, 1734; died, Passy, February
16, 1829. He is considered the founder of symphonic
music in France, and one of the important figures in
the early history of conducting who perfected and
improved orchestral technique. After conducting several less important orchestras—the private band of
La Pouplinière (1751) and the band of Prince Conti
at Chantilly (1762)—he founded and directed the
Concerts des Amateurs which was vitally instrumental
in introducing important symphonic music to France.
In 1773, he reorganized and directed the *Concerts
Spirituels*, and in 1780 he became one of the conductors of the Paris Opéra.

Gui, Vittorio, born, Rome, September 14, 1885. He
began his career in 1907 as conductor at the Teatro
Adriano. For three years thereafter he directed opera
at the San Carlo in Naples. In 1925, he was appointed general music director at the Teatro di Turno.
Since 1933, he has been one of the principal conductors at the annual Spring Florence music festival.

Habeneck, François Antoine, born, Mézières, January 23, 1781; died, Paris, February 8, 1849. For
twenty-three years (1824-1847) he conducted at the
Théâtre de l'Opéra where he gained valuable experience in his art. His enormous importance in baton
history, however, rests in his work with the *Société
des Concerts du Conservatoire* which he founded in

1828, and which he directed for twenty years. (See pages 46-47).

HADLEY, HENRY KIMBALL, born, Somerville, Massachusetts, December 20, 1874. Acquiring his early conductorial experience by directing European orchestras, he became conductor of the Seattle Symphony in 1909. Two years later, he became the principal conductor of the San Francisco Symphony Orchestra. For almost a decade, beginning with 1920, he was an assistant conductor of the New York Philharmonic. More recently, he has conducted the Manhattan Symphony Orchestra in an annual series of winter symphonic concerts in New York. He has been a guest-conductor of major symphony-orchestras in Europe and America.

HAGEMAN, RICHARD, born, Leewarden, Holland. He was an assistant conductor of the Amsterdam Royal Opera at the age of sixteen. His competence with the baton proved to be unmistakable, and so, two years later, he became first conductor. From 1908 until 1921, he was a conductor of the Metropolitan Opera House in New York, directing most of the Sunday night concerts. He has also been a conductor at the Chicago Civic Opera, the Los Angeles Opera Company, and the Ravinia Opera.

HALLÉ, SIR CHARLES, born, Hagen, Westphalia, April 11, 1819; died, Greenheys Lane, Manchester, October 25, 1895. His early conductorial experience included the direction of the Gentlemen's Concerts in Manchester (1845) and of a new choral society (1852). In 1857, he founded the Manchester Symphony Orchestra, and his work there brought him a national reputation. From 1860, he officiated at important concerts, operatic performances and festivals throughout Europe, conducting the Bristol festivals (1873–1893), the Reid concerts at Edinburgh (1868), the London Sacred Harmonic Society and the Liverpool Philharmonic. After his death, the name of his Manchester Orchestra was changed, in his honor, to the Hallé Orchestra.

HANSON, HOWARD, born, Wahoo, Nebraska, October 28, 1896. As director of the Eastman School of Music in Rochester, he was largely responsible for bringing into being the annual festival of modern American music which is each year given under his baton by the Rochester Symphony Orchestra. He has given guest performances with the New York Symphony, the New York Philharmonic, and symphony orchestras of Cleveland, San Francisco, Chicago, Boston, Los Angeles and St. Louis.

HARMATI, SANDOR, born, Budapest, July 9, 1892; died, New York, April 1936. After a short experience as conductor of the Women's String Orchestra in New York and the Morristown Orchestra in New Jersey, he received an appointment as director of the Omaha Symphony Orchestra which he held for five years (1925-1930). He has been a guest conductor of the Pasdeloup orchestra in Paris, the Berlin Philharmonic and leading symphonic organizations in America.

HARRISON, JULIUS ALLEN GREENWAY, born, Stourport, Worcestershire, March 26, 1885. He served his conductorial apprenticeship as an operatic conductor with

the Beecham Opera Company. In 1925, he succeeded
Eugene Goossens as conductor of the Handel Society.
Since that time he has given many commendable oper-
atic performances at the Royal Academy of Music,
and directed symphonic concerts of the Scottish
Orchestra.

HARTY, SIR HERBERT HAMILTON, born, Hillsborough,
Ireland, December 4, 1879. He first gained a great
reputation conducting concerts of the London Symphony Orchestra. In 1920, he was appointed director
of the Hallé Orchestra at Manchester, a position he
has held since that time with enormous distinction.
In 1924, he brought the Hallé Orchestra to London
for a series of symphonic concerts which was sensa-
tionally successful. He visited America in 1934 and
1935 in guest performances with leading symphonic-
organizations.

HASSLEMANS, LOUIS, born, Paris, July 25, 1878. He
made his début as conductor with the Lamoureux orchestra in Paris in 1905. In 1907, he founded and
directed the Hasselmans concerts in Paris which
brought his name to prominence. From 1909 until
1911, he was a conductor at the Opéra Comique.
After directing the Montreal Opera for two years
(1911–1913), the Marseilles *Concerts Classiques*
(1913–1914) and the Chicago Opera (1918–1920),
he joined the company of the Metropolitan Opera
House as one of its principal conductors.

HEGER, ROBERT, born, Strassburg, August 19, 1886.
In 1907, he became conductor of the Strassburg Opera
where he showed sufficient talent to earn for himself

a major post with the Vienna Volksoper four years later. From 1913 to 1921 he conducted the Nuremburg Opera, and from 1921 on he directed opera in Munich. His most important conductorial engagements took place at Nuremberg, the Munich Grand Opera House, the Vienna State Opera, the Royal Opera and Covent Garden at London.

HENSCHEL, SIR ISIDOR GEORGE, born, Breslau, February 18, 1850; died, Aviemore, Scotland, September 10, 1934. He was the first conductor of the Boston Symphony Orchestra, directing this organization during its first three years of existence (1881–1884). From 1885 until 1896 he directed the London Symphony concerts; and in 1893 he became the first conductor of the Scottish Orchestra at Glasgow. In 1930, he returned to America as a guest-conductor of the Boston Symphony Orchestra, in celebration of that orchestra's fiftieth anniversary. (See page 58).

HERTZ, ALFRED, born, Frankfort-on-Main, July 15, 1872. From 1891 until 1902 he enjoyed a prosperous conductorial career in Europe, directing at the Stadt-Theatre at Halle (1891), Altenburg (1892–1895), orchestral concerts in London (1899) and at Breslau (1899–1902). In 1902 he came to America as a conductor of German opera at the Metropolitan Opera House, and it was here that he directed the first performance of *Parsifal* given outside of Bayreuth (1903). He remained at the Metropolitan Opera House until 1915, and resigned in order to become principal conductor of the San Francisco Symphony Orchestra, a post he held for fifteen years.

From 1922 until 1925 he directed summer orchestral concerts at the Hollywood Bowl.

HILLER, JOHANN ADAM (real name, Hüller), born Wendisch-Ossig, Prussia, December 25, 1728; died, June 16, 1794. From 1775, he conducted choral concerts, and in 1776 he established *Concerts Spirituels* in Germany, similar to those held in Paris. From 1781 to 1785 he was principal conductor of the Leipzig Gewandhaus Orchestra, where he established a great reputation as conductor. He was likewise the founder of the German *Singspiel*.

HOESSLIN, FRANZ VON, born, Munich, December 31, 1885. He has had an active career as conductor of opera in Danzig, St. Gallen, Lübeck and Mannheim. In 1922, he was appointed conductor of the Berlin State Opera, and shortly therefore he officiated, for several years, as a principal conductor at the Wagner festivals at Bayreuth.

HOOGSTRATEN, WILLEM VAN, born, Utrecht, March 18, 1884. He gained a European reputation, principally with a Brahms festival which he conducted in Vienna, and a Mozart festival in Salzburg. In 1921, he became one of the principal conductors of the New York Philharmonic. It was in that year that he began conducting the summer concerts at the Lewisohn Stadium, instituting for the first time programs of unquestionably high standard; he has held this position ever since with enormous popularity. Since 1925, he has been the conductor of the Portland Symphony Orchestra. His engagements as guest-conductor have been many, including appearances in Oslo, Stockholm,

Amsterdam, Berlin, Leipzig, Zurich, Vienna, Munich, Philadelphia, Detroit, St. Louis, Los Angeles and New York.

HORENSTEIN, JASCHA, born, Kiev, May 6, 1898. In 1922, he assumed his first conductorial position in Berlin, directing the principal symphony-orchestras in guest performances. His most important post came in 1928, when he became conductor in several theatres in Düsseldorf. Since that time he has led symphony concerts throughout Germany.

ITURBI, JOSÉ, born, Valencia, November 22, 1895, one of the most celebrated pianists and conductors of our time. He has given guest performances in New York, Mexico City, and Philadelphia. During the season of 1936-1937 he acted as the principal conductor of the Rochester Philharmonic Orchestra. (See pp. 273-4).

JAMES, PHILIP, born, New York, 1890. In 1904, he entered upon a conductorial career by directing choral societies in New York. He made his official début as orchestral conductor at the Royal Albert Hall, London, in 1908. After gaining further experience as conductor, by directing the New Jersey Orchestra and the Brooklyn Orchestral Society, he assumed his present post as director of the Bamberger Little Symphony Orchestra which for six years has been broadcasting a weekly symphonic hour over Station W.O.R.

JANSSEN, WERNER, born, New York City, June 1, 1900. His first experience as conductor was at the Roxy Theatre, New York, a position he held for a very short time. In 1930, as a recipient of the *Prix de Rome* he toured Europe, acting as a guest-conductor of im-

ERICH KLEIBER

portant orchestras in Berlin, Budapest, Helsingfors, Riga, Rome and Turin. His European success, procured for him an appointment as one of the conductors of the New York Philharmonic during the season of 1934–1935. He has since been invited to be guest of leading orchestras in America.

JULLIEN, LOUIS ANTOINE. (See pages 80-82).

KAJANUS, ROBERT, born, Helsingfors, December 2, 1856; died, Helsingfors, July 6, 1933. In 1882, he established the choral society at Helsingfors where he gained his early experience with the baton. In 1886, he founded the Philharmonic Orchestra of Helsingfors, and it was here that he gained a wide European reputation as a major symphonic conductor. He was principally celebrated as a conductor of Sibelius' music, whose major works he introduced to the world. In 1932, Kajanus conducted an entire program devoted to Sibelius at Queen's Hall in London.

KINDLER, HANS, born, Rotterdam, January 8, 1893. After serving as a guest-conductor to important European orchestras—in Paris, Brussels, Vienna, Prague, Rome and Milan—he was asked to assume the leadership of the newly-founded National Symphony Orchestra in Washington, D. C. in 1930. He has held the position since that time, elevating the orchestra to a front rank.

KLEIBER, ERICH, born, Vienna, August 5, 1890. (See page 264).

KLEMPERER, OTTO. (See pages 258-263).

KLENAU, PAUL VON, born, Copenhagen, February 2, 1883. In 1907, he launched his career by conducting opera in Freiburg (Baden), assuming a similar post at Stuttgart one year later. He founded the Copenhagen Philharmonic Orchestra in 1920, and it was in the capacity of its director that he proved himself to be one of Europe's eminent conductors. In 1924, he was selected to direct a festival concert in Frankfort in honor of Delius' sixtieth birthday. He likewise distinguished himself as a director of the *Wiener Konzerthausgesellschaft* and of the *Wiener Singakademie*.

KLINDWORTH, KARL, born, Hanover, September 25, 1830; died, Oranienburg, July 27, 1916. Together with Joseph Joachim he directed the Berlin Philharmonic during its first year. For several years he conducted the concerts of the *Wagner-Verein* in Berlin.

KNAPPERTSBUSCH, HANS, born, Elberfeld, March 12, 1888. In 1912, he directed a festival devoted to Wagnerian music-drama in Holland. His success brought him the following year a permanent position at the Elberfeld opera. From 1919 until 1922 he directed opera at Dessau, and then resigned to assume his most important post—that of conductor of the Munich State Opera, which he has held with distinction until the present day.

KNOCH, ERNEST, born, Karlsruhe, August 1, 1875. After serving as an assistant to Felix Mottl at the Karlsruhe Opera (1898), he assumed the post of director of the opera at Strassburg. For a short while, he was an assistant conductor at Bayreuth (1904). For the next ten years, he was a principal conductor of opera at Essen, Cologne, Elberfeld and Rotterdamm. He came to America in 1914 to become one of the conductors of the Century Opera Company in New York. Since that time, he has toured the country frequently with visiting operatic companies, primarily devoted to Wagnerian music-drama.

KOLAR, VICTOR, born, Pesth, February 12, 1888. From 1915 to 1919 he served as assistant to Walter Damrosch on the New York Symphony Society. Since 1919, he has been an assistant conductor to Ossip Gabrilowitsch with the Detroit Symphony Orchestra. He has frequently conducted series of summer concerts at Detroit and Chicago as well as radio concerts.

KOUSSEVITZKY, SERGE. (See pages 227-240).

KRAUSS, CLEMENS, born, Vienna, March 31, 1893. After conducting opera at the German theatre at Riga (1913–1914), Nuremburg (1915–1916) and at Stettin (1916–1921) he became one of the principal conductors at the Vienna State Opera, and of the Vienna Tonkünstlerverein. For five years—from 1924 to 1929—he officiated as Intendant of Opera and director of Museum concerts in Frankfort. From 1929 to 1934 he was principal conductor of the Vienna State Opera, a post he resigned in order to become director of the Berlin State Opera. He was guest conductor of the Munich Festival (1925–1926), of the Salzburg Festival (1926, 1929, 1930–1934), of the New York Philharmonic and the Philadelphia Symphony Orchestra (1929), and of principal orchestras throughout Europe. (See pages 255-256).

KRIPS, JOSEF, born, Vienna, April 8, 1902. In 1920,

he served as choral director at the Volksoper in Vienna, and three years later he became opera-director in Aussig. Since that time he has held the position of Kapellmeister at the Landestheater in Ortmund and Karlsruhe.

LAMOUREUX, CHARLES, born, Bordeaux, September 21, 1834; died, Paris, December 21, 1899. In 1873 he originated the *Société de l'Harmonie Sacree* which devoted itself to the performance of great choral music. After serving for five years as an assistant conductor at the Conservatory concerts (1872–1877), and for one year as an assistant at the Opéra (1876) he was given his first distinguished conductorial position as principal conductor at the Opéra. In 1881 he established the Concerts Lamoureux, and it was as conductor of these concerts that he achieved historical fame. He was a frequent guest-conductor in Rouen and London. (See pages 49-50).

LANGE, HANS. For many years he was employed as violinist in leading symphony orchestras. He first began conducting in Frankfort, assisting Willem Mengelberg in performances of the *Museumgesell-schaft*, and directing the Frankfort Bach Society for three years. In 1923 he came to New York to become assistant concertmaster and assistant conductor of the New York Philharmonic. Since 1931 he has been a regular conductor of the New York Philharmonic. In 1935, he directed a special historical series devoted to music for chamber-orchestra with the Philharmonic Orchestra. (See pages 275-276).

LEGINSKA, ETHEL, born, Hull, England, 1890, dis-

nato Toppo

HANS LANGE

tinguished pianist who, in 1924, turned to conducting. She has directed concerts of the New York Philharmonic, the Boston Symphony, the Boston Women's Symphony and the Women's Symphony Orchestra of Chicago.

LEVI, HERMANN, born, Giessen, November 7, 1839; died, Munich, May 13, 1900. His early important positions as conductor included the direction of opera at Saarbrücken (1859), of German opera at Rotterdamm (1861) and as Kapellmeister at Karlsruhe (1864). From 1872 to 1896, he established a world-wide fame as conductor, in the post of Kapellmeister in Munich. On July 28, 1882 he conducted the world's first performance of *Parsifal*, at Bayreuth. One year later he was selected to direct the music at Richard Wagner's funeral.

LEVIN, SYLVAN. For several years an assistant of Leopold Stokowski with the Philadelphia Symphony Orchestra, he first came to notice in 1934 when he substituted for Stokowski on many of the broadcasts of the Philadelphia Orchestra on the Chesterfield evening quarter-hour. In the Fall of 1934, he was appointed conductor of the York (Pennsylvania) Symphony Orchestra. (See page 276).

LISZT, FRANZ, born, Raiding, October 22, 1811; died, Bayreuth, July 31, 1886, world-famous composer whose name is likewise prominent in baton history. On November 2, 1842 he became Kapellmeister at Weimar, where his baton was instrumental in introducing many new operatic and symphonic works to the music-world. For ten years, Liszt's conducting made Weimar a musical center of Europe. From 1852 on, he directed many music festivals in Karlsruhe, Magdeburg, Aix and Leipzig. In 1870, he directed an important Beethoven festival in Rome. (See pages 84-85).

LULLY, JEAN BAPTISTE, born, at or near Florence, November 29, 1639; died, Paris, March 22, 1687, celebrated composer and prominent conductor of his day. Louis XIV established a band expressly for him to train, and it was here that he gained his first experience as a conductor. For many years he was one of the principal conductors at the Paris Opéra. In 1662, his conductorial talents were singularly honored when he was appointed "*La Charge de Maître de Musique de la Famille Royale.*"

MAGANINI, QUINTO, born, Fairfield, California, November 30, 1897. In 1928, he was invited as a guest conductor to the Mannes concerts in Greenwich and East Orange. He has since that time given guest performances in New York (1928), Paris (1929) and with the San Francisco Symphony Orchestra (1930). He founded the New York Chamber Symphony Orchestra, which for several seasons has performed concerts of unfamiliar old and new music in New York.

MAHLER, GUSTAV. (See pages 122-126).

MANNES, DAVID, born, February 16, 1866. In 1919 he directed symphony-concerts for the benefit of soldiers and sailors at the Metropolitan Museum of Art in New York. In 1920, these concerts were opened to the public at large, and since that time he has annually conducted a series of eight free concerts at the Museum.

MANNS, SIR AUGUST FRIEDRICH, born, Stolzenburg, March 12, 1825; died, London, March 1, 1907. For many years he devoted himself to the direction of band concerts, first at Elbing and Posen (1840), then at Königsberg and Cologne (1848–1851), and finally at the Crystal Palace in London (1855). He changed the band at the Crystal Palace to a full symphony orchestra, and from that time on devoted himself more seriously to the symphonic repertoire. Up to 1901, he had conducted 14,000 concerts—band, symphonic and choral.

MARINUZZI, GIUSEPPE GINO, born, Palermo, March 24, 1882. After conducting operatic performances at the Costanzi in Rome, he came to America in 1920 to succeed Campanini as artistic director of the Chicago Opera. He returned to Italy in 1922, directing in principal opera houses, particularly at the La Scala in Milan where he achieved a great reputation as a conductor of Italian opera.

MASCAGNI, PIETRO, born, Leghorn, December 7, 1863, eminent composer of Italian opera who likewise boasts of a distinguished career with baton. In 1885 he began conducting by directing the town orchestra at Cerignola. From 1895 to 1902 he conducted festivals of orchestral music in Rome. In 1902 he toured America as the conductor of an opera-company in a repertoire of his own works, and eight years later he revisited America. Since that time he has frequently conducted opera and festival concerts in Rome.

MENDELSSOHN, FELIX BARTHOLDY, born, Hamburg, February 3, 1809; died, Leipzig, November 4, 1847, world-celebrated composer and eminent conductor. In 1829, he acquired a permanent place in music history by directing the first performance of Bach's *St. Matthew's Passion* with the *Singakademie*, thereby for the first time bringing Bach from obscurity and neglect to fame and recognition. In 1833, he conducted the Lower Rhine festival at Düsseldorf. Two years later he became the conductor of the Leipzig Gewandhaus Orchestra, and in this position he became one of the most significant names in the early history of conducting. Subsequently, he served as Kapellmeister at the courts of Berlin and Dresden. One year before his death, he conducted at Aix, Düsseldorf, Liège, Cologne and Birmingham. (See pages 79-80).

MENGELBERG, WILLEM, born, Utrecht, March 28, 1871. From 1891 to 1895 he directed the town concerts at Lucerne. In 1895, he was appointed conductor of the Concertgebow Orchestra at Amsterdam, a position he has held ever since; and it has been principally through his efforts and talent that the Concertgebow has taken an imposing position among the great orchestras of the world. From 1911 to 1914 he conducted the London Symphony Orchestra and the Royal Philharmonic regularly. In 1921, he came to America as a guest of the New Symphony Orchestra of New York, and the following year he was appointed one of the permanent conductors of the New York Philharmonic, a position he held for nine years. He has made numerous tours throughout all of Europe with his Concertgebow Orchestra. (See pages 243-252).

MESSAGER, ANDRE CHARLES, born, Montlucon, December 3, 1853. After serving a short apprenticeship as conductor of the Théâtre Eden in Brussels (1880) and as choirmaster at Saint-Marie-des-Batignolles (1882-1884) he was appointed conductor at the Opéra Comique in Paris, a post he held for five years. From 1901 to 1907 he was artistic director at Covent Garden, London, and from 1907 until 1919 artistic director of the Opera in Paris. In 1918 he made an extensive American tour as conductor with a French symphony-orchestra.

MESSNER, JOSEPH, born, Schwaz-Tyrol, Austria, February 27, 1893. He made his début as conductor in Salzburg in 1922. In 1926, he became choirmaster at the Salzburg Cathedral, and since that time he has conducted an annual series of choral performances at the Salzburg Festival. He has been a guest conductor of the Warsaw Philharmonic, the Vienna Philharmonic, and has made extenstive European tours with the Salzburg Cathedral Choir.

MOLINARI, BERNARDINO, born, Rome, April 11, 1880. In 1912 he became the principal conductor of the Augusteo in Rome where he acquired a great reputation with a series of festivals devoted to the music of Scarlatti, Beethoven, Saint-Saëns, Debussy etc. He toured Italy extensively in 1915, and ten years later made a still more extensive tour of Italy, Switzerland, Germany and Czecho-Slovakia. In 1928, he came to America as a guest of the New York Philharmonic, and

THE MAN WITH THE BATON

since that time has directed performances of leading American symphony orchestras. (See pages 254-255).

MONTEUX, PIERRE, born, Paris, April 4, 1875. He served a long apprenticeship as conductor beginning with 1894, directing concerts and opera in Paris, and officiating as a guest conductor in London, Berlin, Vienna and Pesth. In 1916, he came to America with the Russian Ballet, and from 1917 to 1919 was one of the principal conductors at the Metropolitan Opera House. In 1918, he took over Karl Muck's baton with the Boston Symphony Orchestra, remaining its principal conductor until 1924. For several years after that, he was a guest conductor of leading orchestras throughout America. In 1935, he was appointed conductor of the San Francisco Symphony Orchestra and guest-conductor of the Los Angeles Philharmonic.

MÖRIKE, EDUARD, born, Stuttgart, August 16, 1877. For a long period he directed operatic performances in Rostock, Kiel, Stettin and Halle. After assisting at Bayreuth, he went to Paris to help direct the first French performance of *Salomé* by Richard Strauss. In 1925 he was appointed conductor of the *Singakademie* in Dresden.

MOTTL, FELIX, born, Vienna, August 24, 1856; died, Munich, July 2, 1911. After serving as leader of the *Wagnerverein* in Vienna, he went to Bayreuth in 1875 to assist in the first performances there. In 1880, he became Kapellmeister at Karlsruhe, conducting the Philharmonic concerts in that city until 1892. In 1886, he was appointed chief conductor at Bayreuth, where he firmly established himself as one of the foremost Wagnerian conductors of his time. In 1907, he acquired further prestige as Kapellmeister in Munich. He was a guest-conductor in London, Paris and New York.

MUCK, KARL. (See pages 143-159).

NIKISCH, ARTUR. (See pages 127-142).

ORMANDY, EUGENE, born, Budapest, November 18, 1899. After serving as solo concertmaster at the Capitol Theatre in New York in 1921, he became first associate conductor; then conductor with the Judson Radio Program Corp., a guest with the Philadelphia Orchestra, in 1931, permanent conductor of the Minneapolis Symphony Orchestra, and in 1936, the principal conductor of the Philadelphia Orchestra. (See pages 274-275).

PANIZZA, ETTORE, born, Buenos Aires, August 12, 1875. From 1889, he conducted in Italian theatres for several years. In 1907, he was appointed a conductor of Italian opera at Covent Garden, London, and for six years he held this post with distinction. Since 1916, he has been one of the principal conductors at the La Scala in Milan. In 1934 he came to America to become one of the conductors at the Metropolitan Opera House, New York.

PAPI, GENNARO. In 1906, he was chorusmaster at San Severo di Puglia. After experience as assistant conductor in opera houses in Milan, Warsaw, Odessa, London, he came to New York in 1917 and made his début at the Metropolitan Opera House in *Manon*. His performance was so successful that he was retained as a permanent conductor for many years.

THE MAN WITH THE BATON

PARAY, PAUL, born, Treport, May 24, 1886. In 1921, he was an assistant conductor of the Lamoureaux orchestra where he gained attention with vital performances of Ravel, Berlioz and César Franck. In 1923, he became principal conductor of the orchestra, succeeding Camille Chevillard. He has conducted symphony concerts in Vichy.

PASDELOUP, JULES ETIENNE, born, Paris, September 15, 1819; died, Fontainbleau, August 13, 1887. In 1851, he founded the *Société des Jeunes Artistes du Conservatoire,* whose concerts he transferred to the *Cirque d'Hiver* ten years later. For a while, he directed men choral societies in Paris. In 1868 he directed at the Théâtre Lyrique. (See pages 47-48).

PAUMGARTNER, BERNARD, born, Vienna, November 14, 1887. He made his conductorial début in Vienna in 1908, and two years later gave successful performances with the Tonkünstler Orchestra in the same city. He achieved prominence conducting the Mozarteum orchestra at the annual Salzburg festival, and for many years now has been in charge of the performances of the Mozart serenades in the Courtyard of the Archbishop, one of the features of the Salzburg Festival.

PAUR, EMIL, born, Czernowitz, August 29, 1855. His preparatory years as conductor were spent in Kassel and Königsberg. In 1880, he was appointed Kapellmeister at Mannheim and was placed in charge of the subscription concerts. In 1893, he came to America to become conductor of the Boston Symphony Orchestra. From 1898 until 1902 he conducted the New

BIOGRAPHICAL GUIDE

York Philharmonic, and in 1899–1900 he was principal Wagnerian conductor at the Metropolitan Opera
House. For six years (1904–1910) he was conductor
of the Pittsburgh Symphony Orchestra, and then returned to Germany to direct the Berlin State Opera.

PFITZNER, HANS, born, Moscow, May 5, 1869; died, Germany, 1935. In 1894, he assumed his first major post
as conductor, when he became an assistant at the
Stadttheater in Mayence. Then followed an active
career with the baton that included a post at the
Theater des Westens (1903), with the Kaim Orchestra
in Munich (1907) and as director of the Strassburg
Opera. In 1919 he was called upon to conduct the
Munich *Konzertverein*, and one year later he was singularly honored by receiving the appointment of General Music Director of Bavaria. Since that time, he
has intermittently conducted symphonic concerts in
Munich and Berlin.

PIERNÉ, HENRI CONSTANT GABRIEL, born, Metz, August
16, 1863. After being an assistant to Colonne as conductor of his famous orchestra in Paris for seven
years, he became principal conductor in 1910. Since
that time he has conducted Colonne's orchestra with
singular success. In 1925 he became a member of the
Académie des Beaux-Arts, conducting regular concerts of the orchestra at the Institute.

PITT, PERCY, born, London, January 4, 1870; died, England, November 1932. From 1915 to 1920 he was
director of the Beecham Opera Company. For four
years after that he assumed the artistic direction of
the British National Opera Company. In 1922, he

333

associated himself with radio work, becoming artistic director of the British Broadcasting Company. Two years later, he became music director of the Covent Garden Syndicate.

POHLIG, KARL, born, Teplitz, February 10, 1864. After serving as an assistant to Gustav Mahler at the Vienna State Opera (1897), he asumed the position of Kapell-meister at Coburg. In 1900, he became director of the Stuttgart Opera and conductor of symphony concerts in that city. In 1907, he came to America to become conductor of the Philadelphia Symphony Orchestra, a post he held until 1912 when he was succeeded by Leopold Stokowski. Since that time he has held direc-torial posts at the Hamburg Opera and at the Bruns-wick Opera.

POLACCO, GIORGO, born, Venice, April 12, 1875. After conducting operatic performances in Italy, Brussels, Lisbon, Warsaw and St. Petersburg, he came to South America where for eleven years he conducted in opera houses in Buenos Aires and Rio de Janeiro. For three years he was principal conductor at the La Scala in Milan. In 1911, at Puccini's personal request he was placed in charge of the Savage production of the *Girl of the Golden West*. In 1912 he became one of the chief conductors at the Metropolitan Opera House succeeding Toscanini, and in 1918 he officiated over the Chicago Opera Company. His repertoire includes more than 150 operas.

POULET, GASTON, born, Paris, April 10, 1892. After serving a long period with the Poulet String Quartet which he founded, he organized the *Association des Concerts Poulet* which gives annual series of orchestral concerts at the Sarah Bernhardt Theatre in Paris.

POLLAK, EGON, born, Prague, May 3, 1879; died, Germany, June 14, 1933. In 1905, he became first conductor at the Stadttheater in Bremen. From 1910 to 1912 he held a similar post in Leipzig, and five years later he transferred his baton to Frankfort. Shortly before his death he was one of the principal conductors at the Hamburg Opera, and at the annual Munich festival.

PRUWER, JULIUS, born, Vienna, February 20, 1874. From 1894 to 1896 he gained valuable experience as conductor at the Cologne Opera. In 1896 he accepted his most important post to date, as city director of music in Breslau. In 1907, he toured with the Breslau forces throughout Germany in their production of Richard Strauss' *Salomé*. From 1920 to 1923 he was artistic director at Breslau Opera, and since 1925 the permanent conductor of popular concerts of the Berlin Philharmonic.

RABAUD, HENRI BENJAMIN, born, Paris, November 10, 1873. He assumed a conductorial position at the Paris Opéra in 1894. From 1914 to 1918 he was first conductor at the Opéra. In 1918 he came to America to direct the Boston Symphony Orchestra. He returned to Paris the following year to become director of the Paris Conservatory.

RACHMANINOFF, SERGE, born, Onega, Novgorod, March 20, 1873, world-famous pianist and composer, equally distinguished as conductor. In 1912, he became director of opera at Mamontov, after which he conducted at the Royal Opera in Moscow. He has been a guest-conductor of the leading symphonic organizations in Europe and America, principally in his own music.

RAPEE, ERNO, born, Budapest, June 4, 1891. After several years as musical director of the Rivoli Theatre and the Capitol Theatre in New York, he was brought by S. L. Rothafel in 1926 to the new Roxy Theatre as first conductor. At the present time he is director of the symphony orchestra at Radio City, New York, with which organization he has performed frequent symphony concerts over the radio.

REINECKE, KARL HEINRICH, born, Altona, June 23, 1824; died, Leipzig, March 10, 1910. In 1854, he conducted choral and orchestral concerts at Barmen. After one year as conductor of the *Singakademie* in Breslau (1859) he received his most important appointment—as director of the Leipzig Gewandhaus Orchestra. For thirty-five years he held this position with great prestige.

REINER, FRITZ, born, Pesth, December 19, 1888. In 1909, he was chorusmaster at the Komische Opera in Pesth, and from 1911 to 1914 conductor at the Volksoper. For seven years (1914–1921) he enjoyed a distinguished career as principal conductor at the Dresden Opera. He came to America in 1922 to assume the post of principal conductor of the Cincinnati Symphony Orchestra, where he remained for nine years. He has been a guest conductor in Rome, Spain, New York, Philadelphia and Los Angeles. Recently he distinguished himself with operatic performances with the Philadelphia Opera Company. (See page 254).

ARTUR RODZINSKI

RHENÉ-BATON, born, Courseulles-sur-mer, Calvados, September 5, 1879. For a short while (1907) he was director of the chorus of the Opéra-Comique in Paris. Turning to orchestral conducting, he directed the *Concerts Populaires* at Angers, the *Concerts Sainte-Cécile* in Bordeaux, and finally the *Concerts Durand* in Paris where he first came to prominence. In 1910, he conducted the first festival devoted to French music to take place in Germany, at Munich. Two years later, he conducted performances of the Diaghilev Ballet in London, Paris and South America. From 1918 to 1923 he gained further prominence with the baton by directing the Pasdeloup concerts in Paris.

RICHTER, HANS. (See pages 117-121).

RODZINSKI, ARTUR, born, Spalato, Dalmatia, 1894. Stokowski, on a visit to Warsaw, heard Rodzinski's performance of *Die Meistersinger* and was so impressed that he invited the young conductor to be his assistant in Philadelphia. After four years with Stokowski, Rodzinski became conductor of the Los Angeles Philharmonic (1929-1933). In 1933, he became the conductor of the Cleveland Symphony Orchestra, and in 1936 he was appointed one of the conductors of the New York Philharmonic Symphony Society. (See page 276).

RONALD, SIR LANDON, born, London, June 7, 1873. After a career as concert-pianist and accompanist to such world-renowned singers as Melba, Sir Ronald turned to conducting, giving performances at the Lyric Theatre in London, and with the London Symphony Orchestra (1907). He has since been an important conductor of such leading English orchestras as the Liverpool Philharmonic, the Manchester Hallé Orchestra and the Scottish Orchestra, and has given guest performances in principal cities throughout Europe. Since 1908, he has been a conductor of the Royal Albert Hall Orchestra.

Ross, Hugh, born, Langport, England, August 21, 1898. In 1921, he conducted orchestral and operatic performances in London and Oxford. Towards the end of the same year, he became conductor of the Winnipeg Male Choir, making extensive tours with that organization throughout the United States and Canada. For a short period, he served as a guest conductor of the Winnipeg Symphony Orchestra and the Minneapolis Symphony Orchestra. Since 1927, he has been the conductor of the Schola Cantorum in New York.

Rothwell, Walter Henry, born, London, September 22, 1872; died, Los Angeles, March 13, 1927. From 1905 to 1907 he was an assistant of Gustav Mahler at the Hamburg Opera. His early experience as a conductor was procured at Breslau and Vienna. Coming to America, he first toured with the H. W. Savage Co., and then assumed the post of conductor of the St. Paul Symphony Orchestra (1908–1915). In 1917 he was guest-conductor in Cincinnati and Detroit, and two years later he was appointed director of the Los Angeles Philharmonic.

Safonov, Vassily Ilyitch, born, Tertersk, Caucasus, February 6, 1852; died, Kislovodsk, March 1918. For fifteen years (1890–1905) he was director of the

Russian Musical Society concerts in Moscow, where he acquired an imposing reputation as conductor of symphonic music. Esteemed the foremost conductor in Russia at the time, he was invited by the New York Philharmonic to be permanent director for three years (1906–1909). Returning to Russia in 1911, he became director of the Russian Musical Society concerts at Petrograd. He was a frequent guest to principal orchestras in England. During his entire career he attracted much comment because in his conducting he dispensed with the baton.

SALOMON, JOHANN PETER, born, Bonn, February 2, 1745; died, London, November 28, 1815. After serving as concertmaster of a small opera company orchestra belonging to Prince Henry of Prussia, he settled in London, and in 1781 became conductor at Covent Garden. From 1784 to 1786, he conducted symphony concerts in London. In 1813, he was instrumental in the founding of the Royal Philharmonic in London, which he conducted until his death.

SAMINSKY, LAZARE, born, Vale-Gotzulovo, October 27, 1882. He made his first important appearance as conductor in 1909, when he directed the Petrograd Conservatory Orchestra in a program devoted to his own works. In 1913, he conducted his own compositions in Moscow at the invitation of Serge Koussevitzky. He has conducted concerts in principal cities throughout Europe, and has directed special festivals devoted to modern music in Paris in 1923, 1925, 1926, 1928 and 1929. At the present time, he is choral director at the Temple Emanu-El, New York.

SARGENT, HAROLD MALCOM WATTS, born, Stamford, Lincolnshire, April 29, 1895. In 1921 he conducted at a Queen's Hall Promenade Concert a Program devoted to his own works. His second important appearance as conductor took place in 1924, when he directed the first performance of Vaughan-Williams' opera, *Hugh the Drover*, at His Majesty's Theatre. Since that time he has conducted symphony concerts in London (1925), and Manchester, and has directed a London season of the D'Oyly Carte Opera Co. (1926). He has conducted several series of children concerts at Westminster.

SCHALK, FRANZ, born, Vienna, May 27, 1863; died, Vienna, September 3, 1931. After receiving a conductorial training from Anton Bruckner, he became a conductor at the Vienna Opera (1904), finally rising to the position of principal conductor. From 1907 to 1911, he directed opera at Covent Garden, London, and from 1914 until 1918 was associated with Richard Strauss at the Imperial Opera in Vienna. Upon Strauss' resignation in 1924, Schalk became the sole director. He has also conducted the Vienna Philharmonic, and for many years was associated with the Salzburg Festival, of which he was one of the originators.

SCHEEL, FRITZ, born, Lübeck, November 7, 1852; died, Philadelphia, March 12, 1907. When he was seventeen years old, he was engaged in orchestra work as a concertmaster at Bremerhaven. In 1873, he began directing summer concerts in Schwerin, and from 1890 to 1893 conducted orchestral concerts in Hamburg.

He came to America in 1893, and two years later founded the San Francisco Symphony Orchestra which he directed for four years. In 1899, he conducted summer concerts in Philadelphia with such success that, the following year, he was appointed principal conductor of the Philadelphia Orchestra.

SCHELLING, ERNEST, born, Belvedere, New Jersey, July 26, 1876. He has made guest-appearances with the Philadelphia and the Boston Symphony Orchestras. He has distinguished himself particularly with his direction of the annual series of children's concerts with the New York Philharmonic, the Philadelphia and the Los Angeles Philharmonic Orchestras.

SCHERCHEN, HERMANN, born, Berlin, June 21, 1891. After conducting symphony concerts at Riga, he came to Berlin in 1918 where he founded the *Neue Musik-gesellschaft*. In 1921 he conducted the New Grotrian-Steinweg Orchestra in Leipzig, and the following year he was called to Frankfort to direct the museum concerts. In 1928 he was appointed conductor of the Philharmonic concerts in Köngsberg, and has since conducted orchestral performances of the annual festival conducted by the International Society of Modern Music. He has also inaugurated a school of conducting which each year brings him to another principal city, and which has increased his prestige immeasurably in the world of music.

SCHILLINGS, MAX VON, born, Düren, April 19, 1868; died, Berlin, July 24, 1933. In 1868 he served as assistant stage director at Bayreuth, and by 1902 he had risen to the position of chorus master. He went to Stuttgart in 1908, where his conducting received such acclaim that three years later he was appointed general music director—a post he held for seven years. In 1919, he was called to Berlin to become general director of the State Opera. When Hitler came to power, Schillings was given the position of principal conductor at Charlottenburg, which he held until his death. He came to America in 1930 as a conductor of the German Grand Opera Company.

SCHINDLER, KURT, born, Berlin, February 17, 1882. In 1902, he conducted at the Stuttgart Opera, and the following year he brought his baton to Würzburg. Coming to America in 1905, he became assistant conductor at the Metropolitan Opera House for three years. In 1909 he founded the Macdowell Chorus in New York. Three years later, he became director of the Schola Cantorum, New York, holding this position until 1926.

SCHNEEVOIGT, GEORGE, born, Viborg, November 8, 1872. For a short period he conducted at the Riga Exposition. From 1904 until 1908 he was head of the Kaim orchestra in Munich. In 1912 he was called to Helsingfors to direct the Symphony Orchestra. In 1918 he founded the Philharmonic Orchestra of Osolo. He came to America six years later as a guest-conductor of the Boston Symphony Orchestra, and since that time has directed the Los Angeles Philharmonic for two seasons.

SEIDL, ANTON, born, Pesth, May 7, 1850; died, New York, March 28, 1898. From 1879 until 1882 he was conductor at the Leipzig Opera House. In 1882 he took a long tour through Europe as a conductor of Angelo Neumann's opera troupe, in performances of the *Nibelungen Ring*, and it was at this time that he first came to the fore. For a short period in 1883 he conducted at the Bremen Opera House. Two years later, he came to America to become principal German conductor at the Metropolitan Opera House. In 1891, he became conductor of the New York Philharmonic. Shortly before his death he conducted opera at Covent Garden in London, and at Bayreuth.

SERAFIN, TULLIO, born, Cavarzere, Italy, September 8, 1878. He made his début at the Communale Theatre in Ferrara in 1900. There followed several engagements as conductor in Turin (1903) at the Augusteo in Rome (1906) and at the La Scala in Milan (1909). After conducting opera in Buenos Aires, London and Madrid, he came to New York in 1924 to become permanent conductor at the Metropolitan Opera House. He resigned this position in 1935, and returned to Italy to be director at the Teatro Reale in Rome.

SEVITZKY, FABIEN, born, Wyshny, Russia, September 30, 1893. In 1914, his first appearance as conductor took place with the Moscow Imperial Theatre Orchestra. In 1925, he founded and conducted the Philadelphia Chamber Sinfonietta, which gave concerts of music for chamber orchestra in principal cities in America.

SHAVITCH, VLADIMIR, born, South America, July 20, 1888. After conducting the Rochester Philharmonic for one year (1923), he was appointed conductor of the Syracuse Symphony Orchestra. Five years later, he received an appointment as conductor of the Moscow State Opera. He has been a guest conductor of the London Symphony Orchestra, the Berlin Symphony Orchestra, and of principal orchestras in Paris, Madrid, Moscow, Leningrad, Detroit, San Francisco and Los Angeles.

SHILKRET, NATHANIEL, born, New York, January 1, 1895. For fourteen years he has been musical director of the R.C.A. Victor Company. He created the Victor Salon Orchestra which he has conducted for many years in recordings of symphonic and popular music. He has directed many popular radio broadcasts, and has made extensive recordings.

SLONIMSKY, NICOLAS, born, Petrograd, April 15, 1894. He has conducted the Boston Symphony Chamber Orchestra with considerable success, and in recent years has directed programs of modern American music in Paris.

SMALLENS, ALEXANDER, born, Petrograd, 1889. He served a long apprenticeship as conductor of opera, first as assistant conductor of the Boston Opera (1911), and then as a principal conductor of the Century Opera Company, the Colon Opera in Buenos Aires and the National Theatre in Havana. From 1919 until 1922 he was a conductor of the Chicago Opera Company, where he conducted the world première of Prokofieff's *Love Of Three Oranges* at the express request of the composer. After directing operatic performances at the Volksoper and Staatsoper in Berlin, and at the Royal Opera in Madrid, he returned to America to be director at the Philadelphia

Civic Opera Company (1923–1930). During the summer seasons of 1934 and 1935, he directed operatic performances at the Lewisohn Stadium in New York.

SMITH, DAVID STANLEY, born, Toledo, July 6, 1877. As dean of the music department of Yale University, he organized the New Haven Symphony Orchestra and has directed it for several years. He has been a guest conductor of the New York Philharmonic, the Cleveland and Detroit Symphony Orchestra in performances of his own music.

SODERO, CESARE, born, Naples, August 2, 1886. He was an operatic conductor at the age of fourteen. At maturity, he was appointed a guest-conductor at the San Carlo Opera Company, and permanent conductor with the Aborn English Opera. For six years, he directed symphony concerts over the National Broadcasting Company.

SOKOLOFF, NIKOLAI, born, Kiev, May 28, 1886. As a boy, he toured with the Municipal Orchestra of Kiev as violinist. Coming to America in 1898, he joined the violin section of the Boston Symphony Orchestra. After returning to Europe for a period of musical study, he assumed his first conductorial position when he was called upon to direct the San Francisco Symphony Orchestra in 1916. In 1918 he organized the Cleveland Symphony Orchestra, and remained its principal conductor for more than ten years. In 1922, he was invited as the first American conductor to direct the London Symphony Orchestra at the National Welsh Festival. He has given guest performances with leading orchestras in England, Russia and the United States. In 1930, he founded the New York Orchestra which he has since been directing.

SPOHR, LUDWIG, born, Brunswick, April 5, 1784; died, London, October 22, 1859. In 1809 he received his first important assignment as conductor when he was called to direct the first German festival at Frankenhausen. From 1812 until 1815 he conducted performances at the Theatre-an-der-Wien, and for the following two years broadened his prestige by directing concerts in Italy and Holland. After two years as operatic conductor in Frankfort, he was invited as a guest of the Royal Philharmonic where he made conductorial history by directing performances with a baton. Shortly before his death, he served as Kapellmeister at Kassel. (See pages 78-79).

SPONTINI, GASPARO LUIGI, born, Jesi, November 14, 1774; died, Majolati, January 14, 1851. For a short period, in 1800, he directed court performances at Palermo. Then, after giving performances throughout Italy, he was called to Paris to conduct Italian Opera at the Odéon, a position he held with great distinction for two years (1810-1812). In 1820, he was appointed Kapellmeister at Berlin, and after that he conducted operatic performances in leading opera-houses in Germany.

STAMITZ, JOHANN WENZEL ANTON, born, Deutschbrod, June 19, 1717; died, Mannheim, March 27, 1757. In 1745 he was appointed conductor of the Mannheim orchestra, and it was in this position that he not only established the "Mannheim school of conducting" but also developed his orchestra as one of the most technically perfect of the time. He toured throughout Germany with the Mannheim Orchestra, and everywhere created a sensation. (See pages 75-76).

STEINBACH, EMIL, born, Lengenzieden, November 14, 1849; died, Mayence, December 6, 1919. From 1871 until 1874 he was assistant conductor in Mannheim. In 1877 he became first Kapellmeister at Mayence. As conductor of Wagnerian Opera at Covent Garden, London, in 1893 he established his reputation as an important operatic conductor.

STEINBACH, FRITZ, born, Grünsfeld, June 17, 1885; died, Munich, August 13, 1916. From 1880 until 1886, he was assistant conductor at Mayence. Revealing unmistakable talents in this direction, he was appointed conductor of the Meiningen Orchestra, where he acquired a great reputation, particularly after extensive tours with the orchestra. From 1902 unitl 1914, he was conductor of the Gürzenich concerts.

STIEDRY, FRITZ, born, Vienna, October 11, 1883. After a short period as conductor in Dresden (1907) he accepted important engagements in Teplitz, Posen and Prague. In 1914 he became conductor of the Berlin State Opera. Ten years later, he succeeded Weingartner as director of the Vienna State Opera. In 1928, he returned to the Berlin State Opera where he has remained ever since.

STOCK, FREDERICK, born, Jülich, November 11, 1872. In 1900 he became an assistant to Theodore Thomas with the Chicago Symphony Orchestra. Upon Thomas' death in 1905 Stock was appointed principal conductor, and he has held this position since that time with constantly increasing prestige. In 1929, he directed the Cincinnati May Festival, and the following year he was called upon to direct the North Shore Festival in Evanston. He has been a guest conductor of the New York Philharmonic Orchestra. (See page 57).

STOESSEL, ALBERT, born, St. Louis, October 11, 1894. During the World War, he served as bandmaster. After the War, he became assistant conductor of the Oratorio Society of New York, rising to full conductorship in 1921. He has more recently conducted operatic performances at the Juilliard School of Music in New York.

STOKOWSKI, LEOPOLD. (See pages 197-226).

STRANSKY, JOSEF, born, Bohemia, September 9, 1872; died, New York, March, 1936. In 1898, he directed performances of German Opera in Prague, and in 1903 at the Hamburg Opera. In 1909, he turned to symphonic music, first conducting the Blüthner Orchestra in Berlin and then, the following year, the *Musikfreunde* concerts in Dresden. He came to America in 1911 to become principal conductor of the New York Philharmonic, remaining in this position until 1923 when he retired from all musical activity.

STRARAM, WALTER, born, London, July 9, 1876; died, Paris, November 24, 1933. In 1909 he was assistant conductor of the Manhattan Opera Company. Returning to Paris, he founded the Walter Straram concerts which he directed with great success until his death.

STRAUSS, RICHARD, born, Munich, June 11, 1864, world-famous composer, equally eminent as conductor. After being an assistant to Hans von Bülow at Meiningen, he became Kapellmeister in 1886. From 1889 until 1894 he occupied a similar post at Weimar, resigning in order to accept the much more significant position of court-director at Munich. In the Summer of 1894, he conducted several performances at Bayreuth, and the following year replaced Hans von Bülow as director of the Berlin Philharmonic. In 1898 he became principal conductor of the Berlin Opera, rising to the post of general director in 1908. From 1919 until 1924, he conducted at the Vienna State Opera. Since that time he has been a guest-conductor to opera-houses in Munich, Berlin, Vienna and Bayreuth, distinguishing himself particularly with his remarkable performances of Mozart.

STÜCKEN, FRANK VAN DER, born, Fredricksburg, Texas, October 15, 1858. After intensive European study, he became Kapellmeister of the Stadttheater in Breslau in 1881. Returning to America, he directed the Arion chorus of New York in 1884, and three years later directed symphony concerts at Steinway Hall. From 1895 until 1907 he was conductor of the Cincinnati Symphony Orchestra.

TAFFANEL, CLAUDE PAUL, born, Bordeaux, September 16, 1844; died, Paris, November 22, 1908. In 1892 he became conductor at the Opéra, and in the same year became director of the Conservatory concerts—a position he held with great esteem until his death.

TCHEREPNINE, NIKOLAI, born, Petrograd, May 15,

1873. After directing opera at the Marinsky Theatre in Moscow, he came to Paris to conduct at the Opéra Comique, where he introduced Rimsky-Korsakoff's *Snow Maiden*. From 1909 until 1919, he was principal conductor of the Diaghilev Ballet.

THOMAS, THEODORE. (See pages 53-57).

TOSCANINI, ARTURO. (See pages 169-196).

VERBUGGHEN, HENRI, born, Brussels, August 1, 1874; died, United States, 1934. Before coming to America, he served as an assistant conductor of the Scottish Orchestra (1903) and as conductor of the Choral Union of Glasgow (1911). He came to America in 1922, when he became conductor of the Minneapolis Symphony Orchestra, and founded the Minneapolis Chorus. He has directed Beethoven and Brahms festivals in London, and has made successful guest-appearances in Brussels, Munich, Berlin and Russia.

WAGNER, RICHARD, born, Leipzig, May 22, 1813; died, Venice, Febraury 13, 1883, one of the world's greatest composers, who has likewise earned a permanent place in conductorial history. In 1833, he served as chorus-master at the Würzburg Theatre, and for the following three years he directed performances at the Magdeburg Theatre. From 1836 until 1839 he directed symphony concerts at Königsberg and at the Riga Theatre, attracting considerable attention because of the authority and strength of his performances. For a short period he was Kapellmeister at Dresden (1842), directing symphony and choral concerts and distinguishing himself particularly with his interpretation of Beethoven. In 1855, he was invited

to direct concerts of the London Philharmonic, and
five years later he gave guest performances in Paris,
Brussels, Vienna, Prague and Russia. In 1864, he
assumed the position of director of the Munich Opera.
(See pages 84-85).

WAGNER, SIEGFRIED, born, Triebschen, June 6, 1869;
died, Bayreuth, August 1930. For a short period, in
1893, he directed concerts of symphonic music. Then,
after serving as an assistant conductor at Bayreuth
(1894), he rose to the ranks of principal conductor,
and from 1896 until his death in 1930 he was one of
the important conductors of the annual Wagnerian
festival.

WALLENSTEIN, ALFRED, born, Chicago, October 7, 1898.
After studying the violoncello in Leipzig under Julius
Klengel, he returned to America in 1914 to become
violoncellist in the San Francisco Symphony Orchestra. There followed a long and successful career as
orchestra performer which brought him to the Chicago
Symphony Orchestra (1920-1928) and, finally, to the
New York Philharmonic. Recently he has turned to
the baton, directing weekly symphonic concerts over
the radio (W.O.R.) and giving guest performances
with the Los Angeles Philharmonic. In 1935, he was
appointed music director of radio station W.O.R.

WALTER, BRUNO. (See pages 258-264).

WEINGARTNER, FELIX. (See pages 160-166).

WEISBACH, HANS, born, Germany, July 19, 1885. In
1911, he officiated as assistant conductor of the *Rühl-
schen Gesangverein* in Frankfort. Eight years later
he was appointed music director in Hagen. In 1924,

he became director of the *Konzertgesellschaft* and the *Stadt Singverein* in Barmen. In 1926, he became musical director of Düsseldorf, and one year later he was appointed first conductor of opera in that city.

WOLLE, JOHN FREDERIC, born, Bethlehem, Pennsylvania, April 4, 1863; died, Pennsylvania, 1932. From 1905 until 1907, he conducted symphony and choral concerts at Berkeley, California. In 1911 he began to conduct choral societies in and near Bethlehem, and it was as a result of these efforts that he succeeded in establishing the Bethlehem Bach Choir which acquired a national reputation by virtue of its annual Bach festival. Wolle also toured to Philadelphia and New York with his Bach Choir.

WOOD, SIR HENRY JOSEPH. (See pages 44-45).

YSAYE, EUGENE, born, Liège, July 16, 1858; died, Brussels, May 14, 1931, one of the foremost violin virtuosos of his time, and celebrated as a conductor. In 1894, he founded the *Société des Concerts Ysaÿe* in Brussels which he conducted for several years with distinction. In 1918, he gave several guest-performances with the Cincinnati Symphony Orchestra and was so successful that he was immediately appointed permanent conductor. He held this position until 1922.

ZASLAWSKY, GEORGES. In 1920, he gave guest performances in Berlin, Paris, Prague and Buenos Aires creating a favorable impression. He came to New York in 1926 and gave a special concert with the New York Philharmonic. In 1927, he founded the short-lived Beethoven Symphony Orchestra which he conducted until its demise.   Since that time he has been conducting concerts in Europe, principally in Vienna.

ZEMLINSKY, ALEXANDER VON, born, Vienna, October 4, 1872.   After conducting operatic performances at the Karl Theatre in Vienna (1900), he was appointed first conductor of the Vienna Volksoper (1906), and then principal conductor of the Vienna Hofoper (1908). In 1909 he went to Mannheim, and three years later was given the principal conductorial post in Prague. In 1927, he became first conductor of the Berlin State Opera, holding that position until political developments in Germany, as a result of Hitler's ascent to power, compelled him to resign.

BARBIROLLI, JOHN, born, London, December 1899. After touring Great Britain, France, Belgium, Germany and Spain as a member of the International String Quartet, he began his conductorial career in 1925 by founding and directing the Barbirolli Chamber Orchestra.   In 1926, he was appointed conductor of the British National Opera Company, and in 1927 he became a conductor of the London Symphony Orchestra.   In recent years he has also conducted the British Broadcasting Corporation Orchestra, the Halle Orchestra of Manchester and other important British organizations.   In 1936, he was engaged as one of the principal conductors of the New York Philharmonic Symphony to succeed Arturo Toscanini. Late in 1936, it was announced that Barbirolli had been appointed the permanent conductor of the New York Philharmonic for a period of three years.   (See pages 270-272).

BIBLIOGRAPHY

A SELECT BIBLIOGRAPHY

I.

THE HISTORY OF CONDUCTING

CHYBINSKI, ADOLF, *Beitrage zur Geschichte des Takt-schalgens*. Leipzig. Breitkopf und Hartel. 1912.

DANDELOT, ARTHUR, *La société des concerts du Conservatoire*. Paris. G. Harvard fils. 1898.

DÖRFFEL, A., *Geschichte der Gewandhauskonzerte*. Leipzig. Concert direction. 1884.

FOSTER, M. B., *History of the Philharmonic Society of London*. London. John Lane. 1912.

HOGARTH, GEORGE, *The Philharmonic Society of London*. London. Bradbury and Evans. 1862.

HUNEKER, JAMES GIBBONS, *The Philharmonic Society of New York*. New York. The Philharmonic Society. 1917.

LINNEMANN, RICHARD, *Der 150 Jahre Leipziger Gewandhaus*. Leipzig. Brandstetter. 1931.

LÖBMANN, HUGO, *Zur Geschichte des Taktierens und Dirigirens*. Düsseldorf. L. Schwann. 1913.

NEWMARCH, ROSA, *Quarter of a Century of Promenade Concerts*. London. 1920.

SCHÜNEMANN, GEORG, *Geschichte des Dirigirens*. Leipzig. Breitkopf und Hartel. 1913.

SCHWARTZ, RUDOLPH, *Zur Geschichte des Taktschlagens*. Leipzig. Jahrbuch Peters. 1908.

VOGL, EMIL, *Zur Geschichte des Taktschlagens.* Leipzig. Jahrbuch Peters. 1899.

II.

TECHNIQUE OF CONDUCTING; THE ORCHESTRA; INSTRUMENTATION, ETC.

BACHRACH, A. L., *The Musical Companion.* London. Victor Gollancz. 1934.

BERG, DAVID ERIC, *Early and Classic Symphonies and the Functions of a Conductor.* New York. Caxton Press. 1927.

BERLIOZ, HECTOR, *Art of Conducting.* New York. Carl Fischer. 1926.

———, *Treatise on Modern Instrumentation.* London. Novello, Ewer and Co. 1882.

COERNE, LOUIS ADOLPHE, *Evolution of Modern Orchestration.* New York. Macmillan. 1908.

COLLES, H. C., *Symphony and Drama: 1850-1900* (Oxford History of Music, vol. 7). London. Oxford University Press. 1934.

GEHRKENS, K. W., *Essentials in Conducting.* Boston. Oliver Ditson. 1919.

PEMBAUER, JOSEF, *Uber das Dirigiren.* Leipzig. F.E.C. Leuckart. 1907.

SAMINSKY, LAZARE, *Music of Our Day.* New York. Thos. Y. Crowell Company. 1932.

SCHERCHEN, HERMANN, *Treatise on Conducting.* London. Oxford University Press. 1934.

WAGNER, RICHARD, *On Conducting.* London. William Reeves. 1897.

WEINGARTNER, FELIX, *On Conducting*. London. B. and H. 1906.

III.

CONDUCTORS

ALDRICH, RICHARD, *Musical Discourses*. London. Oxford University Press. 1928.

APTHORP, W. F., *Conductors and Conducting*. New York. Scribner's. 1895.

BERLIOZ, HECTOR, *Memoirs*. New York. A. A. Knopf. 1932.

BÜLOW, MARIE VON, *Hans von Bülow in Leben und Wort*. Stuttgart. J. Engelhorns. 1925.

CHEVALLEY, HEINRICH, *Artur Nikisch: Leben und Wirken*. Berlin. H. Behrens. 1922.

COWEN, SIR FREDERIC H., *My Art and Friends*. London. Edward Arnold. 1913.

CROGER, THOMAS R., *Notes on Conductors and Conducting*. London. W. Reeves. 1904.

DAMROSCH, WALTER, *My Musical Life*. New York. Scribner's. 1926.

DER MOULIN ECKART, RICHARD MARIA FERDINAND, GRAF, *Hans von Bülow*. Munich. Rösel und Cie. 1921.

DETTE, ARTHUR, *Artur Nikisch*. Leipzig. Joachim. 1922.

ENGEL, GABRIEL, *Gustav Mahler*. Bruckner Society of America. 1932.

FULLER-MAITLAND, J. A., *The Consort of Music*. London. Oxford University Press. 1915.

GREW, SIDNEY, *Favorite Musical Performers*. London. T. N. Foulis. 1923.

HADDEN, J. CUTHBERT, *Conductors and Conducting*. London. T. N. Foulis. 1924.

————, *Modern Musicians*. London. T. N. Foulis. 1914.

HENSCHEL, SIR GEORG, *Musings and Memories*. London. Macmillan. 1918.

KRAUSS, EMIL, *Weingartner als Schaffen der Künstler*. Berlin. Gose und Tetzlaff. 1904.

KREBS, KARL, *Meister der Taktstocks*. Berlin. Schuster und Loeffler. 1902.

LASER, ARTHUR, *Der Moderne Dirigent*. Leipzig. Breitkopf und Hartel. 1904.

LITTLEHALES, LILLIAN, *Pablo Casals*. New York. W. W. Norton. 1929.

LOURIÉ, ARTHUR, *Serge Koussevitzky and His Epoch*. New York. A. A. Knopf. 1931.

NEWMARCH, ROSA, *Sir Henry J. Wood*. London. John Lane. 1904.

NICOTRA, TOBIAS, *Arturo Toscanini*. New York. A. A. Knopf. 1929.

PARKER, HENRY TAYLOR, *Eighth Notes*. New York. Dodd Mead. 1922.

PRUNIÈRES, HENRI, *La vie illustré et libertine de Jean-Baptiste Lully*. Paris. Librarie Plon. 1909.

RIESENFELD, PAUL, *Felix Weingartner*. Breslau. Schelsische Verlag. 1906.

RUSSELL, CHARLES EDWARD, *The American Orchestra and Theodore Thomas*. New York. Doubleday, Page. 1927.

SERÉ, OCTAVE, *Musiciens français d'aujourd 'hui*. Paris. Mercure de France. 1921.

SOLLITT, EDNA NICHOLSON, *Mengelberg and the Symphonic Epoch*. New York. Ives Washburn. 1930.

SORDET, DOMINIQUE, *Douze chefs d'orchestre*. Paris. Fischbacher. 1924.

SPECHT, RICHARD, *Wilhelm Furtwängler*. Vienna. WILA. 1925.

————, *Gustav Mahler*. Berlin. Schuster und Loeffler. 1918.

SPOHR, LOUIS, *Autobiography*. London. Longmans, Green. 1865.

STANFORD, SIR CHARLES VILLIERS, *Interludes, Records and Reflections*. London. John and Murray. 1922.

STEFAN, PAUL, *Gustav Mahler*. New York. G. Schirmer. 1913.

STEINER, A., *Hans von Bülow*. Zurich. Hug. 1906.

THOMAS, THEODORE, *A Musical Autobiography*. Chicago. A. C. McClurg. 1905.

WEINGARTNER, FELIX, *Lebenserrinerungen*. Vienna. WILA. 1923.

WEISSMAN, ADOLF, *Der Dirigent im XX Jahrhundert*. Berlin. Propyläen. 1925.

WHELBOURN, HUBERT, *Celebrated Musicians, Past and Present*. London. T. Werner Laurie. 1930.

IV.

DICTIONARIES, ETC.

EINSTEIN, ALFRED, *Das neue Musiklexikon*. Berlin. Max Hesser. 1926.

Grove, George, *Dictionary of Music and Musicians.* New York. Macmillan Co. 1934.

Hull, Arthur Eaglefield, *Dictionary of Modern Music and Musicians.* New York. E. P. Dutton. 1924.

Key, Pierre, *Who's Who in Music.* New York. Pierre Key. 1931.

Pratt, W. S., *New Encyclopedia.* New York. Macmillan. 1934.

Riemann, Hugo, *Musiklexikon* (11th edition). Leipzig. M. Hesse. 1929.

V.

MUSIC MAGAZINES

Allgemeine Musikzeitung.
Chesterian.
Disques.
Monthly Musical Record.
Music and Letters.
Musical America.
Musical Courier.
Musical Record.
Musical Standard.
Musical Times.
Musical Quarterly.
Die Musik.
Musikblätter des Anbruch.
La Revue Musicale.
Sackbut.
Zeitschrift für Musik.

INDEX

INDEX

Abendroth, Hermann, 295.
Accidentals, elimination of, 28.
Albrecht, Karl, 295.
Alfano, Franco, 182.
America, outstanding orchestras, 51-67.
Ansermet, Ernest, 44, 295.
Arbós, Enrique Fernández, 46, 253, 254; biography, 296.

B. B. C. Symphony Orchestra, London, 45.
Bach, Johann Sebastian, 39; use of string instruments, 36; as conductor, 72, 75; *Brandenburg Concerto,* 73; Stokowski's transcriptions of, 203, 223.
Bach, Philip Emanuel, 72.
Bähr, Johann, 70.
Balance, problem of, 105.
Bamboscheck, Giuseppe, 296.
Barbirolli, John, 270.
Barlow, Howard, 297.
Barrère, Georges, 297.
Barzin, Leon, 277, 297.
Bass-clarinet, 27, 37.
Bass-drum, 31, 37.
Bass-tuba, 30.
Bassoon, 28.
Baton, use of: history, 77, 83; technique, 83, 103; gesturing with, 282.
Bayreuth, first festival inaugurated by Hans Richter, 117; Dr. Muck's performances, 158; Toscanini's, 173, 187, 194.
Beecham, Sir Thomas, 44, 221, 253; appraisal of, 257; gestures, 284, 291; biography, 297.
Beethoven, Ludwig van, instruments employed by, 26, 28, 30, 31, 36; development of orchestra, 36; relations with Royal Philharmonic Society: sale of *Ninth Symphony,* 43; its first performance, 43, 76; reputation as conductor, 74; von Bülow's performance of, 116.
Bekker's Dictionary, cited, 103n.
Bells, 32.
Benedict, Sir Julius, 298.
Bennett, Sir William Sterndale, 44; biography, 298.
Bergmann, Carl, 52, 55; biography, 299.
Berlin Philharmonic Orchestra, 50.
Berlioz, Hector Louis, treatise on instrumentation, 34, 83; as conductor, 84, 85; biography, 299; mentioned, 37, 38, 49, 82, 100.
Bibliography, 357-362.
Biographical guide to conductors, 295-353.
Black, Frank, 300.
Blech, Leo, 300.
Bodanzky, Artur, 267; his New Symphony Orchestra, 56, 243, 244; appraisal of, 99; biography, 300.
Boehm action in woodwinds, 38.
Book list, 357-362.
Boston Symphony Orchestra, 57-59; conducted by Nikisch, 134; by Karl Muck, 148, 150, 155; plight during years after World War, 227; under leadership of Serge Koussevitzky, 227, 236-240, 242.
Boult, Sir Adrian Cedric, 283, 301; on Nikisch, 128.

365

INDEX

Brahms, Johannes, von Bülow's eulogy, 115; tradition for performance of music of, 116; rebukes Hans Richter, 121; influence upon Nikisch, 129, 132, 139.

Brass instruments, 29, 37.

Brico, Antonia, 277, 301.

Broadcasting, Stokowski's experiments, 197, 207.

Bülow, Hans von, 85; quoted, 86; career and methods, 111-116; associations with Weingartner, 161.

Busch, Fritz, 253, 257; biography, 302.

Busser, Henri Paul, 302.

Cameron, Basil, 303.

Campanini, Cleofante, 303.

Casals, Pablo, 303; quoted, 92.

Casella, Alfredo, 304.

Castanets, 31.

Cavaliere, instruments employed by, 34.

Celeste, 31.

Chavez, Carlos, 304.

Chevillard, Camille, 50, 304.

Chicago Symphony Orchestra, 56-57.

Child-prodigies, 87, 128.

Chimes, 32.

Chorley, H. F., quoted, 82.

Cincinnati Symphony Orchestra, 60, 114n, 256; conducted by Stokowski, 211.

Clarinet, 27, 37.

Clavier, time-beating with, 72.

Clementi, Muzio, 41.

Coates, Albert, 44, 77n, 253; biography, 305.

Code of conduct for conductors, 74.

Colles, H. C., quoted, 38.

Collingwood, Lawrence, 305.

Colonne, Edouard, 48, 305.

Colors, Stokowski's experiments with, 208.

Concertgebow Orchestra, 243, 249.

Concertmaster, 24; dispensed with, by Stokowski, 209.

Concerts du Châtelet, 48.

Concerts du Conservatoire, 46.

Concerts Golschmann, Paris, 256.

Concerts Koussevitzky, 235.

Concerts Populaires, 48.

Conducting, art of, 13-19, 23, 106; in nineteenth century and today, 17; development of the art, 68-86; artistic liberation, 84; what conducting is, 87-107.

Conductor, art of interpretation, 14-19; technique, 17, 92, 101-106; exponents of modern music, 47, 54, 62, 66, 212, 220, 264; preeminent Wagnerites, 50, 55, 63, 65, 98, 99, 117, 129, 149, 158, 173, 187, 194; as time-beater, 69-73; personal element; tempers and whims; code of conduct for, 74; eighteenth-century standards, 76; growing importance and prestige, 77; use of baton, 77, 83, 103, 282; present-day types, 80; exhibitionists, 80, 113, 198, 205, 211, 279-292; child-prodigies, 87; demands upon conductor, 89; methods, 89-92; relationship with men of orchestra, 89, 112, 119, 123, 140, 144, 164, 185, 191, 195, 204, 221, 245, 251; methods during rehearsals, 91, 124, 138, 140, 144, 146, 164, 184, 189, 195, 217, 220, 237, 246, 251; necessary qualifications, 93-100; conducting from memory, 96, 112, 114, 121, 133, 135, 177, 205, 285-289; *tempo* and rhythm, 101; gesturing, 104, 282-285; balance, 105; world-famous leaders, Hans von Bülow, 111; Hans Richter, 117; Gustav Mahler, 122; Artur Nikisch, 127; Dr.

INDEX

INDEX

INDEX

370

INDEX

INDEX

372

INDEX

373

INDEX

374